Autism

Sara Miller McCune founded SAGE Publishing in 1965 to support the dissemination of usable knowledge and educate a global community. SAGE publishes more than 1000 journals and over 800 new books each year, spanning a wide range of subject areas. Our growing selection of library products includes archives, data, case studies and video. SAGE remains majority owned by our founder and after her lifetime will become owned by a charitable trust that secures the company's continued independence.

Los Angeles | London | New Delhi | Singapore | Washington DC | Melbourne

Autism

Trevor Cotterill   A Student's Guide

Los Angeles | London | New Delhi
Singapore | Washington DC | Melbourne

Los Angeles | London | New Delhi
Singapore | Washington DC | Melbourne

SAGE Publications Ltd
1 Oliver's Yard
55 City Road
London EC1Y 1SP

SAGE Publications Inc.
2455 Teller Road
Thousand Oaks, California 91320

SAGE Publications India Pvt Ltd
B 1/I 1 Mohan Cooperative Industrial Area
Mathura Road
New Delhi 110 044

SAGE Publications Asia-Pacific Pte Ltd
3 Church Street
#10-04 Samsung Hub
Singapore 049483

Editor: Delayna Spencer
Editorial assistant: Bali Birch-Lee
Production editor: Martin Fox
Marketing manager: Lorna Patkai
Cover design: Wendy Scott
Typeset by: C&M Digitals (P) Ltd, Chennai, India
Printed in the UK

Library of Congress Control Number: 2022937823

British Library Cataloguing in Publication data

A catalogue record for this book is available from the
British Library

ISBN 978-1-5297-0648-2
ISBN 978-1-5297-0647-5 (pbk)

At SAGE we take sustainability seriously. Most of our products are printed in the UK using responsibly sourced
papers and boards. When we print overseas we ensure sustainable papers are used as measured by the PREPS
grading system. We undertake an annual audit to monitor our sustainability.

Contents

About the author

Trevor Cotterill is currently Senior Lecturer in Education and SEND, and Programme Leader for the BA (Hons) Special Educational Needs and Disabilities degree at the University of Derby. He has over 40 years' experience across a range of educational contexts, including Secondary, FE and HE sectors and teaches on undergraduate and post graduate programmes. His publications cover a broad range of issues associated with aspects of SEND including autism, ADHD, chromosomal diversity and associated pedagogy, alongside areas such as the marketisation of education, play and assessment.

ONE

Introduction

This chapter takes an historical perspective and focuses upon some of the most prominent individuals associated with the development of autism as a concept, including Kanner and Asperger, and the rise of emotional and social theories proposed by individuals such as Bettleheim and Rimland. The 1970s saw the development of experimental studies into autism such as those conducted by Hermelin and O'Connor, and twin studies. The 1980s heralded the behavioural interventionist approach, such as that proposed by Lovaas, but it was the 1990s that saw a different approach in the form of theories such as Theory of Mind and advocates such as Uta Frith, Alan Leslie and Simon Baron-Cohen. The Diagnostic and Statistical Manual of Mental Disorders 5th edition (American Psychiatric Association, 2013) and the International Classification of Diseases (ICD) 11th revision (World Health Organization, 2019) diagnostic criteria have undergone numerous revisions to accommodate how our understanding of autism has developed over time. Research into autism has yielded much information, such as the role of the interplay between genetics and environmental factors, and the current view is that autism exists as a spectrum referred to as the Autism Spectrum Disorder (ASD) and is a developmental disability that can cause significant social, communication and behavioural challenges (Centers for Disease Control and Prevention [CDC], 2022), or autism is a lifelong developmental disability which affects how people communicate and interact with the world (National Autistic Society [NAS], 2022).

There are other names for autism used by some people, such as:

- Autism spectrum condition (ASC) – used instead of ASD by some people.
- Asperger's (or Asperger syndrome) – used by some people to describe autistic people with average or above average intelligence (NHS, 2022).

This book will use the term 'autism' to refer to any of the above, unless a specific term is used, for example with respect to research. It also uses the terms autistic adult/people/child/young person, or person/child on the autism spectrum as this is informed by research, which indicates that there is a growing preference for positive identity first language, particularly among autistic adults (NAS, 2022).

Over the past 70 years, the concept of autism has undergone several changes but there are several interesting accounts of children who were markedly unusual in their abilities and interactions that have been noted through the centuries. Perhaps the most famous of these is Victor, a youngster who was discovered in 1797 near St-Sernin-sur-Rance, France, having spent several years living in isolation (Lane, 1977). Jean Itard, a physician, worked tirelessly over many years with Victor, focusing on socialising him. Although Victor's expressive language did not develop, his understanding of the world and of other people improved considerably. Several reports of 'feral' children of varying reliability (Newton, 2002) are included in the literature on autism, although, as with Victor, it is difficult to differentiate the effects of early deprivation/privation. Children whose abilities and behaviour accord with our current understanding of autism have also been described by some early psychiatrists. Psychiatrists such as Haslem (1809) and Maudsley (1879) had patients who spoke of themselves in the third person, were solitary, had a very narrow range of deep interests and did not form attachments to caregivers (Wolff, 2004).

Early recognition

The concept of autism was coined in 1911 by the German psychiatrist Eugen Bleuler to describe a symptom of the most severe cases of schizophrenia, a concept he had also created. According to Bleuler, autistic thinking was characterised by infantile wishes to avoid unsatisfying realities and replace them with fantasies and hallucinations. 'Autism' defined the subject's symbolic 'inner life' and was not readily accessible to observers (Bleuler, 1950). In the 1940s, two clinicians working independently outlined the conditions we know as autism and Asperger syndrome. Kanner's (1943) case studies of 11 children identified language problems; atypical use of nonverbal communication, such as eye gaze and gesture; narrowly restricted interests and a desire for sameness; and atypical reactions to sensory stimuli. The children's apparent aloofness and isolation from the human world led him to coin the phrase 'autistic aloneness'.

Hans Asperger, a paediatrician working in Vienna during the same period as Kanner was active in the USA, described a behaviour pattern very similar to Kanner's description, which he called 'autistic psychopathy' (Asperger, 1944). Asperger highlighted important features in common, but the children generally having fluent speech and vocabulary, even if they used it oddly, talking at length about their favourite topic or interest. Rather than seeming unaware of the existence of others, their reactions to others appeared strange and antisocial.

It was only in the 1980s that psychiatrist Lorna Wing highlighted the remarkable similarity between Asperger's and Kanner's clinical observations and 'Asperger syndrome' (AS) was recognised as a diagnostic subtype of autism. Wing also introduced the term 'autism spectrum' to reflect the variation on the core symptom profile. In 1992, the World Health Organization published the International Classification of

Diseases (ICD) and included the syndrome and two years later, the DSM did the same. However, currently ICD-11 and DSM-5 subsume AS within the autism spectrum. Interestingly, Czech (2018) and Sheffer (2018) provide evidence that Asperger collaborated with the Nazi regime, despatching some children in his care to a 'euthanasia clinic' where they met their death, but this is disputed by some scholars who say the stain on Asperger's name shouldn't erase his contributions to the understanding of autism (Furfaro, 2018).

Relationships in the family and parenting styles have also been sought as to the reason for the characteristics seen in children, particularly parents who were emotionally unavailable, the so-called 'refrigerator mother' (Bettelheim, 1967). Kanner, initially favouring a biological explanation of autism, began to consider autism as a form of withdrawal from the emotional coldness he had perceived in some mothers. Rimland (1964) began to collect scientific and medical evidence to challenge Bettelheim's approach and suggested that autism was a neurological disorder, and not due to faulty relationships.

A neurodevelopmental disorder

Hermelin and O'Connor (1970) suggested that autistic children were more likely to respond to tactile and visual stimulation than auditory stimulation and that the developmental process in all children was driven by a hierarchical structure of sensory systems. Central to this thinking was the cognitive deficit of autism which saw researchers focusing on the study of language and regarding autism as a 'communication disorder' rather than a 'psychotic disorder'. The exact form of the central sensory disorder which caused autism was not known, but the view developing was that it was not caused by emotional reactions or hallucinations but was instead characterised by a deficit in certain aspects of linguistic thought. The language 'deviance' and impaired usage of spoken language and gesture seen in autistic children was different from the problems seen in other language-disordered children (Bartak et al., 1975).

Twin studies carried out by Folstein and Rutter (1977) found that when one member of an identical twin pair (MZ) had autism, the second twin was more likely to have some form of autism than when the twins were non-identical. The concordance for cognitive abnormalities was 82 per cent in MZ (identical) pairs and 10 per cent in DZ (non-identical) pairs and concluded that brain injury in the infancy period may lead to autism on its own or in combination with a genetic predisposition. Wing and Gould (1979) introduced the concept of the 'autism spectrum', which saw autism moving from being recognised as a discrete disorder to that of a continuum of strengths and needs. Autism was now framed as a developmental disorder and they proposed the idea of a triad of impairments characterised by patterns of social interaction, social communication, and social imagination, each with their own subgroups.

Diagnosis and classification

The first edition of DSM (DSM-I) (APA, 1952) saw autism under the term Schizophrenic reaction, childhood type. The second edition of the DSM (DSM-II) (APA, 1968) defined autism as a psychiatric condition – a form of childhood schizophrenia marked by a detachment from reality. DSM-III (APA, 1980) established autism as its own separate diagnosis and described it as a 'pervasive developmental disorder' distinct from schizophrenia and listed specific criteria required for a diagnosis. It defined three essential features of autism: a lack of interest in people; severe impairments in communication; and bizarre responses to the environment, all developing in the first 30 months of life. DSM-IV (APA, 1994) was the first edition to categorise autism as a spectrum (Zeldovich, 2018).

Wing and Gould (1979) also argued that the 'pattern of impairments and behaviour problems' previously being termed childhood psychosis, childhood autism, or childhood schizophrenia needed to be reconceptualised as problems of social impairment (Wing and Gould, 1979). Key features of the so-called triad of impairment autism were defined as: 'absence or impairment of social interaction', 'absence or impairment of development of verbal or nonverbal language', or 'repetitive, stereotyped activities of any kind'. Cognitive psychology researchers (Baron-Cohen et al., 1985) also argued that autistic children lacked a 'theory of mind', the ability to attribute autonomous mental states to the self and others so as to predict and explain actions following, and that autistic children displayed an 'input processing deficit' described as 'weak central coherence' (Frith, 2003).

Autism is now recognised as a neurodevelopmental disorder in which deficits of communication, social interaction, restricted and repetitive behaviours are displayed, significantly impacting on a person's functioning, with a range of differing symptoms leading to the understanding of it as existing within a spectrum of strengths and weaknesses (Bourgeron, 2016). Previously the triad of impairment comprising social interaction, communication, and restricted, repetitive behaviours has now seen the move towards recognising the interrelated nature of social interaction and communication resulting in the amalgamation of these two areas into one, that of social communication. The addition of a new symptom relating to sensory issues was included following significant evidence of it being a common feature (Fung and Hardan, 2014). ICD-11 recognises that these characteristics may not occur until social demands increase later in life (WHO, 2019), whereas DSM-5 identifies those difficulties in social communication to be present in early development (APA, 2013).

Future diagnostic rates may reduce due to these changes; the removal of the previously distinct subtypes may present challenges to practitioners aiming to easily identify specific traits and areas of deficit (Fung and Hardan, 2014). DSM-5 recognises severity levels and the presence (or lack) of intellectual disability aims to clarify these diagnoses. However, Happé and Frith (2020) imply the removal of confusing low- and high-functioning labels serves little purpose when considering the wider and conflicting behaviours and provisions required to support those with autism in daily life.

Neurodiversity

The dominant image of autism up to the 1980s was that of a person lacking the self-insight and communicative skills necessary to tell others what it is like to be autistic. In the mid-1990s, the emergence of the internet provided a more accessible text-based means of communication and empowered a growing number of autistic people to connect and share ideas with one another (Dekker, 2020). Autistic culture, the autistic self-advocacy movement, and the assertion that autism is a valid way of being gave rise to the neurodiversity movement. Kapp (2020) argues that a central premise of the neurodiversity movement is that variations in neurological development and functioning across humans are a natural and valuable part of human variation and therefore not necessarily pathological and that autism is simply another form of variation between individuals (Blume, 1998). Many autistic people have adopted the neurodiversity framework, coining the term 'neurotypical' to describe the majority brain and seeing autism as an example of diversity in the set of all possible diverse brains, none of which is normal and all of which are simply different (Salman, 2019). Leadbitter et al. (2021) suggest that this movement should involve partnerships with autistic people, alongside caregivers and other stakeholders; reflection by intervention researchers and practitioners upon how their intervention practices align with a neurodiversity framework; greater regard within intervention programmes to natural autistic developmental processes, coping strategies, autonomy and wellbeing; and increased efforts to develop and validate tools to measure autistic prioritised outcomes.

However, the concept of neurodiversity as applied to autism is criticised for being skewed towards the 'high-functioning' individuals of the autistic spectrum or those with milder forms of the condition. Some parents of autistic children and parent-led organisations, autism researchers and autistic people have accused neurodiversity advocates of presenting a sanitised view of what autism can be like and deflecting attention and resources away from the struggles of more severely affected individuals and their families (Hughes, 2020). In the UK, there is an increased understanding among researchers that there needs to be more meaningful involvement of autistic people in research (Fletcher-Watson et al., 2019) and a greater emphasis on participatory and action research models with autistic viewpoints and experiences at the centre (Lam et al., 2020). Lam et al. (2020) suggest that research that meaningfully includes autistic individuals and captures their perspectives of positive wellbeing is essential for stakeholders to better understand how to provide services that respond to the needs and wants of the autistic community. (See Chapter 2 for more information on neurodiversity.)

In conclusion, Happé and Frith (2020) suggest that there have been several major changes in how autism is thought of, operationalised, and recognised:

- from a narrow definition to wide diagnostic criteria;
- from a rare to a relatively common condition, although still under-recognised in women;

- from something affecting children, to a lifelong condition;
- from something discrete and distinct, to a dimensional view;
- from one thing to many 'autisms';
- from a focus on 'pure' autism, to recognition that complexity and comorbidity is the norm;
- from conceptualising autism purely as a 'developmental disorder', to recognising a neurodiversity perspective, operationalised in participatory research models.

References

American Psychiatric Association (1952). *Diagnostic and Statistical Manual of Mental Disorders* (1st edition). Washington, DC: American Psychiatric Publishing.

American Psychiatric Association (1968). *Diagnostic and Statistical Manual of Mental Disorders* (2nd edition). Washington, DC: American Psychiatric Publishing.

American Psychiatric Association (1980). *Diagnostic and Statistical Manual of Mental Disorders* (3rd edition). Washington, DC: American Psychiatric Publishing.

American Psychiatric Association (1994). *Diagnostic and Statistical Manual of Mental Disorders* (4th edition). Washington, DC: American Psychiatric Publishing.

American Psychiatric Association (2013). *Diagnostic and Statistical Manual of Mental Disorders* (5th edition). Washington, DC: American Psychiatric Publishing.

Asperger, H. (1944). Die 'Autistischen Psychopathen' im Kindesalter. [The 'Autistic Psychopaths' in Childhood]. *Archiv für Psychiatrie und Nervenkrankheiten*, 117, pp. 76–136.

Baron-Cohen, S., Leslie, A. M. and Frith, U. (1985). Does the autistic child have a 'theory of mind'? *Cognition*, 21 (1), pp. 37–46.

Bartak, L., Rutter, M. and Cox, A. (1975). A comparative study of infantile autism and specific developmental receptive language disorder: I. The children. *The British Journal of Psychiatry*, 126, pp. 127–45.

Bettelheim, B. (1967). *The Empty Fortress: Infantile autism and the birth of the self.* New York: Free Press.

Bleuler, E. (1950). *Dementia Praecox or the Group of Schizophrenias.* New York: International Universities Press.

Blume, H. (1998). *Neurodiversity. On the neurological underpinnings of geekdom.* [online] Available at: www.theatlantic.com/magazine/archive/1998/09/neurodiversity/305909/ [Accessed 20.03.2022].

Bourgeron, T. (2016). Current knowledge on the genetics of autism and propositions for future research. *Comptes Rendus Biologies*, 339 (7–8), pp. 300–7.

Centers for Disease Control and Prevention (CDC) (2022). *Autistic Spectrum Disorder.* [online] Available at: https://www.cdc.gov/ncbddd/autism/index.html [Accessed 12.02.2022].

Czech, H. (2018). Hans Asperger, National Socialism, and 'race hygiene' in Nazi-era Vienna. *Mol Autism*, 9 (29), pp. 1–43.

Dekker, M. (2020). From exclusion to acceptance: Independent living on the Autistic Spectrum. In S. Kapp (Ed.), *Autistic Community and the Neurodiversity Movement: Stories from the frontline*. Singapore: Springer Nature, pp. 41–9.

Fletcher-Watson, S., Adams, J., Brook, K., Charman, T., Crane, L., Cusack, J., Leekam, S., Milton, D., Parr, J. R. and Pellicano, E. (2019). Making the future together: Shaping autism research through meaningful participation. *Autism*, 23 (4), pp. 943–53.

Folstein, S. and Rutter, M. (1977). Infantile autism: A genetic study of 21 twin pairs. *J Child Psychol Psychiatry*, 18 (4), pp. 297–321.

Frith, U. (2003). *Autism: Explaining the enigma* (2nd edition). Oxford: Blackwell.

Fung, L. K. and Hardan, A. Y. (2014). Autism in DSM-5 under the microscope: Implications to patients, families, clinicians, and researchers. *Asian J Psychiatr*. 11, pp. 93–7.

Furfaro, H. (2018). *New evidence ties Hans Asperger to Nazi eugenics program*. [online] Available at: www.spectrumnews.org/news/new-evidence-ties-hans-asperger-nazi-eugenics-program/ [Accessed 04.03.2022].

Happé, F. and Frith, U. (2020). Annual Research Review: Looking back to look forward – changes in the concept of autism and implications for future research. *Journal of Child Psychology and Psychiatry*, 61 (3), pp. 218–232.

Hermelin, B. and O'Connor, N. (1970). *Psychological Experiments with Autistic Children*. Oxford: Pergamon Press.

Hughes, J. (2020). Does the heterogeneity of autism undermine the neurodiversity paradigm? *Bioethics*, 35 (1), pp. 47–60.

Kanner, L. (1943). Autistic disturbances of affective contact. *Nervous Child*, 2, pp. 217–50.

Kapp, S. K. (2020). Introduction. In S. Kapp (Ed.), *Autistic Community and the Neurodiversity Movement*. Singapore: Palgrave Macmillan.

Lam, G. Y. H., Holden, E., Fitzpatrick, M., Mendez, L. R. and Berkm, K. (2020). 'Different but connected': Participatory action research using Photovoice to explore wellbeing in autistic young adults. *Autism*, 24 (5), pp. 1246–59.

Lane, H. (1977). *The Wild Boy of Aveyron*. London: Allen and Unwin.

Leadbitter K., Buckle K. L., Ellis C. and Dekker M. (2021). Autistic self-advocacy and the neurodiversity movement: Implications for autism early intervention research and practice. *Frontiers in Psychology*, 12, 635690.

National Autistic Society (NAS) (2022). *What is Autism?* [online]. Available at: www.autism.org.uk/advice-and-guidance/what-is-autism [Accessed 03.02.2022].

National Health Service (NHS) (2022). *Signs of Autism*. [online]. Available at: www.nhs.uk/conditions/autism/signs/ [Accessed 01.02.2022].

Newton, M. (2002). *Savage Girls and Wild Boys: A history of feral children*. London: Faber and Faber.

Rimland, B. (1964). *Infantile Autism: The syndrome and its implications for a neural theory of behavior*. New York: Appleton-Century-Crofts.

Salman, S. (2019). Simon Baron-Cohen: Neurodiversity is the next frontier. But we're failing autistic people. [online] Available at: www.theguardian.com/society/2019/oct/02/simon-baron-cohen-autism-neurodiversity-brains-money [Accessed 12.02.2022].

Sheffer, E. (2018). *Asperger's Children: The origins of autism in Nazi Vienna*. New York: W. W. Norton and Company.

Wing, L. and Gould, J. (1979). Severe impairments of social interaction and associated abnormalities in children: Epidemiology and classification. *Journal of Autism and Developmental Disorders*, 9 (1), pp. 11–29.

Wolff, S. (2004). The history of autism. *European Child and Adolescent Psychiatry*, 13, pp. 201–8.

World Health Organization (2019). *International Statistical Classification of Diseases and Related Health Problems* (11th edition).

Zeldovich, L. (2018). *The evolution of 'autism' as a diagnosis, explained*. [online] Available at: www.spectrumnews.org/news/evolution-autism-diagnosis-explained/ [Accessed 20.03.2022].

TWO
Researching autism

Introduction

This chapter examines the methods used by researchers into autism. These include techniques such as observations, experiments, research into genetics, such as families and twin studies, and brain imaging. These areas are discussed in detail elsewhere in the book. The focus of the chapter is to outline the standing of current research methods involving techniques in identifying the complexities surrounding autism; for example, sensory issues and Sensory Integration (SI) will be discussed and evaluated. Much of this chapter focuses upon how research is and should be carried out with autistic people. As such, it emphasises participatory autism research, the impact that having an autistic child has on families and the use of Interpretive Phenomenological Analysis (IPA) as a method in studying the lived experience of autistic individuals. It briefly identifies possible new research in diagnostics and testing and debates the Polyvagal Theory (Porges, 2007), which suggests that autism is a learnt response to early stressors.

───────────────────── Learning objectives ─────────────────────

This chapter will:

- Introduce you to a range of methods used in researching autism
- Invite you to consider research surrounding the role of sensory issues and Sensory Integration (SI)
- Introduce you to the importance in undertaking participatory autism research, the impact of autism on families and the use of Interpretive Phenomenological Analysis (IPA) in examining the lived experience
- Invite you to review the importance of Polyvagal Theory in our understanding of autism

───────────────────── Key terms ─────────────────────

Research, sensory issues in autism, Sensory Integration, participatory autism research, families, Interpretive Phenomenological Analysis, lived experience, Polyvagal Theory

―――――――――――― Pause for reflection ――――――――――――

- What do you think are the main methods for researching autism?
- What would be your research priorities if you were an autistic individual, a family member, or a scientist?

Sensory issues

Sensory issues are common in people with autism and are even included in the diagnostic criteria for autism spectrum disorder. Autistic people might have sensitivities to sights, sounds, smells, tastes, touch, and balance. In DSM-5 (APA, 2013) sensory issues became an official part of the diagnosis of autism and it is described as hyper- or hypo-reactivity to sensory input or unusual interests in sensory aspects of the environment (e.g. apparent indifference to pain/temperature, adverse response to specific sounds or textures, excessive smelling or touching of objects, visual fascination with lights or movement). Autistic people can experience hypersensitivity (over-responsiveness), for example to bright lights or certain light wavelengths (e.g. fluorescent lights), certain sounds, smells, textures and tastes, and sensory overload and avoidance may occur. Hyposensitivity may also be experienced such as a constant need for movement; difficulty recognising sensations like hunger, illness, or pain; or attraction to loud noises, bright lights, and vibrant colours. Sensory seeking may occur by making loud noises, touching people or objects, or rocking back and forth, for example.

Many autistic people use stimming as a form of sensory seeking to keep their sensory systems in balance, such as hand flapping, making repetitive noises, or rocking back and forth and covering ears or eyes. Repetitive movements, sounds or fidgeting can help people with autism stay calm, relieve stress, or block out uncomfortable sensory input. Certain behaviours may show when they are experiencing a sensory issue such as increased movement, for example jumping, spinning, or crashing into things; increased stimming; difficulty communicating or responding as the brain shifts resources to deal with sensory input or escalating, overwhelming emotions or need to escape a situation.

Many theories relating to autism are based on the premise that autistic individuals process sensory information in a way that is different from others. Early research was based on observations of hypo- or hyper-arousal and unusual reactions to sensory input and many of the current theories of autism reflect the theme that sensory atypicalities are core symptoms of autism. There are many ways in which research has been carried out in this area, including questionnaires, autobiographical accounts, and retrospective video observations.

Parents of infants with autism often report sensory peculiarities early in the development of their infants which may be features of autism in the first two years of life. For example, they may be easily distressed or preoccupied by innocuous sights, sounds, odours, and textures, and are not responsive to other more meaningful sensations such as the sound of their name (Baranek, 1999). Atypical sensory perceptual behaviours appear to persist throughout the development of individuals with autism. Based on a review of research that included anecdotal and clinical reports, the prevalence of sensory sensitivities among persons with autism was estimated to be between 30 and 100 per cent (Dawson and Watling, 2000) and that it may help individuals cope with their sensory environment by either generating or avoiding sensory stimulation.

Traditionally, clinicians used parental questionnaires such as Sensory Profile (SP) to assess the sensory profile of autistic children (Dunn and Westman, 1997). Kientz and Dunn (1997) compared the SPs of 32 autistic children (3–13 years) with that of typically developing (TD) children (3–10 years) and found significantly more (85 per cent of the items) hypo- or hyper-responses (e.g. preoccupations with sensory features, perceptual distortions, paradoxical responses to sensory stimuli). Rogers et al. (2003) found that such groups had significant differences in their sensitivity to touch, taste and smell. Sigman and Capps (1997) suggest that autistic people may not be impaired but rather react to stimuli in very idiosyncratic ways such as smelling non-edible objects and attending to objects out of the corner of their eyes.

Autobiographical accounts provide another relevant source of information on the subjective sensory-perceptual experience of autistic people. The personal accounts include examples from vision, sound, taste, smell, proprioception, and kinaesthetic stimulation of sensory distortions difficulties. Jones et al. (2003) conducted a qualitative analysis of the numerous first-hand web page accounts of sensory disturbances and discovered reports of aversive experiences, coping mechanisms, pleasurable experiences, and awareness of being different. Fascinations with certain smells, movements, and engaging in sensory stereotypes were sources of interest and pleasure. These sensory experiences and the coping behaviours that they elicit may evoke positive or negative feelings about the self; however, reports of one individual with autism may change significantly over time (O'Neill and Jones, 1997). Systematic observation and analysis of home videos of infants who are later diagnosed with autism provide another source of information on sensory issues in autism. Ornitz (1969) concluded that a profound disturbance of perception is found in both autistic children and schizophrenic adults, and that this perceptual dysfunction may be common to, and underlie, the divergent clinical pathology present in these conditions.

Sensory Integration (SI)

Sensory Integration (SI) theory is based on the understanding that interferences in neurological processing and integration of sensory information disrupt the construction of purposeful behaviours, with Watling and Dietz (2007) finding that subjective data suggest that Ayres' sensory integration may produce an effect that is evident during treatment sessions and in home environments. Ayres (1979) refers to the term sensory integration as the ability to produce appropriate motor and behavioural responses to stimuli and she observed hyper- and hypo-responses to sensory stimuli in autistic individuals. Specifically, she noted that these individuals exhibited problems in registration (signal detection and interpretation), in modulation (signal inhibition or propagation), in interacting with certain objects and/or in motivation. Ayres and Tickle (1980) investigated sensory disturbances in autism and their responses to SI therapy specifically. In this retrospective study, the authors found that individuals with hyper-reactivity had better outcomes than those who were hypo-reactive and proposed that children who register sensory input respond better to therapy than those who do not. They implicated the limbic system and suggested that some autistic children do not register sensory inputs properly; and as a result, these children allocate attention differently from neurotypical children.

Ayres (1979) also hypothesised that registration problems are in the limbic system and proposed that autistic children not only fail to register sensory input properly but also have trouble modulating input that they do register. She suggested that over- or under-activity of these systems may manifest in fight, fright or flight reactions to light touch that most others would consider non-noxious. She described motivation as the desire or willingness to respond to a stimulus that has been registered or to ignore it and proposed that autistic children have a motivation deficit. Much of the technology used today to study brain structure and function was not available to Ayres when she developed her theoretical explanations and interventions, but there are several methods available now such as structural and functional Magnetic Resonance Imaging (MRI), eye-tracking systems and electroencephalogram (EEG). With the advancement of neuroimaging and other innovative technologies, scientists have begun to map the structure and function of the brain areas that may underlie sensory processing deficits in autism. Ayres' predictions about sensory registration, modulation and motivation are strongly supported by the findings of various studies. Kilroy et al. (2019) reviewed studies of sensory processing and sensory integration that used a variety of modern neuroimaging technologies and techniques to examine components related to sensory processing and provide preliminary evidence to support Ayres.

Ayres (1979) conceptualised an intervention approach now referred to as Ayres' Sensory Integration (ASI) to treat the sensorimotor foundations of academic skills and other higher order abilities (i.e. planning and organisation). The therapy involves the client interacting with a combination of equipment such as scooters and swings, providing the opportunity to obtain and process enhanced sensory input and develop normal levels of arousal and security when interacting with their environment.

The intervention approach was founded on the hypothesis that sensory integration (SI) disturbance and other processing abnormalities were, in part, the result of abnormal brain functioning. Treatment is designed to provide controlled sensory experiences so that an adaptive motor response is elicited and uses planned, controlled sensory input in accordance with the needs of the child and is characterised by an emphasis on sensory stimulation and active participation of the client and involves client-directed activities. In each session, a trained therapist artfully engineers the characteristics of the environment to create the 'just-right challenge' (Baranek, 2002). The goals of treatment are to improve sensory modulation related to behaviour and attention and to increase abilities for social interactions, academic skills and independence through better SI. The activities provided are meant to help the nervous system modulate, organise and integrate information from the environment, resulting in future adaptive responses (Baranek, 2002).

In a pilot study (Pfeiffer et al., 2011), autistic children aged 6–12 were randomly assigned to a fine motor or SI treatment group. Pre-tests and post-tests measured social responsiveness, sensory processing, functional motor skills, and social-emotional factors. Results identified significant positive changes in Goal Attainment Scaling scores for both groups; more significant changes occurred in the SI group, and a significant decrease in autistic mannerisms occurred in the SI group. A systematic review (Schoen et al., 2019) found that ASI intervention meets the criteria for an evidence-based practice for 4–12-year-old autistic children and that it meets the criteria for an evidence-based practice according to the CEC Standards for Evidence-Based Practices in Special Education (Cook et al., 2015; Council for Exceptional Children [CEC], 2014); and the FPG Child Development Institute Guidelines (Wong et al., 2015).

Case study

Maryam is a 13-year-old girl who attends mainstream secondary school. She is living with selective mutism in school, and she has now refused to complete work, participate, or stay in class, which may be due to a change in the group she works with. When she is calm, Maryam has a good understanding of language, can follow instructions, and participate in interactions in both home and school settings. When under stress she will sometimes 'freeze' or become very upset when asked to go for a break with the others and will engage in pacing backwards and forwards. She has difficulty managing with sudden, loud and background noises and becomes stressed or anxious. She will become very upset in a crowded or busy environment. She may not always register auditory cues particularly at home but will notice small changes within the environment and others moving about when shopping or within the classroom.

(Continued)

- How do these behaviours relate to the discussion at the beginning of this chapter?
- If you were a teaching assistant or classroom teacher, how might you support Maryam with the issues outlined?

Participatory autism research

In the past decade, there has been increasing concern about the disconnect between researchers and the autism community (Pellicano and Stears, 2011; Milton and Bracher, 2013; Woods and Waltz, 2019). This disconnect may be due to several factors, including a lack of involvement of the autism community in research, poor dissemination of findings to the community, and use of demeaning language about autistic people (Gowen et al., 2019). This, alongside a history of controversial claims from scientists (from 'refrigerator mothers' to claims that vaccines cause autism), has contributed to growing distrust of autism researchers by autistic self-advocates (Dawson et al., 2004), hence the move towards participatory research. Participatory autism research refers to ways of involving autistic people and their allies (e.g. family members) in making decisions about research. These decisions can include what research gets done, how it gets done and how research findings are used (Pickard et al., 2021).

Research into autism has often been guided by the interests of researchers and funders rather than autistic people and their allies (Cusack and Sterry, 2016). Arnstein (1969) proposes a ladder of participation, in that power varies across different types of participation: from no power (e.g. therapy), through tokenism (e.g. consultation), to shared power (e.g. partnership). However, this model has been critiqued for its failure to recognise that participation itself can be a goal and that process and diversity of experience matter as much as outcome (Tritter and McCallum, 2006). Also, much of the research into autism it could be argued involves no power, or only tokenistic forms of power, for the autistic community and their allies (Nicolaidis et al., 2019). Fletcher-Watson et al. (2019) identify five topics relevant to building a community of practice in participatory research: Respect, Authenticity, Assumptions, Infrastructure and Empathy. Autistic people should be respected as equal partners, taking their voices seriously and allowing them to be heard. Tokenistic involvement should be avoided by working with autistic people who are skilled, invested in, and/or knowledgeable about the specific topic being studied. Authenticity also requires that collaborators recognise and attempt to address imbalances of power, such as those that exist between academic and non-academic partners, and between autistic and non-autistic people.

Nicolaidis et al. (2019) suggested that despite growing appreciation of the need for research on autism in adulthood, few survey instruments have been validated for use with autistic adults. They suggested that to understand what can improve the lives of autistic adults, researchers need to collect survey data directly from autistic adults. Participants often said that, if taking a survey that used the original instruments, they would experience confusion, frustration, anxiety, or anger. They repeatedly stated that, faced with such measures, they would offer unreliable answers, leave items blank, or just stop participating in the study. Common concerns included the use of difficult vocabulary, confusing terms, complex sentence structure, convoluted phrasings, figures of speech, or imprecise language. Partners struggled with response options that used vague terms. They also felt anxious if their answer might not be completely accurate or if their responses could vary in different situations and often the surveys did not completely capture the intended idea. Sometimes, instruments used offensive language or ideas. To support autism researchers in making their work more participatory, best practice guidelines have been proposed (Fletcher-Watson et al., 2018; Nicolaidis et al., 2019).

Common adaptations included:

- adding prefaces to increase precision or explain context;
- modifying items to simplify sentence structure;
- substituting difficult vocabulary words, confusing terms, or figures of speech with more straightforward terms;
- adding hotlinks that define problematic terms or offer examples or clarifications;
- adding graphics to increase clarity of response options; and
- adding new items related to autism-specific aspects of the construct.

Participatory research involves incorporating the views of the autism community about what research gets done, how it is done and how it is implemented (Cornwall and Jewkes, 1995). Specific manifestations of participatory research include the involving of autistic researchers, partnership with autistic people or allies in research and engagement with the community (Fletcher-Watson et al., 2018). However, despite a multitude of benefits, there is evidence to suggest that participatory research is not yet the standard, but rather the exception. Unfortunately, in the rare circumstances where there is autism community involvement, at present, this is rarely more than tokenistic (Fletcher-Watson et al., 2018; Michael, 2021).

There are multiple factors that can complicate attempts to adopt collaborative research practices (Pickard et al., 2021; Redman et al., 2021). One key reason is that the infrastructure of scientific research is not conducive to participatory working, in several ways. First, there are significant time and funding constraints within academic environments that may prohibit a participatory working style. Second, participatory approaches are not incentivised, for instance in terms of career progression, within the current academic structure (Pickard et al., 2021). Finally, some early career researchers feel that there is an absence of support for participatory working from more senior academics (Fletcher-Watson et al., 2019; Pickard et al., 2021).

In addition, researchers may not engage in participatory practices because they believe effective participatory research requires them to have strong relationships with the community, and forging these relationships takes time (Pickard et al., 2021). However, participatory research can enhance rapport and trust between researchers and the autism community (Gowen et al., 2019). Pavlopoulou et al. (2020) adopted a participatory approach throughout the entirety of the research process to investigate facilitators of sleep for autistic adolescents. At the onset of the study, a consultation group provided input on study objectives, research design, procedures and tools, ideas for public engagement, and other areas relating to the specifics of the project. The consultation group created visual aids that were then used for dissemination at a community exhibition alongside panel discussions and workshops involving various members of the autism community (parents, psychologists, autistic people, etc.).

Pause for reflection

- Why do you think that participatory research is important in contributing to our understanding of autism?
- What ethical issues could be important to follow if you were involved in such research?

Examples of participatory research

The work of Cassidy et al. (2021) constitutes a good example of effective participatory research. Autistic people identified a need for better tools to assess suicidality in autism. Following this, the authors conducted two studies to adapt the suicidal behaviour questionnaire to improve the clarity and relevance of the items to autistic adults. Three focus groups identified potential issues with the original version of the questionnaire (that was designed for non-autistic adults) and suggested adaptations. Following this, autistic and non-autistic adults completed the initial adapted version of the questionnaire to explore the equivalence of the tool between groups and identify problematic items. Cognitive interviews were undertaken, and a large sample of autistic and non-autistic adults provided qualitative feedback and completed the finalised version of the questionnaire on each item of the original and refined versions of the tool. Lastly, a focus group discussed the findings from the project and potential next steps at an open public engagement event, thus providing the community with an active role in the dissemination of findings.

Long and Clarkson (2017) aimed to gain the perspective of autistic people with learning disabilities on their experiences of support services (for example regarding support for their health and wellbeing, support for communication and involvement, the presence of low stress service environments, etc.). Importantly, participants were given the opportunity to communicate in a way that accommodated communicative differences. By accommodating these communication differences, the authors were able to better understand the autistic participants' experiences of their support services, thus allowing their voices to be heard and changes to be implemented accordingly.

Families

The experiences of autistic individuals and their families are on the rise (Bayat, 2007; Bradford, 2010) and reasons include the increase in individuals being diagnosed with autism. Duchan and Patel (2012) refer to the evolution of the concept of autism and changing criteria for diagnosis, while Fombonne (2002) found a prevalence of 10 per 10,000 for autism. Some researchers have found that sibling cohesion is negatively affected by the presence of children with disabilities in families. Angell et al. (2012) found that autistic children infrequently quarrelled with their siblings, that they enjoyed mutual activities, and that they were friends with their siblings. However, sibling participants focused on their embarrassment or frustration with their siblings' aggressive or socially inappropriate behaviour. Also, sibling participants told the researchers that their parents had taught them some strategies to use to calm or redirect their siblings when needed and that they used positive reinforcement to encourage their siblings to exhibit prosocial behaviour. They also directly taught their siblings new skills that helped them function more effectively in social situations.

Two types of family coping strategies are described in the literature: problem-focused coping strategies and emotion-focused coping strategies. Vernhet et al. (2019) carried out a systematic review and found that parents of an autistic child used more avoidance strategies and less social support-seeking strategies than those of typical children. Furthermore, problem-focused coping protects parental stress and quality of life, while, on the contrary, emotion-focused coping is a risk factor for alteration. Children may also employ coping strategies such as removing themselves from their siblings to defuse potentially conflictual situations. As participants aged, they described their coping strategies with more complexity.

Crowell et al. (2019) focus upon issues such as deficits in social communication and restrictive, repetitive behavioural patterns which emerge early in a child's development. While parents do not cause these difficulties, impairments in social relatedness can strain parent–child interactions and parental stress can have negative transactional effects that impede development. They suggest that parents may not fully accept or understand the disorder; they may be distressed and have

(Continued)

competing demands on their resources, such as other children or jobs. Many may also share some of their children's characteristics. Parents tend to report lower parental self-efficacy or belief in their ability to effectively parent their child. They also tend to have a decreased sense of agency, in assuming that they play a less active role in their child's development, resulting in emotional distress, including guilt, depressive symptoms and feelings of helplessness.

Stress may be a factor in relation to the impact of a diagnosis on the family. One example might be the view that a community may have on their child, when the family are out shopping, or when visiting friends or relatives. One interesting view is that parents may grieve in not having a neurotypical child (Hartmann, 2012) and they are faced with the loss of lifestyle changes and drastic changes in their family dynamics that may be produced from an autism diagnosis. Diagnosis of autism could be perceived as a loss for the family leading to both joy and acceptance on the one hand, but also the fact that their lives might be changed (Hooyman and Kramer, 2006). Siblings also may experience stress such as the embarrassment around peers, alongside concern regarding the future of their brother/sister's autism (Orsmond and Seltzer, 2007).

—————————— Key research in the field ——————————

Cheuk, S. and Lashewicz, B. (2015). How are they doing? Listening as fathers of children with autism spectrum disorder compare themselves to fathers of children who are typically developing. *Autism*, 20 (3), pp. 343–52.

Aim

Although fathers are increasingly hands-on in raising children, research focus on parenting children with autism spectrum disorder continues to be skewed toward experiences of mothers. This research sought to contribute understandings of how fathers of children with autism spectrum disorder perceive themselves to be managing, and to comparisons fathers of children with autism spectrum disorder make between their parenting experiences and experiences of fathers of typically developing children.

Method

A purposive sample of 28 fathers of children (aged 2–13 years) with autism spectrum disorder living in an urban centre in Western Canada participated in in-depth interviews about their parenting successes and challenges.

Results

The study found fathers speak of universal fathering experiences yet articulate their own sense of loss and efforts to come to terms with unanticipated demands associated with autism spectrum disorder. Fathers of children with autism spectrum disorder felt 'pangs of jealousy' toward fathers of typically developing children, yet they were keenly attentive to their own child's development and conveyed a sense of gratitude for their child's capabilities and personality amidst an appreciation for trials and triumphs of fathering in general and fathering a child with autism spectrum disorder.

Conclusions

The authors conclude that the study of fathers builds understandings of fathering within its own right rather than as relative to mothering. They recommend continued study of fathers' needs in terms of support for their own fathering as well as what support they may have to offer other fathers.

The lived experience

In a qualitative meta-synthesis report, DePape and Lindsay (2016) found that when autistic children, adolescents and adults talked about their experiences, four themes emerged: perception of self; interactions with others; experiences at school; and factors related to employment. In the first theme, they found autistic individuals experienced a range of effects associated with their disorder and their identity. Some did not want to understand the implications of their disorder, whereas others struggled with it, especially in adolescence. Interestingly, many adults reported accepting their disorder, such that they could not imagine their life without autism. The second theme saw mixed experiences in their relationship with others. Starting with family, individuals reported they were an important source of social support but acknowledged that their disorder affected family dynamics. Friends were another important component of the lived experience of autistic individuals. Some had friends at school while others reported being teased or bullied by their classmates and many individuals felt different compared with their classmates, with this feeling heightened when teachers provided extra help to them in the classroom.

In the third theme, school and some teachers played a critical role by providing them with much-needed support in the classroom. However, some teachers were perceived as lacking an understanding of autism. Some individuals had issues related to the curriculum, such as problems with time management or feeling bored with the material. Work was an important factor in the lived experience, particularly finding a job that matched their interests and skill sets and some had experienced success in jobs that they were particularly well suited for. However, autistic adults reported unemployment or under-employment, as well as a lack of opportunity for career advancement, and social aspects of a job were also challenging for some.

─────────────────────────── Pause for reflection ───────────────────────────

- What contribution do you think that life stories play in our understanding of the experience of autistic people?
- How could the contributor record such stories and how would you analyse these?

───

Interpretative Phenomenological Analysis (IPA)

One qualitative methodological approach that views participants as the experts of their own personal and social worlds and seeks to establish an equality of voice between the researcher and the researched is Interpretative Phenomenological Analysis (IPA) (Smith et al., 2009). IPA requires researchers to consider the impact of their own experiences, thoughts and preconceptions related to the area under discussion. The focus of IPA studies is on the meanings that individuals attribute towards an experience (Langdridge, 2007). Layers of analysis are introduced as the researcher then reflects on the participants' reflections to illuminate where an ordinary everyday experience becomes an experience of importance.

To construct an understanding of an individual's lived experience, IPA is informed by three key areas of philosophy of knowledge: phenomenology, hermeneutics and idiography. This distinct combination produces a rich and descriptive qualitative analysis, with lived experience as the centre point for a process of sense-making of the phenomena in question (Smith et al., 2009).

Phenomenology is concerned with the study of lived experiences and how individuals understand such experiences. Interest is given to what events, relationships, etc. constitute everyone's lived world. Hermeneutics contributes towards the interpretative phase of this methodology. Hermeneutics further enhances phenomenology by seeking to describe the meaning behind an individual's lived experience. IPA shares the view with hermeneutics that humans endeavour to make sense of their experiences (Willig, 2012).

Smith and Osborn (2003) declare that a sense of self-awareness and self-conscious reflections should be maintained throughout ongoing interpretation of the accounts; this is to ensure that any pre-determined assumptions will be modified as new information is collated. The hermeneutic circle engages with non-linear thinking, which implies that to understand any given part, you look to the whole; to understand the whole, you look to the parts. This focus on generating rich and detailed knowledge of an individual's subjective lived experience demands a small sample size to ensure each case is analytically approached in-depth (Pietkiewicz and Smith, 2012). Different levels of analysis are applied within this interpretative methodology, which allows for points of interest to be highlighted to add to the overall interpretation; these points of interest can also be known as 'gems'. Smith (2011) proposes a spectrum of gems, from the shining gem, which is clearly apparent, to the suggestive gem, which requires some investigation and interpretation, to the secret gem, which requires a great deal of investigation and interpretation.

Examples of autism research involving IPA

Table 2.1 Examples of autism research involving IPA

Dewinter et al. (2017)	How adolescent boys with autism experience their sexuality revealed three major themes relating to (a) how they experience sexual feelings, think about sexuality, and think about themselves as sexual beings; (b) how they perceive messages relating to sexuality in their surroundings; and (c) how they experience finding and having a partner and partnered sex.
Huws and Jones (2015)	Perceptions and social comparisons of autistic young people. Three underlying themes were identified: changes over time, degrees of autism and of ability. When comparing how they perceived themselves now, and how they perceived themselves in the past, the young people viewed themselves more positively in the present and to locate themselves as being in a better position than other autistic individuals.
MacLeod et al. (2018)	They consulted with 16 autistic UK higher education (HE) students about their experiences of success. Participants offered counter-narratives to deficit-based interpretations of autism, giving accounts of making themselves 'extra-visible' as autistic to assert their rights.
Petalas et al. (2012)	Experiences of sibling relationships among adolescents who had a brother with autism yielded six themes: difficulties and negative impact of their brother's condition on themselves and their family; how others' reactions to their brother negatively affected them as siblings; how their histories contextualised their present circumstances; the varying degrees of acceptance and tolerance towards their brothers; positive perceptions and experiences with their brothers; and their thoughts and worries about the future.
Tierney et al. (2016)	Social coping strategies of girls on the autism spectrum. Ten autistic adolescent female participants were interviewed to explore their experiences of managing their social relationships. The results showed that participants were motivated to develop and maintain friendships, but during adolescence this became increasingly difficult. Consequently, they developed explicit strategies to manage these relationships, including masking and imitation.

———————————————— Case study ————————————————

Autism narratives are not just stories or histories, describing a given reality. They are creating the language in which to describe the experience of autism, and hence helping to forge the concepts in which to think about autism (Hacking, 2009). There are several autobiographies written by autistic individuals, including:

(Continued)

Williams, D. (1999). *Nobody Nowhere: The Remarkable Autobiography of an Autistic Girl*. London: Jessica Kingsley.

James, L. (2018). *Odd Girl Out*. Basingstoke: Pan Macmillan.

Robison, J. E. (2007). *Look Me in the Eye: My Life with Asperger's*. New York: Crown Publishers.

Grandin, T. (2006). *Thinking in Pictures*. London: Bloomsbury Publishing.

- Read one of the autobiographies and identify any themes which the author is using to interpret their experiences.
- What interpretations do you bring to the reading?

New research in diagnostics and testing

Autism can be challenging to detect, especially in very young children, and early diagnosis and treatment interventions can lead to better long-term outcomes for autistic people. Miron et al. (2021) researched the importance of 'Prolonged Auditory Brainstem Response in Universal Hearing Screening of Newborns' with autism. Children with autism spectrum disorder have slow brain responses to sounds. They examined these brain responses from newborns' hearing tests and found that those who were later diagnosed with autism also had slower brain responses to sounds.

Clinicaltrials (2022) are currently running the Children's Autism Metabolome Project (CAMP-01) in an aim to identify metabolic signatures in blood plasma and/or urine using a panel of biomarker metabolites that differentiate autistic children from children with delayed development (DD) and/or typical development (TD), to develop an algorithm that maximises sensitivity and specificity of the biomarker profile, and to evaluate the overall algorithm as a diagnostic tool. It also seeks to define metabolites capable of classifying subtypes of autism. Their hope is that, once they identify causative factors, researchers could then develop screening tests for earlier detection and more targeted treatments for symptoms and health conditions related to autism. However, the Autistic Self Advocacy Network (2022) suggest that autism does not need to be cured. Instead of wasting time and money on something that is not possible and that autistic people do not want, we should focus on supporting autistic people to live good lives. Some scientists speculate that gene variants cause autism, while others believe environmental factors, such as exposure to toxins, contribute to this neurotype. Still others theorise imbalances in the intestinal microbiome may be at play.

Current research on genes

Hiramoto et al. (2021) discovered a decrease in the integrity of myelin, a protective sheath surrounding nerve cells in the brain, in mice with a syndromic form of autism. The study showed a gene variant-based malfunction in oligodendrocytes, which are cells that produce myelin. This malfunction may lead to insufficient myelin production in the nerve cells and disrupt nerve communication in the brain, impairing brain development. Creighton et al. (2021) have demonstrated that rare variants in the ANK2 gene, consistently found in individuals with autism spectrum disorder, can alter the architecture and organisation of neurons, potentially contributing to autism and neurodevelopmental comorbidities. Multiple genetic studies have consistently identified rare variants in ANK2 in autistic individuals, making it one of the high-confidence risk genes associated with the condition.

Other avenues of research on autism include investigations into gene variants that could play a role in the development of autism. Satterstrom et al. (2020) analysed the DNA of more than 35,584 people worldwide, including 11,986 autistic individuals and identified variants in 102 risk genes linked with an increased probability of developing autism – 53 of the genes identified were mostly associated with autism and no other developmental condition. The gene variants the scientists identified mainly reside in the cerebral cortex, which is responsible for complex behaviours. These variants may play a role in how the brain neurons connect and help turn other genes on or off – a possible factor that may contribute to autism. The 102 new genes fell primarily into one of two categories. Many play a role in the brain's neural connections and the rest are involved primarily in switching other genes on and off in brain development. Interestingly, they are expressed both in excitatory neurons, which are active in sending signals in the brain, and in inhibitory neurons that squelch such activity. Many of these genes are also commonly expressed in the brain's cerebral cortex, the outermost part of the brain that is responsible for many complex behaviours. Overall, these findings underscore that autism does exist on a spectrum.

The Spectrum 10K study led by Simon Baron-Cohen, director of the Autism Research Centre (ARC) at the University of Cambridge, UK, is a £3 million project which is funded by the London-based biomedical funding charity Wellcome and is the largest genetic study of autism in the United Kingdom. It aims to collect DNA samples, together with information on participants' mental and physical health, from 10,000 autistic people and their families. This will be used to study the genetic and environmental contributions to autism, and to co-occurring conditions such as epilepsy and gut-health problems. However, the study has been voluntarily paused, following criticism that it failed to properly consult the autism community about the goals of the research. Concerns about the study include fears that its data could potentially be misused by other researchers seeking to 'cure' or eradicate autism. To address these misgivings, the Spectrum 10K team is now planning a consultation with hundreds of autistic people and their families and intends to create a representative committee to oversee the project's data-sharing strategy.

Exploring contributing factors

A multiyear study funded by the Centers for Disease Control and Prevention (CDC) is underway to learn more about factors potentially linked to autism. The Study to Explore Early Development (SEED) (CDC, 2021) is currently the largest study in the United States to help identify factors that may put children at risk for autism and other developmental disabilities. Understanding the risk factors that make a person more likely to develop autism will help us learn more about the causes. The research goals for SEED include learning about physical and behavioural characteristics of autistic children, children with other developmental disabilities, and children without a developmental delay or disability and health conditions. For example, researchers have found that exposure to a type of air pollution called particulate matter during an infant's first year also increased the likelihood of the infant later receiving a diagnosis of autism (McGuinn et al., 2020). The conclusion is that there is a positive association between early life air pollution exposure and autism, with a potentially critical window of exposure during the late prenatal and early postnatal period.

Autism and the gut microbiome

The gastrointestinal, or gut, microbiome is another area of interest to researchers looking for factors that contribute to autism. Several studies have established a link between imbalances in the gut biome and autism. There is also growing evidence that balancing the populations of gut microbes can help correct these disparities and improve some of the unwanted symptoms and behaviours linked to autism. Kang et al. (2017) found that microbiota transfer therapy (MTT) in autistic children improved gut microbiota diversity and symptoms associated with autism and that, after the MTT treatment, participants experienced more gut bacterial diversity. Also observed in the participants treated with MTT was a decrease in gastrointestinal (GI) symptoms, as well as improved language, social interaction and behavioural symptoms.

In a follow-up investigation, they found that the participants who received MTT treatment still experienced fewer GI issues and a continued improvement of autism-related symptoms. Buffington et al. (2021) found that mice that lack CNTNAP2, a gene linked to autism, have an unusual population of microbes in their intestines. They also displayed some social behaviours like those seen in some autistic people. When the mice were treated with *Lactobacillus reuteri*, a common bacterium missing from their microbiome, and a strain of gut bacteria commonly found in wild-type mice, their social behaviours improved. However, Yap et al. (2021) argue that if researchers find changes in the gut microbiome of people on the autism spectrum it may be due to 'fussy eating', which is more common among autistic children due to sensory sensitivities or restricted and repetitive interests. Their research found that children with an autism diagnosis tended to be pickier eaters, which led them to have a less-diverse microbiome, which in turn was linked to more-watery stools.

They suggest that behaviour and dietary preferences affect the microbiome, rather than the other way around.

———————————————— Exercise ————————————————

In the journal *Outlook*, Svoboda (2020) poses the question: Could the gut microbiome be linked to autism? Read the article and answer the following questions:

• Who were the first researchers to propose the link between gut microbiome and autism and what were their findings?
• How has current research been undertaken and what are the findings?
• Why might it be a 'muddied outlook'?

The article can be accessed via the Nature website: www.nature.com/articles/d41586-020-00198-y

Polyvagal Theory

The Polyvagal Theory (Porges, 2011) suggests autism is a learnt response to early stressors – the result of a child being in a prolonged state of 'fight or flight' while their nervous system is still developing. The 'high alert vagal symptoms' may explain the many difficulties experienced by autistic individuals and that people on the spectrum have a reduced capacity to engage with the world because they have not learned to process complex social data. As a result, they may continue reading threats in the environment and jump quickly into fight, flight or freeze responses. When the body system is immobilised, it becomes painful or agitated; digestion is difficult, and the focus turns inward compromising the interaction with the outside world. As a result, the natural integration of the social engagement system doesn't take place as it should and subsequently, the child may not learn how to use their system, ending up on 'autopilot'.

In response to stress in utero or at birth or emotional trauma, the vagus is disposed towards immobilisation and the child's nervous system does not get fully developed. The child's system is in a state of distress. The baby misses out on the full integration of all that the social system has to offer and the senses are all offline. Using a case study approach, Muscatello et al. (2021) linked atypical physiological reactivity in autism during relatively benign social situations. They argued that their results demonstrated evidence for reduced parasympathetic functioning, especially in older autistic youth, during a naturalistic interaction with a same-aged peer. As children are confronted with frequent social encounters with peers, the implications for atypical physiological arousal to these daily occurrences are numerous. They concluded that physiological regulation, age and social functioning likely influence stress responses to peer interactions for autistic youth.

———————————————————— Key points ————————————————————

- Alongside the established methods for researching autism, the importance of autistic people as researchers and sources of experience is becoming more recognised
- As well as an understanding of communication and interaction issues in autism, the impact of sensory issues has also been investigated
- Research carried out needs to be open to scrutiny and evidence-based practice arising from it needs to be examined
- New research in diagnostics and testing is shedding new light on autism, such as the importance of genes, contributing factors and gut microbiome, but these are not without controversy
- Unlike the relationship between genes, the brain, and other factors, one interesting theory suggests that autism is a learnt response to early stressors

———————————————————— Questions to consider ————————————————————

- How should researchers collaborate to extend our understanding of autism?
- What do you think are the most important areas in which to research and why?
- What is the likely impact of new research, not only on our understanding of autism but also on autistic individuals, their families and allies?

———————————————————— Further reading ————————————————————

Muscatello, R. A., Vandekar, S. N. and Corbett, B. A. (2021). Evidence for decreased parasympathetic response to a novel peer interaction in older children with autism spectrum disorder: A case-control study. *J Neurodevelop Disord*, 13 (1), 6.

This study supports a growing literature linking atypical physiological reactivity in ASD during relatively benign social situations. The results uniquely demonstrate evidence for reduced para-sympathetic functioning, especially in older youth with ASD, during a naturalistic interaction with a same-aged peer. As children are confronted with frequent social encounters with peers, the implications for atypical physiological arousal to these daily occurrences are numerous. Chronic stress might increase susceptibility to several conditions, including gastrointestinal problems and internalising disorders, and impaired social engagement behaviours may increase social isolation and loneliness thereby increasing the risk for depression or suicidality.

O'Leary, S. and Moloney, M. (2020). Understanding the experiences of young children on the autism spectrum as they navigate the Irish Early Years' education system: Valuing voices in child-centered narratives. *International Journal of Qualitative Methods*, 19, pp. 1–11.

This article focuses upon narrative inquiry as a means of including the voice and experience of young autistic children and their families as they navigate the Irish Early Years' education system (both preschool and primary school). It focuses on the need to acknowledge and appreciate the experiences of these children within their homes and educational settings, their immediate microsystem. Six parents shared stories of navigating the Irish Early Years' education system with their young child on the autism spectrum and their children's voices were incorporated into these narratives using visual storytelling methods.

Tavassoli, T., Miller, L. J., Schoen, S. A., Nielsen, D. M. and Baron-Cohen, S. (2013). Sensory over-responsivity in adults with autism spectrum conditions. *Autism*, 18 (4), pp. 428–32.

Anecdotal reports and empirical evidence suggest that sensory processing issues are a key feature of autism spectrum conditions. This study set out to investigate whether adults with autism spectrum conditions report more sensory over-responsivity than adults without autism spectrum conditions. Another goal of the study was to identify whether autistic traits in adults with and without autism spectrum conditions were associated with sensory over-responsivity. Adults with autism spectrum conditions reported more sensory over-responsivity than control participants across various sensory domains (visual, auditory, tactile, olfactory, gustatory, and proprioceptive). Sensory over-responsivity correlated positively with autistic traits (Autism Spectrum Quotient) at a significant level across groups and within groups. Adults with autism spectrum conditions experience sensory over-responsivity to daily sensory stimuli to a high degree.

References

American Psychiatric Association (2013). *Diagnostic and Statistical Manual of Mental Disorders* (5th edition). Washington, DC: American Psychiatric Publishing.

Angell, M. E., Meadan, H. and Stoner, J. B. (2012). Experiences of siblings of individuals with autism spectrum disorders. *Autism Res Treat*, 949586.

Arnstein, S. R. (1969). A ladder of citizen participation. *J Am Inst Plann*, 35 (4), pp. 216–24.

Autistic Self Advocacy Network (2022). *Clinical trials*. [online] Available at: https://clinicaltrials.gov/ct2/show/NCT02548442 [Accessed 12.03.2022].

Ayres, A. J. (1979). *Sensory Integration and the Child*. Los Angeles, CA: Western Psychological Services.

Ayres, A. J. and Tickle, L. S. (1980). Hyper-responsivity to touch and vestibular stimuli as a predictor of positive response to sensory integration procedures by autistic children. *Am J Occup Ther*, 34 (6), pp. 375–8.

Baranek, G. T. (1999). Autism during infancy: A retrospective video analysis of sensory-motor and social behaviors at 9–12 months of age. *J Autism Dev Disord*, 29 (3), pp. 213–24.

Baranek, G. T. (2002). Efficacy of sensory and motor interventions for children with autism. *J Autism Dev Disord*, 32 (5), pp. 397–422.

Bayat, M. (2007). Evidence of resilience in families of children with autism. *Journal of Intellectual Disability Research*, 51, pp. 702–14.

Bradford, K. (2010). Brief education about autism spectrum disorders for family therapists. *Journal of Family Psychotherapy*, 21(3), pp. 161–79.

Buffington, S. A., Dooling, S. W., Sgritta, M., Noecker, C., Murillo, O. D., Felice, D. F., Turnbaugh, P. J. and Costa-Mattioli, M. (2021). Dissecting the contribution of host genetics and the microbiome in complex behaviors. *Cell*, 184 (7), pp. 1740–56.

Cassidy, S. A., Bradley, L., Cogger-Ward, H. and Rodgers, J. (2021). Development and validation of the suicidal behaviours questionnaire – autism spectrum conditions in a community sample of autistic, possibly autistic and non-autistic adults. *Molecular Autism* 12 (46).

Centers for Disease Control and Prevention (CDC) (2021). *Study to Explore Early Development (SEED)*. [online] Available at: www.cdc.gov/ncbddd/autism/seed.html [Accessed 12.02.2022].

Cheuk, S. and Lashewicz, B. (2015). How are they doing? Listening as fathers of children with autism spectrum disorder compare themselves to fathers of children who are typically developing. *Autism*, 20 (3), pp. 343–52.

Clinicaltrials (2022). *Children's Autism Metabolome Project (CAMP-01)*. [online] Available at: https://clinicaltrials.gov/ct2/show/NCT02548442 [Accessed 12.01.2022].

Cook, B. G., Buysse, V., Klingner, J., Landrum, T., McWilliam, R. A., Tankersley, M. and Test, D. (2015). CEC's standards for classifying the evidence base of practices in special education. *Remedial and Special Education*, 34 (4), pp. 220–34.

Cornwall, A. and Rachel Jewkes, R. (1995). What is participatory research?, *Social Science & Medicine*, 41(12), pp. 1667–1676.

Council for Exceptional Children (2014). Standards for evidence-based practices in Special Education. *Teaching Exceptional Children*, 46 (6), pp. 206–12.

Creighton, B. A., Afriyie, S., Ajit, D., Casingal, C. R., Voos, K. M., Reger, J., Burch, A. M., Dyne, E., Bay, J., Huang, J. K., Anton, E. S., Fu, M. M. and Lorenzo, D. N. (2021). Giant ankyrin-B mediates transduction of axon guidance and collateral branch pruning factor sema 3A. *Elife*.

Crowell, J. A., Keluskar, J. and Gorecki, A. (2019). Parenting behavior and the development of children with autism spectrum disorder. *Compr Psychiatry*, 90, pp. 21–9.

Cusack, J. P. and Sterry, R. (2016). *Your Questions Shaping Future Autism Research*. London: Autistica.

Dawson, G. and Watling, R. (2000). Interventions to facilitate auditory, visual, and motor integration in autism: A review of the evidence. *J Autism Dev Disord*, 30, pp. 415–21.

Dawson, G., Toth, K., Abbott, R., Osterling, J., Munson, J., Estes, A. and Liaw, J. (2004). Early social attention impairments in autism: Social orienting, joint attention, and attention to distress. *Dev Psychol*, 40 (2), pp. 271–83.

DePape, A.-M. and Lindsay, S. (2016). Lived experiences from the perspective of individuals with autism spectrum disorder: A qualitative meta-synthesis. *Focus on Autism and Other Developmental Disabilities*, 31 (1), pp. 60–71.

Dewinter, J., De Graaf, H. and Begeer, S. (2017). Sexual orientation, gender identity, and romantic relationships in adolescents and adults with autism spectrum disorder. *J Autism Dev Disord*, 47, pp. 2927–34.

Duchan, E. and Patel, D. R. (2012). Epidemiology of autism spectrum disorders. *Pediatr Clin North Am*, 59 (1), pp. 27–43.

Dunn, W. and Westman, K. (1997). The sensory profile: The performance of a national sample of children without disabilities. *American Journal of Occupational Therapy*, 51 (1), pp. 25–34.

Fletcher-Watson, S., Adams, J., Brook, K., Charman, T., Crane, L., Cusack, J., Leekam, S., Milton, D., Parr, J. R. and Pellicano, E. (2018). Making the future together: Shaping autism research through meaningful participation. *Autism*, 23 (4), pp. 943–53.

Fletcher-Watson, S. and Happé, F. (2019). *Autism: A new introduction to psychological theory and current debate*. London: Routledge.

Fombonne, E. (2002). Epidemiological trends in rates of autism. *Mol Psychiatry*, 7 (2), pp. 4–6.

Gowen, E., Taylor, R., Bleazard, T., Greenstein, A., Baimbridge, P. and Poole, D. (2019). Guidelines for conducting research studies with the autism community. *Autism Policy Pract*, 2, pp. 29–45.

Grandin, T. (2006). *Thinking in Pictures*. London: Bloomsbury Publishing.

Hacking, I. (2009). Autistic autobiography. *Philosophical Transactions of the Royal Society: Biological Sciences*, 364 (1522), pp. 1467–73.

Hartmann, A. (2012). *Autism and its Impact on Families*. Master of Social Work Clinical Research Papers 35. Available at: https://sophia.stkate.edu/msw_papers/35 [Accessed 24.03.2022]

Hiramoto, T., Sumiyoshi, A., Yamauchi, T., Tanigaki, K., Shi, Q., Kang, G., Ryoke, R., Nonaka, H., Enomoto, S., Izumi, T., Bhat, M. A., Kawashima, R. and Hiroi, N. (2021). Tbx1, a gene encoded in 22q11.2 copy number variant, is a link between alterations in fimbria myelination and cognitive speed in mice. *Molecular Psychiatry*. Advance online publication. https://doi.org/10.1038/s41380-021-01318-4

Hooyman, N. and Kramer, B. (2006). *Living Through Loss: Interventions across the life span*. New York: Columbia University Press.

Huws, J. C. and Jones, R. S. (2015). 'I'm really glad this is developmental': Autism and social comparisons – An interpretative phenomenological analysis. *Autism*, 19 (1), pp. 84–90.

James, L. (2018). *Odd Girl Out*. Basingstoke: Pan Macmillan.

Jones, R. S. P., Quigney, C. and Huws, J. C. (2003). First-hand accounts of sensory perceptual experiences in autism: A qualitative analysis. *Journal of Intellectual and Developmental Disability*, 28 (2), pp. 112–21.

Kang, D. W., Adams, J. B., Gregory, A. C., Borody, T., Chittick, L., Fasano, A., Khoruts, A., Geis, E., Maldonado, J., McDonough-Means, S., Pollard, E. L., Roux, S., Sadowsky, M. J., Lipson, K. S., Sullivan, M. B., Caporaso, J. G. and Krajmalnik-Brown, R. (2017). Microbiota Transfer Therapy alters gut ecosystem and improves gastrointestinal and autism symptoms: An open-label study. *Microbiome*, 5 (1), 10.

Kientz, M. A. and Dunn, W. (1997). A comparison of the performance of children with and without autism on the Sensory Profile. *Am J Occup Ther*, 51 (7), pp. 530–7.

Kilroy, E., Aziz-Zadeh, L. and Cermak. S. (2019). Ayres' theories of autism and sensory integration revisited: What contemporary neuroscience has to say. *Brain Sci*, 9 (3), 68.

Langdridge, D. (2007). *Phenomenological Psychology: Theory, research and method*. Harlow, UK: Pearson.

Long, J. and Clarkson, A. (2017). Towards meaningful participation in research and support practice: Effecting change in autism services. In D. Milton and N. Martin (Eds), *Autism and Intellectual Disability in Adults, Vol. 2*. Hove: Pavilion Publishing, pp. 41–5.

MacLeod, A., Allan, J., Lewis, A. and Robertson, C. (2018). 'Here I come again': The cost of success for higher education students diagnosed with autism. *International Journal of Inclusive Education*, 22 (6), pp. 683–97.

McGuinn, L. A., Windham, G. C., Kalkbrenner, A. E., Bradley, C., Di, Q., Croen, L. A., Fallin, M. D., Hoffman, K., Ladd-Acosta, C., Schwartz, J., Rappold, A. G., Richardson, D. B., Neas, L. M., Gammon, M. D., Schieve, L. A. and Daniels, J. L. (2020). Early life exposure to air pollution and autism spectrum disorder: Findings from a multisite case-control study. *Epidemiology*, 31 (1), pp. 103–14.

Michael, C. (2021). Is being othered a co-occurring condition of autism? *Autism Adulth*, 3 (2), pp. 118–19.

Milton, D. and Bracher, M. (2013). Autistics speak but are they heard? *Medical Sociology online*, 7 (2), pp. 61–9.

Miron, O., Delgado, R. E., Delgado, C. F., Simpson, E. A., Yu, K. H. and Gutierrez, A., et al. (2021). Prolonged auditory brainstem response in universal hearing screening of newborns with autism spectrum disorder. *Autism Res*, 14, pp. 46–52.

Muscatello, R. A, Vandekar, S. N and Corbett, B. A. (2021). Evidence for decreased para-sympathetic response to a novel peer interaction in older children with autism spectrum disorder: A case-control study. *J Neurodev Disord*, 13 (1), 6.

Nicolaidis, C., Raymaker, D., Kapp, S. K., Baggs, A., Ashkenazy, E., McDonald, K., Weiner, M., Maslak. J., Hunter, M. and Joyce, A. (2019). The AASPIRE practice-based guidelines for the inclusion of autistic adults in research as co-researchers and study participants. *Autism*, 23 (8), pp. 2007–19.

O'Neill, M. and Jones, R. S. (1997). Sensory-perceptual abnormalities in autism: A case for more research? *J Autism Dev Disord*, 27 (3), pp. 283–93.

Ornitz, E. M. (1969). Disorders of perception common to early infantile autism and schizophrenia. *Comprehensive Psychiatry*, 10 (4), pp. 259–74.

Orsmond, G. I. and Seltzer, M. M. (2007). Siblings of individuals with autism spectrum disorders across the life course. *Ment Retard Dev Disabil Res Rev*, 3 (4), pp. 313–20.

Pavlopoulou, G., Wood, R. and Papadopoulos, C. (2020). *Impact of Covid-19 on the experiences of parents and family carers of autistic children and young people in the UK*. UCL Research Briefing.

Pellicano, E. and Stears, M. (2011). Bridging autism, science and society: Moving towards an ethically informed approach to autism research. *Autism Res*, 4 (4), pp. 271–82.

Petalas, M. A., Hastings, R. P., Nash, S., Reilly, D. and Dowey, A. (2012). The perceptions and experiences of adolescent siblings who have a brother with autism spectrum disorder. *J Intellect Dev Disabil*, 37 (4), pp. 303–14.

Pfeiffer, B. A., Koenig, K., Kinnealey, M., Sheppard, M. and Henderson, L. (2011). Effectiveness of sensory integration interventions in children with autism spectrum disorders: A pilot study. *Am J Occup Ther*, 65 (1), pp. 76–85.

Pickard, H., Pellicano, E., den Houting, J. and Crane, L. (2021). Participatory autism research: Early career and established researchers' views and experiences. *Autism*, 23, pp. 477–93.

Pietkiewicz, I. and Smith, J. A. (2012). A practical guide to using interpretative phenomenological analysis in qualitative research psychology. *Psychological Journal*, 20 (1), pp. 7–14.

Porges, S. W. (2007). The polyvagal perspective. *Biological Psychology*, 74, pp. 116–43.

Porges, S. W. (2011). *The Polyvagal Theory: Neurophysiological foundations of emotions, attachment, communication, and self-regulation*. New York: W. W. Norton.

Redman, S., Greenhalgh, T., Adedokun, L., Staniszewska, S., Denegri, S. and Co-production of Knowledge Collection Steering Committee (2021). Co-production of knowledge: The future. *BMJ*, 372: n434.

Robison, J. E. (2007). *Look Me in the Eye: My life with Asperger's*. New York: Crown Publishers.

Rogers, S. J., Hepburn, S. L., Stackhouse, T. and Wehner, E. (2003). Imitation performance in toddlers with autism and those with other developmental disorders. *J Child Psychol Psychiatry*, 44 (5), pp. 763–81.

Satterstrom, F. K., Kosmicki, J. A., Wang, J., Breen, M. S., De Rubeis, S., An, J. Y., Peng, M., Collins, R., Grove, J., Klei, L., Stevens, C., Reichert, J., Mulhern, M. S., Artomov, M., Gerges, S., Sheppard, B., Xu, X., Bhaduri, A., Norman, U., Brand, H., Schwartz, G., Nguyen, R., Guerrero, E. E., Dias, C.; Autism Sequencing Consortium; iPSYCH-Broad Consortium, Betancur, C., Cook, E. H., Gallagher, L., Gill, M., Sutcliffe, J. S., Thurm, A., Zwick, M. E., Børglum, A. D., State, M. W., Cicek, A. E., Talkowski, M. E., Cutler, D. J., Devlin, B., Sanders, S. J., Roeder, K., Daly, M. J. and Buxbaum, J. D. (2020).

Large-scale exome sequencing study implicates both developmental and functional changes in the neurobiology of autism. *Cell*, 180 (3), pp. 568–84.

Schoen, S. A., Lane, S. J., Mailloux, Z., May-Benson, T., Parham, L. D., Smith Roley, S. and Schaaf, R. C. (2019). A systematic review of ayres sensory integration intervention for children with autism. *Autism Res*, 12 (1), pp. 6–19.

Sigman, M. and Capps, L. (1997). *Children with Autism: A developmental perspective*. Cambridge, MA: Harvard University Press.

Smith, J. A. (2011). Evaluating the contribution of interpretive phenomenological analysis. *Health Psychology Review*, 5, pp. 9–27.

Smith, J. A. and Osborn, M. (2003). Interpretative phenomenological analysis. In J. A. Smith (Ed.), *Qualitative Psychology: A practical guide to research methods*. London: SAGE Publications, pp. 51–80.

Smith, J. A., Flowers, P. and Larkin, M. (2009). *Interpretative Phenomenological Analysis: Theory, method and research*. London: SAGE Publications.

Tierney, S., Burns, J. and Kilbey, E. (2016). Looking behind the mask: Social coping strategies of girls on the autistic spectrum. *Research in Autism Spectrum Disorders*, 23, pp. 73–83.

Tritter, J. Q. and McCallum, A. (2006). The snakes and ladders of user involvement: Moving beyond Arnstein. *Health Policy*, 76 (2), pp. 156–68.

Vernhet, C., Dellapiazza, F., Blanc, N., Cousson-Gelie, F., Miot, S., Roeyers, H. and Baghdadli, A. (2019). Coping strategies of parents of children with autism spectrum disorder: A systematic review. *European Child and Adolescent Psychiatry*, 28 (6), pp. 747–58.

Watling, R. L. and Dietz, J. (2007). Immediate effect of Ayres's sensory integration-based occupational therapy intervention on children with autism spectrum disorders. *Am J Occup Ther*, 61 (5), pp. 574–83.

Williams, D. (1999). *Nobody Nowhere: The remarkable autobiography of an autistic girl*. London: Jessica Kingsley.

Willig, C. (2012). Perspectives on the epistemological bases for qualitative research. In H. Cooper, P. M. Camic, D. L. Long, A. T. Panter, D. Rindskopf and K. J. Sher (Eds), *APA Handbook of Research Methods in Psychology, Vol. 1. Foundations, planning, measures, and psychometrics*. Washington, DC: American Psychological Association, pp. 5–21.

Wong, C., Odom, S. L., Hume, K. A., Cox, A. W., Fettig, A., Kucharczyk, S., Brock, M. E., Plavnick, J. B., Fleury, V. P. and Schultz, T. R. (2015). Evidence-based practices for children, youth, and young adults with autism spectrum disorder: A comprehensive review. *J Autism Dev Disord*, 45 (7), pp. 1951–66.

Woods, R. and Waltz, M. (2019). The strength of autistic expertise and its implications for autism knowledge production: A response to Damian Milton. *Autonomy, the Critical Journal of Interdisciplinary Autism Studies*, 1 (6).

Yap, C. X., Henders, A. K., Alvares, G. A., David, L. A., Wood, D. L. A., Krause, L., Tyson, G. W., Restuadi, R., Wallace, L., McLaren, T., Hansell, N. K., Cleary, R. D., Grove, R., Hafekost, C., Harun, A., Holdsworth, H., Jellett, R., Khan, F., Lawson, L. P., Leslie, J., Mira Levis Frenk, A., Masi, A., Nisha, E., Mathew, N. E., Muniandy, M., Nothard, M., Miller, J. L., Nunn, L., Holtmann, G., Strike, L. T., de Zubicaray, G. I., Thompson, P. M., McMahon, K. L., Wright, M. J., Visscher, P. M., Dawson, P. A., Dissanayake, C. V., Eapen, A., Heussler, H. S., McRae, A. F., Whitehouse, A. J. O., Wray, N. R. and Gratten, J. (2021). Autism-related dietary preferences mediate autism-gut microbiome associations. *Cell*, 184 (24), pp. 5916–31.

THREE

Issues and debates surrounding autism

Introduction

There are many contemporary issues and debates within the field of autism which have an impact on the standing of and educational implications for practitioners working with individuals and their families. Many are well documented, including the debate surrounding vaccination and the impact on autism, others are less so. This chapter addresses three of these:

- Parents seeking a cure for their child's autism look for treatments and interventions.
- Why are more boys diagnosed with autism than girls?
- What is the experience of autism being diagnosed in adulthood?

———————————————— Learning objectives ————————————————

This chapter will:

- Invite you to consider the reasons why there is a gender difference in autism
- Invite you to evaluate the merits of two therapies designed to 'cure' some of the characteristics associated with autism
- Introduce you to the role of camouflaging in relation to gender differences in the diagnosis of autism
- Help you to consider the impact of adult diagnosis of autism

———————————————— Key terms ————————————————

Hyperbaric oxygen therapy, CEASE therapy, autism and gender, extreme male brain theory, camouflaging, adult diagnosis of autism

---
Pause for reflection

- Why do you think there are so many debates surrounding this area of need?
- Who contributes to the discourses surrounding these debates?
- Can you think of any myths that are still perpetuated in relation to autism?

Exploring the explicit goals of a cure

The Westminster Commission for Autism (2018) found that autistic people had been offered treatments such as crystal therapy, ear candles, vitamins, spiritual intervention, aromatherapy, chelation, juice plus diet, hyperbaric oxygen therapy, exorcism, stem-cell transplants, exposure therapy (including slapping), rerum, acupuncture, DAN (defeat autism now) therapy, MMS (bleach), turpentine and many more. Recent media reports also highlight examples of people selling, promoting, and using harmful interventions for autism. The Commission recommended the following guiding principles:

1 The intervention is based on a good understanding of autism.
2 The people who deliver the intervention know the person well and respect their feelings and views.
3 The person's capacity for consent is considered.
4 The intervention is adapted to the needs of the person receiving it.
5 The intervention is based on a theory that is logical and scientifically feasible.
6 Research evidence shows the intervention can work for people on the autism spectrum.
7 The intervention works in the real world, not just in a research laboratory.
8 The intervention is delivered by, or supported by, appropriately qualified and experienced professionals.
9 The people delivering the intervention follow established guidance.
10 The intervention is carefully monitored and reviewed on a regular basis.
11 The intervention provides significant benefits.
12 The intervention does not cause significant physical or emotional harm.
13 The benefits outweigh any costs (including risks).
14 The intervention is good value for the money and time invested.

In the next section, we examine two controversial and debated therapies associated with attempting to 'cure' autistic characteristics.

Hyperbaric oxygen therapy

Traditionally, hyperbaric oxygen treatment (HBOT) is indicated in several clinical disorders include decompression sickness, healing of problem wounds and arterial gas embolism. However, some investigators (Rossignol et al., 2012) have used HBOT to 'treat' autistic individuals, suggesting that several autistic individuals possess certain physiological abnormalities that HBOT might ameliorate, including cerebral hypoperfusion, inflammation, mitochondrial dysfunction, and oxidative stress. Rossignol and Frye (2011) argue that evidence from many fields of medicine has documented multiple non-CNS physiological abnormalities associated with autism, suggesting that, in some individuals, autism arises from systemic, rather than organ-specific, abnormalities. Specifically, in recent decades, research and clinical studies in autism have implicated physiological and metabolic systems that transcend specific organ dysfunction, such as cerebral hypoperfusion, immune dysregulation, inflammation, oxidative stress, and mitochondrial dysfunction (Ming et al., 2008).

Herbert (2005) suggests that autism may arise from, or at least involve, systemic physiological abnormalities rather than being a purely CNS disorder, at least in a subset of autistic individuals. She believes that these physiological problems may cause many of the other problems found in people on the autism spectrum, such as poor eye contact, poor socialisation, and lack of attention. Herbert also thinks that hyperbaric therapy can be used to reduce or overcome the underlying physiological problems and that this can lead to a reduction in the behavioural problems. It has become increasingly common for parents of children with autism to supplement behaviour analytic interventions with therapies that have not yet been subjected to adequate scientific scrutiny and controlled evaluations of unproven therapies can be challenging (Lerman et al., 2008).

There are approximately 75 organisations providing hyperbaric therapy in the UK. These include NHS hospitals, Multiple Sclerosis National Therapy Centres as well as various organisations affiliated to the British Hyperbaric Association (2021). As you would expect in the debate surrounding therapies and autism, there is conflicting research evidence. On the one hand, Bent et al. (2012) sought to determine whether HBOT leads to parental-reported behavioural changes and alterations in cytokines in autistic children. Ten children completed 80 sessions of HBOT and all improved by 2 points on the clinician-rated CGI-I scale (much improved) as well as several parent-completed measures of behaviour. Chungpaibulpatana et al. (2008) reported 75 per cent of children showed improvement while 25 per cent did not seem to respond to the treatment. Other research points to inconsistent effects, suggesting that there were no benefits. Rossignol et al. (2012) concluded many of the reviewed studies suffered from limitations, including the lack of control children, an open-label design, a small number of participants, a retrospective design, and the use of parent-rated scales. None of the studies reported measurements of the long-term effects of HBOT beyond the study period, so it is not known if any of the reported improvements were long lasting.

Several studies on the use of HBOT in autistic children and young people are currently underway and early results are promising. Xiong et al. (2016) argue that to date, there is no evidence that hyperbaric oxygen therapy improves core symptoms and associated symptoms of autism It is important to note that adverse effects (minor-grade ear barotrauma events) can occur. Given the absence of evidence of effectiveness and the limited biological plausibility and possible adverse effects, the need for future randomised control trials (RCTs) of hyperbaric oxygen therapy must be carefully considered. There is currently sufficient research evidence to suggest that hyperbaric therapy is ineffective as an intervention for individuals on the autism spectrum (Podgórska-Bednarz and Perenc, 2021). NICE (2013) go further in stating that hyperbaric oxygen therapy should not be used to manage autism in any context in children and young people. Jepson et al. (2011) examined the effects of a full 40 hours of HBOT on directly observed behaviour across a total of 16 participants with autism spectrum disorders and found no consistent effects across any group or within any individual participant, demonstrating that HBOT was not an effective treatment for the participants in this study.

CEASE therapy

The Complete Elimination of Autistic Spectrum Expression (CEASE) therapy was developed by Dr Tinus Smits (1946–2010) in the Netherlands. Smits had practised as a non-medically trained homeopath for many years before he studied medicine. He then developed his own ideas about autism and wrote several books about his theory. Smits never published a single scientific paper in the peer-reviewed literature and, as a homeopath, he believed that 'like cures like' – a substance that causes symptoms in a healthy person can be used to cure these symptoms when they occur in a patient. Smits thus claimed that autism must be cured by ingesting homeopathic doses of the substances which allegedly caused the condition. Step by step, all assumed causative factors including vaccines, conventional medication, environmental toxins, etc. are 'detoxified' with homoeopathically prepared remedies made from all the substances that were administered prior to the onset of autism. The therapy itself consists of alternative medicine remedies and high amounts of dietary supplements such as vitamin C or zinc. Children are given 200 times more vitamin C as well as four to five times more zinc compared to the standard set by the Department of Health.

There are numerous and obvious problems with CEASE therapy. Ernst (2018) argues that the problem with this therapy is that it flies in the face of science. There is no reason to believe that autism is caused by the exposure to toxins. In fact, CEASE turns out to be a layered monster of bogus assumption. The first layer is a false theory of the pathogenesis of autism; the second is the 'like cures like' myth of homeopathy; the third is the notion that 'potentisation' (dilution) renders substances not less but more potent; the fourth is the nonsensical concept of detoxification. The notion that one can 'detox' the body in the suggested fashion is not in line with our current knowledge of physiology and there is no evidence that the CEASE therapy might cure autism or any other condition. The Professional Standards Authority (PSA) for Health and Social Care (2020) stated that advertising or undertaking CEASE therapy or putting across anti-vaccination messages posed a risk to public health. Blakely (2020) writes in *The Times* that the PSA renewed its accreditation despite a plea from the NHS that it be revoked. The NHS imposed several conditions, including that any member of the society stop offering CEASE therapy, a supposed cure for autism that relies on the idea that it is caused by vaccinations.

───────────────── Exercise ─────────────────

The CEASE Therapy website can be accessed online at: www.cease-therapy.com/

- What steps are involved in the treatment?
- What evidence does the website cite for the success of CEASE?
- How do the case studies support their point of view?

Gender issues and autism: Male bias research?

For decades, autism has been considered a predominantly male disorder. Previously, the gender ratio was considered among researchers as 4:1 (Fombonne, 2009; Werling and Geschwind, 2013). However, contemporary investigation into this male bias brings the ratio to between 3:1 and 2:1 (Smith, 2019). What factors may be involved in these differences?

───────────── Pause for reflection ─────────────

Before you read the next section, why do you think that the number of females with an autism diagnosis is much lower than in males? Can you think of at least two reasons why the ratio is changing?

Diagnosis

There is growing evidence that the number of girls and women with the condition may have been vastly underestimated. The prevalence of autism is considerably higher in males than females, especially in individuals with a higher IQ (Werling and Geschwind, 2013). According to the most recent report from the United States Centers for Disease Control and Prevention, one in 38 boys and one in 152 girls aged eight years were diagnosed with autism (Baio et al., 2018). The same report revealed that, although the average prevalence of males to females with a diagnosis is 4:1, a significantly higher proportion of autistic males have average or above average IQ as compared to females. Given the noted gender imbalance, there is a distinct possibility that the typical presentation of autism is biased towards males (Kirkovski et al., 2013). Females may need to exhibit a greater number of or more intense symptoms to receive a diagnosis given that many diagnostic tools were originally tested with male participants (Kreiser and White, 2014). A suggestion is the view that females are currently being misdiagnosed or not diagnosed at all due to the male bias assessment methods and that females mask the deficit in social development and communication (Kirkovski et al., 2013). As the DSM-5 currently requires an autistic child to present characteristics from all areas of the dyad of impairments, including social communication aspects, this could be suggested as the cause for the higher prevalence of males than females. Recent research, based on active screening rather than clinical or school records, found a ratio of 3:1. Fletcher-Watson and Happé (2019) believe this could fall further – potentially to as low as 2:1 – as the diagnostic process becomes better tailored to identifying autism in girls and women.

Interestingly, Hull and Mandy (2017) discuss further implications of a missed diagnosis in autistic females such as developing a mental health disorder. It is suggested that there are three disorders which if diagnosed with, should also be assessed for high-functioning autism. The three disorders are Anorexia Nervosa (AN), anxiety and Gender Dysphoria. Hull and Mandy (2017) report, unlike autism, AN is predominantly diagnosed among females, which could suggest that the missed diagnosis of autism within females could effectively be diagnosed as AN, having shared traits such as the inability to regulate emotions and repetitive behaviours.

Camouflaging

Research indicates that females camouflage autistic symptoms more than males, potentially contributing to the difference in prevalence. Schuck et al. (2019) found camouflaging was found to be more common in autistic females, and not associated to social phobia. Furthermore, camouflaging correlated negatively with emotional expressivity in females, but not males. Young et al. (2018) suggest that autistic females in primary schools have the same social deficit as boys but they mask their social deficit and often mimic peer behaviours due to the female's desire for social communication and interaction being greater than autistic males. Parish-Morris et al. (2017) relate the female ability to mask the social communication and interaction deficit to 'linguistic camouflage' in the form of conversation pauses.

They showed that females were more likely to use the 'Um' expression during conversation pauses than males, enabling the speaker to hold the conversation for longer than otherwise. It is thought that females mimicking peers in how they fill a conversation pause enables them to hold a longer conversation, thus having them appear to have no social communication deficit at all. The gender difference in camouflaging may be due at least in part to the societal pressures and expectations that females face to conform to gender roles (Kreiser and White, 2014; Young et al., 2018). Autistic females may face more stigma and rebuke for exhibiting characteristics that are stereotypically more male, such as being disruptive or less empathic (Goldman, 2013). Thus, symptoms might be more difficult to detect in females and, consequently, a significant portion of females may be misdiagnosed, diagnosed after a significant delay, or not diagnosed at all, resulting in lack of treatment and support.

Camouflaging can take the form of blending and masking strategies, allowing social interactions with their, often typically developing, peer group. These methods have allowed females to conceal their social anxiety to a reasonable extent and adopt and copy similar social traits to typical learners (Smith, 2019). Rowe (2013) describes through her personal experience of living with Asperger's, the use of camouflaging as the normal mask and although camouflaging techniques have been observed in both sexes, it appears to be more commonly used among females with ASD (Parish-Morris et al., 2017; Rowe, 2013). Methods of camouflaging are varied among individuals, and develop through exposure, age and time; some may force eye contact, suppress behaviours that deviate from the social norm, remove themselves from environments they consider a sensory overload and display false emotion, all to conceal a more socially undesirable presentation (Hull and Mandy, 2017; Hull et al., 2019).

Although the camouflaging techniques adopted by autistic individuals can result in a social benefit, in comparison, the long-term impacts of disguising the characteristics could be detrimental for development. If females appear to be socially competent and intellectual at a young age the likelihood of identification is lower, as social deficits play a huge role in the diagnostics of autism, and females who cover specific traits with confidence could go under the typical diagnostic radar (Hull et al., 2019). This newer knowledge could provide some explanation for the previous male diagnostic bias. Furthermore, there is sufficient evidence to suggest that disguising autistic symptoms can result in mental health problems, increased stress, anxiety and depression (Hull et al, 2019). Again, this can stem from a lack of required support, stunting development and from suppression of true self (Cage and Troxell-Whitman, 2019).

Extreme Male Brain Theory

It is believed by Baron-Cohen et al. (2011) that the cause for male vulnerability to autism is due to Extreme Male Brain (EMB) theory. Wen and Wen (2014) explain EMB to be a result of parental exposure to high levels of testosterone which impacts the functional development of an unborn child. It is further suggested that the exposure of high levels of Androgen Receptors (AR) during foetal development create 'masculine behavioural' traits within a child. Wen and Wen (2014) describe 'masculine behavioural' traits to be linked to higher ability and interest within systemising and limited cognitive empathy, traits which are also more associated with the general male population rather than females. They report that autistic individuals have a deficit within cognitive empathy development suggesting the exposure to testosterone levels, regardless of a child's gender, is a cause of autism.

Greenberg et al. (2018) further support the EMB theory and conducted a study involving 670,000 participants, including 36,648 autistic individuals. The results showed that 40.23 per cent of neurotypical males compared to 25.58 per cent neurotypical females were considered as systemisers, leaning towards the masculine stereotyping.

These results could support the stereotypical assumptions that males are inheritably more inclined to systemise rather than empathise and that EMB theory accounts for the difference of gender prevalence rates. However, Krahn and Fenton (2012) argue that Baron-Cohen's (2002) EMB hypothesis is heavily based upon stereotypical assumptions, for example that males are more inclined to engage in aggressive behaviours while females are more nurturing. They argue that extreme male brain theory does not consider sociological perspectives on gender. Associating empathising with females and systemising with males adds to the view that autism is fundamentally masculine and, therefore, boys are more likely to be diagnosed with the condition and this could have an impact on the support and provision available for girls.

Case study

Janet is aged 13. She enjoys school but has difficulty if routine changes and finds transitions between lessons difficult. Although quiet and shy, she does not ask for help, or becomes avoidant, to mask difficulty in her understanding. Socially, she mirrors the behaviours of her peers, but also tries to control them by using scripted responses. Emotionally, she camouflages emotions or masks her autistic characteristics. This constant social imitation and mirroring leaves her exhausted, unable to take part in lessons, becoming anxious and shutting down in a corner and crying.

- Research what support a teacher or support a member of staff could offer to Janet and her parents, in respect to learning, emotions and social skills.

Key research in the field

Milner, V., McIntosh, H., Colvert, E. and Happé, F. (2019). A qualitative exploration of the female experience of autism spectrum disorder (ASD). *J Autism Dev Disord*, 49 (6), pp. 2389–402.

Objective

A qualitative study which explored female presentation and experience of autism spectrum disorder. This study aimed to gather information from a range of perspectives, both diagnosed and self-diagnosed reports before, during and after diagnosis, as well as positive aspects of an autism diagnosis from both autistic females and parents of autistic females.

Method

Participants were 18 females with a clinical diagnosis of autism (n = 16) or self-diagnosed autism (n = 2), and four mothers of autistic girls recruited via four routes: adverts on social media, word of mouth, through contacts at a secondary school and through a tertiary referral autism diagnostic clinic. Participants were invited to attend group discussions at the research centre, but when this was inconvenient for the participant, in-home individual discussions and/or telephone discussions were offered.

Both group and individual discussions were offered using a topic guide covering three overarching themes: diagnostic pathway, impact of autism, and resilience and coping. All discussions were audio recorded and transcribed verbatim, using thematic analysis to identify themes in the data.

Findings

Five themes were identified: fitting in with the norm, potential obstacles for autistic women and girls, negative aspects of autism, the perspective of others, and positive aspects of having autism. The women and girls in this study reported adopting strategies to mask and camouflage their autistic behaviours. Evidence from the discussions supported the premise that autistic females struggle to initiate and maintain relationships and resolve conflicts within friendships. There was a general lack of understanding about female autism symptomology, including camouflaging behaviour and interest in social relationships, which was suspected to lead to many women receiving a late or delayed diagnosis. Despite a largely negative view towards their experiences of autism, an encouraging finding is that the females identified several positive aspects of being autistic.

Conclusion

By capturing qualitative accounts of the female experiences of autism, the hope was to contribute to a greater understanding of the obstacles and challenges faced by women and girls at various stages of having an autism diagnosis. The reporting of several positive aspects of autism, often underreported in the literature, was an interesting conclusion.

The experience of autism being diagnosed in adulthood

Geurts and Jansen (2012) found that the most common initial reasons for autistic adults to seek help were social problems, mood disturbance and anxious feelings. Receiving a diagnosis of autism has a huge impact on the life of an individual and those close to them (Midence and O'Neill, 1999; Punshon et al., 2009) and a positive diagnostic experience can influence reactions to the news and subsequent coping strategies (Hasnat and Graves, 2000). Among adults, strong post-diagnostic support has been shown to improve quality of life (Renty and Roeyers, 2006), reduce levels of anxiety and depression (National Autistic Society, 2008) and decrease the use of high-cost acute hospital services (National Audit Office, 2009). Delayed diagnosis into adulthood is common, and self-diagnosis is a growing phenomenon. Fear of not being believed by professionals was identified as the most frequently occurring and most severe barrier (Lewis, 2017). Adults who receive a diagnosis may already be experiencing social problems, anxiety and mood disturbances (Bishop-Fitzpatrick et al., 2018), without any focus upon autism. Additionally, adults face isolation and poor employment prospects (Howlin and Moss, 2012).

Camm-Crosbie et al. (2019) found that autistic people are at high risk of mental health problems, self-injury and suicidality. They conducted an online survey to explore autistic people's experiences of treatment and support for these difficulties, including mental health problems, self-injury and suicidality. Three underlying themes were identified: difficulties in accessing treatment and support; lack of understanding and knowledge of autistic people with co-occurring mental health difficulties; and appropriate treatment and support, or lack of, impacted autistic people's wellbeing and likelihood of seeing suicide as their future. Research by Murphy et al. (2016) concluded that health services research for autistic adults is urgently warranted. Research was required to better understand the needs of autistic adults, including health, aging, service development, transition, treatment options across the lifespan, sex, and the views of autistic people.

Stagg and Belcher (2019) interviewed nine adults over the age of 50, who had recently been diagnosed with autism. Results of a thematic analysis showed that the participants had received treatment for anxiety and depression. They also reported autistic behaviours in their childhood and growing up they felt isolated and alien and that receiving a diagnosis was seen as a positive step and allowed for a recon-figuration of self and an appreciation of individual needs. The participants all appeared to have had characteristic symptoms of autism as children, such as exhib-iting repetitive behaviours and experiencing social isolation. Many were pushed to seek a diagnosis, albeit late, after concerns over social functioning and relationships became 'untenable'. Diagnosis came with a combination of emotions, including feel-ings of vindication and overall clarity. Post-diagnosis, participants said they had better self-awareness, and were more readily able to take control of their lives and address previously difficult situations. While participants reported greater self-awareness after their diagnosis, the study also suggests that professional help should immediately follow a diagnosis to help the patient best cope.

Taylor's (1983) cognitive adaptation model suggests that individuals faced with life-changing information need to re-evaluate their sense of self and their possible futures. This re-evaluation involves three mechanisms: meaning making; taking con-trol; and self-esteem building. The model suggests that individuals need to examine the causes of the life-changing event and consider how this change alters their cur-rent meaning system. They need to re-evaluate and gain control over their current circumstances and build self-esteem (Stagg and Belcher, 2019) and comparing one-self to others undergoing the same situation is helpful in this respect.

Crane et al. (2018) researched aspects of the diagnostic process that are working well, and areas in which improvements are needed. Using thematic analysis, three key themes were identified: the process of understanding and accepting autism; multiple barriers to satisfaction with the diagnostic process; and inadequate post-diagnostic support provision. Lewis (2017) found that delayed diagnosis into adulthood is common, and self-diagnosis is a growing phenomenon. Analysing the data from individuals who were self-diagnosed or formally diagnosed, fear of not being believed by professionals was identified as the most frequently occurring and most severe barrier. Interestingly, Portway and Johnson (2005) found that young adults who were believed to have Asperger syndrome subjectively felt different and perceived themselves to be different from the norm but did not exhibit outward difficulties enough to be recognised, diagnosed, or supported through intervention. This othering is an important point in that without a label to help them to understand their behaviour, it could lead to misunderstanding others and being misunderstood, bullying, isolation, loneliness and few close, confiding friendships. NICE (2016) has released guidance specifically to help practitioners identify the signs of autism in adults and suggests to consider assessment for possible autism when a person has one or more of the following:

- persistent difficulties in social interaction;
- persistent difficulties in social communication;
- stereotypic (rigid and repetitive) behaviours, resistance to change or restricted interests.

And one or more of the following:

- problems in obtaining or sustaining employment or education;
- difficulties in initiating or sustaining social relationships;
- previous or current contact with mental health or learning disability services;
- a history of a neurodevelopmental condition (including learning disabilities and attention deficit hyperactivity disorder) or mental disorder.

—————————————— Pause for reflection ——————————————
- How might some of the characteristics be identified or measured?
- How do these characteristics compare to the signs of autism in children?

Bargiela et al. (2016) investigated the female autism phenotype and its impact upon the under-recognition of autism spectrum conditions (ASC) in girls and women. Fourteen women with ASC (aged 22–30 years) diagnosed in late adolescence or adulthood gave in-depth accounts of: 'pretending to be normal'; of how their gender led various professionals to miss their ASC; and of conflicts between ASC and a traditional feminine identity. Experiences of sexual abuse were widespread in this sample, partially reflecting specific vulnerabilities from being a female with undiagnosed ASC.

Leedham et al. (2020) found that females often receive autism spectrum condition diagnoses later than males, leaving needs misunderstood. Eleven autistic females diagnosed over the age of 40 years completed semi-structured interviews, analysed using Interpretative Phenomenological Analysis. Four superordinate themes emerged:

- A hidden condition (pretending to be normal and fitting in; mental health and mislabelling).
- The process of acceptance (initial reactions and search for understanding; re-living life through a new lens).
- The impact of others post-diagnosis (initial reactions; stereotyped assumptions).
- A new identity on the autism spectrum (negotiating relationships, connections, and community; changing wellbeing and views of the self; the meaning of diagnosis).

Findings highlighted several factors not previously identified that affect late diagnosis in females, including widespread limited understanding of others. Diagnosis was experienced by several participants as facilitating transition from being self-critical to self-compassionate, coupled with an increased sense of agency. Participants experienced a change in identity that enabled greater acceptance and understanding of the self. However, this was painful to adjust to at such a late stage.

Case study

For most of his life, Stephen struggled to fit in. Although he was good with words and conversations which he felt in charge of, he had few friends and lacked empathy and social skills. Throughout school he felt increasingly depressed and although he performed well in coursework and exams, he felt isolated from his peers.

Now aged 21, he left school with high grades in his GCSEs and A levels but felt that he would struggle at university and decided to apply for an Apprenticeship. In the first few months, he is finding the work rewarding if he is focused upon the task. However, he still struggles with relationships with both peers and clients, finds it difficult to join in, cannot read people's emotions and show empathy. 'I have had enough, I thought work would be different to school.'

He is thinking of seeking help and support for a diagnosis.

- What advice would you give to both Stephen and his employer about the merits and issues surrounding diagnosing autism as an adult?

—————————————— Key points ——————————————

- There are many therapies and treatments which pertain to 'cure' the characteristics associated with autism
- Many of these are regarded as unethical and lacking in research evidence to support their claims
- There are several reasons which could explain the difference in diagnosis of autism in relation to girls and boys
- Social camouflaging has been researched in relation to these differences
- There are several reasons as to why adults may seek a diagnosis of autism, and this may have an impact upon their life experience

—————————————— Questions to consider ——————————————

- What other reasons may there be behind the gender differences in autism?
- Do you think that there needs to be more scrutiny of interventions such as diet and food additives in relation to autism?
- What do you think may be the longer-term social, educational and employment consequences of the issues discussed in this chapter on the life of an adult on the autism spectrum?

—————————————— Further reading ——————————————

Hendrix, S. (2015). *Women and Girls with Autism Spectrum Disorder: Understanding life experiences from early childhood to old age.* London: Jessica Kingsley Publishers.

The difference that being female makes to the diagnosis, life and experiences of a person with an Autism Spectrum Disorder (ASD) has largely gone unresearched and unreported until recently. In this book, Hendrix has collected both academic research and personal stories about girls and women on the autism spectrum to present a picture of their feelings, thoughts and experiences at each stage of their lives. Outlining how autism presents differently and can hide itself in females and what the likely impact will be for them throughout their lifespan, the book looks at how females with ASD experience diagnosis, childhood, education, adolescence, friendships, sexuality, employment, pregnancy and parenting, and aging.

Kalyva, E. (2011). *Autism: Educational and therapeutic approaches.* London: SAGE.

There are many different approaches and therapies available for children, young people and adults on the autistic spectrum, and the amount of information available on each one can be daunting for professionals and parents alike. This book offers concise and clear explanations of a variety of proposed interventions and their effectiveness.

Murphy, C. M., Wilson, C. E., Robertson, D. M., Ecker, C., Daly, E. M., Hammond, N., Galanopoulos, A., Dud, I., Murphy, D. G. and McAlonan, G. M. (2016). Autism spectrum disorder in adults: Diagnosis, management, and health services development. *Neuropsychiatric Disease and Treatment,* 12, pp. 1669–86.

(Continued)

This article reviews available evidence regarding the aetiology, legislation, diagnosis, management, and service provision for autistic adults and considers what is needed to support adults with ASD as they age. They conclude that health services research for autistic adults is urgently warranted. Research is required to better understand the needs of adults, including health, aging, service development, transition, treatment options across the lifespan, sex, and the views of autistic people. Additionally, the outcomes of recent international legislative efforts to raise awareness of autism and service provision for adults are to be determined. Future research is required to identify high-quality, evidence-based, and cost-effective models of care. Furthermore, future health services research is also required at the beginning and end of adulthood, including improved transition from youth to adult health care and increased understanding of aging and health in older adults.

References

Baio, J., Wiggins, L., Christensen, D. L., Maenner, M. J., Daniels, J., Warren, Z., Kurzius-Spencer, M., Zahorodny, W., Robinson Rosenberg, C., White, T., Durkin, M. S., Imm, P., Nikolaou, L., Yeargin-Allsopp, M., Lee, L. C., Harrington, R., Lopez, M., Fitzgerald, R. T., Hewitt, A., Pettygrove, S., Constantino, J. N., Vehorn, A., Shenouda, J., Hall-Lande, J., Van Naarden Braun, K. and Dowling, N. F. (2018). Prevalence of autism spectrum disorder among children aged 8 years. *Autism and Developmental Disabilities Monitoring Network*, 67 (6), pp. 1–23.

Bargiela, S., Steward, R. and Mandy, W. (2016). The experiences of late-diagnosed women with autism spectrum conditions: An investigation of the female autism phenotype. *J Autism Dev Disord*, 46 (10), pp. 3281–94.

Baron-Cohen, S. (2002). The extreme male brain theory of autism. *Trends in Cognitive Sciences*, 6 (6), pp. 248–54.

Baron-Cohen, S., Lombardo, M. V., Auyeung, B., Ashwin, E., Chakrabarti, B. and Knickmeyer, R. (2011). Why are autism spectrum conditions more prevalent in males? *PLoS Biol*, 9 (6).

Bent, S., Bertoglio, K., Ashwood, P., Nemeth, E. and Hendren, R. L. (2012). Brief report: Hyperbaric oxygen therapy (HBOT) in children with autism spectrum disorder: A clinical trial. *J Autism Dev Disord*, 42 (6), pp. 1127–32.

Bishop-Fitzpatrick L., Mazefsky, C. A. and Eack, S. M. (2018). The combined impact of social support and perceived stress on quality of life in adults with autism spectrum disorder and without intellectual disability. *Autism*, 22 (6), pp. 703–771

Blakely, R. (2020). Society of Homeopaths rebuked over bogus autism remedies. [online] Available at: www.thetimes.co.uk/article/homeopaths-ordered-to-stop-offering-autism-treatment-bvvh0cmbn [Accessed 24.03.2022].

British Hyperbaric Association (2021). [online] Available at: www.ukhyperbaric.com/ [Accessed 21.11.2021].

Cage, E. and Troxell-Whitman, Z. (2019). Understanding the reasons, contexts and costs of camouflaging for autistic adults. *J Autism Dev Disord*, 49 (5), pp. 1899–911.

Camm-Crosbie, L., Bradley, L., Shaw, R., Baron-Cohen, S. and Cassidy, S. (2019). 'People like me don't get support': Autistic adults' experiences of support and treatment for mental health difficulties, self-injury and suicidality. *Autism*, 23, pp. 1431–41.

Chungpaibulpatana, J., Sumpatanarax, T., Thadakul, N., Chantharatreerat, C., Konkaew, M. and Aroonlimsawas, M. (2008). Hyperbaric oxygen therapy in Thai autistic children. *J Med Assoc Thai*, 91 (8), pp. 1232–8.

Crane, L., Batty, R., Adeyinka, H., Goddard, L., Henry, L. A. and Hill E. L. (2018). Autism diagnosis in the United Kingdom: Perspectives of autistic adults, parents and professionals. *J Autism Dev Disord*, 48 (11), pp. 3761–72.

Ernst, E. (2018). *Seven things you might want to know about 'CEASE' therapy (as practised by homeopaths and naturopaths).* [online] Available at: https://edzardernst. com/2018/05/seven-things-you-might-want-to-know-about-cease-therapy-as-practised-by-homeopaths-and-naturopaths/ [Accessed 11.01.2021].

Fletcher-Watson, S. and Happé, F. (2019). *Autism: A new introduction to psychological theory and current debate.* London: Routledge/Taylor & Francis Group.

Fombonne, E. (2009). Epidemiology of pervasive developmental disorders. *Pediatr Res*, 65 (6), pp. 591–8.

Geurts, H. M. and Jansen, M. D. (2012). A retrospective chart study: The pathway to a diagnosis for adults referred for ASD assessment. *Autism*, 16 (3), pp. 299–305.

Goldman, S. (2013). Opinion: Sex, gender and the diagnosis of autism – A biosocial view of the male preponderance. *Research in Autism Spectrum Disorders*, 7 (6), pp. 675–9.

Greenberg, D. M., Warrier, V., Allison, C. and Baron-Cohen, S. (2018). Testing the empathizing–systemizing theory of sex differences and the extreme male brain theory of autism in half a million people. *PNAS Proceedings of the National Academy of Sciences of the United States of America*, 115 (48), 12152–12157.

Hasnat, M. and Graves, P. (2000). Disclosure of developmental disability: A study of parent satisfaction and the determinants of satisfaction. *Journal of Paediatrics and Child Health,* 36 (1), pp. 32–35.

Herbert, M. (2005). A brain disorder, or a disorder that affects the brain? *Clinical Neuropsychiatry*, 2 (6), pp. 354–79.

Howlin, P. and Moss, P. (2012). Adults with autism spectrum disorders. *Can J Psychiatry*, 57 (5), pp. 275–83.

Hull, L. and Mandy, W. (2017). Protective effect or missed diagnosis? Females with autism spectrum disorder. *Future Neurology*, 12 (3), pp. 159–69.

Hull, L., Mandy, W., Lai, M. C., Baron-Cohen, S., Allison, C., Smith, P. and Petrides, K. V. (2019). Development and validation of the Camouflaging Autistic Traits Questionnaire (CAT-Q). *J Autism Dev Disord*, 49 (3), pp. 819–33.

Jepson, B., Granpeesheh, D., Tarbox, J., Olive, M. L., Stott, C., Braud, S., Yoo, J. H., Wakefield, A. and Allen, M. S. (2011). Controlled evaluation of the effects of hyperbaric oxygen therapy on the behavior of 16 children with autism spectrum disorders. *J Autism Dev Disord*, 41 (5), pp. 575–88.

Kirkovski, M., Enticott, P. G. and Fitzgerald, P. B. (2013). A review of the role of female gender in autism spectrum disorders. *J Autism Dev Disord*, 43 (11), pp. 2584–603.

Krahn, T. M. and Fenton, A. (2012). The extreme male brain theory of autism and the potential adverse effects for boys and girls with autism. *J Bioeth Inq*, 9 (1), pp. 93–103.

Kreiser, N. L. and White, S. W. (2014). ASD in females: Are we overstating the gender difference in diagnosis? *Clin Child Fam Psychol Rev*, 17 (1), pp. 67–84.

Leedham, A., Thompson, A. R., Smith, R. and Freeth, M. (2020). 'I was exhausted trying to figure it out': The experiences of females receiving an autism diagnosis in middle to late adulthood. *Autism*, 24 (1), pp. 135–46.

Lerman, D. C., Sansbury, T., Hovanetz, A., Wolever, E., Garcia, A., O'Brien, E. and Adedipe, H. (2008). Using behavior analysis to examine the outcomes of unproven therapies: An evaluation of hyperbaric oxygen therapy for children with autism. *Behavior Analysis in Practice*, 1 (2), pp. 50–8.

Lewis, L. F. (2017). A mixed methods study of barriers to formal diagnosis of autism spectrum disorder in adults. *J Autism Dev Disord*, 47 (8), pp. 2410–24.

Midence, K. and O'Neill, M. (1999). The experience of parents in the diagnosis of autism. *Autism*, 3, pp. 273–85.

Milner, V., McIntosh, H., Colvert, E. and Happé, F. (2019). A qualitative exploration of the female experience of autism spectrum disorder (ASD). *J Autism Dev Disord*, 49 (6), pp. 2389–402.

Ming, X., Brimacombe, M., Chaaban, J., Zimmerman-Bier, B. and Wagner, G. C. (2008). Autism spectrum disorders: Concurrent clinical disorders. *J Child Neurol*, 23 (1), pp. 6–13.

Murphy, C. M., Wilson, C. E., Robertson, D. M., Ecker, C., Daly, E. M., Hammond, N., Galanopoulos, A., Dud, I., Murphy, D. G. and McAlonan, G. M. (2016). Autism spectrum disorder in adults: Diagnosis, management, and health services development. *Neuropsychiatr Dis Treat*, 7 (12), pp. 1669–86.

National Audit Office (2009). *Supporting People with Autism through Adulthood*. London: Stationery Office.

National Autistic Society (2008). *I Exist: The message from adults with autism in England*. London: The National Autistic Society.

NICE (2013). *Do not use recommendation*. [online] Available at: www.nice.org.uk/donotdo/do-not-use-hyperbaric-oxygen-therapy-to-manage-autism-in-any-context-in-children-and-young-people [Accessed 17.01.2022].

NICE (2016). *Recognition, referral, diagnosis and 7 management of adults on the autism spectrum*. [online] Available at: www.nice.org.uk/guidance/cg142/documents/autism-in-adults-full-guideline2 [Accessed 02.12.2021].

Parish-Morris, J., Liberman, M. Y., Cieri, C., Herrington, J. D., Yerys, B. E., Bateman, L., Donaher, J., Ferguson, E., Pandey, J. and Schultz, R. T. (2017). Linguistic camouflage in girls with autism spectrum disorder. *Mol Autism*, 30 (8), 48.

Podgórska-Bednarz, J. and Perenc, L. (2021). Hyperbaric oxygen therapy for children and youth with autism spectrum disorder: A review. *Brain Sciences*, 11 (7), 916.

Portway, S. M. and Johnson, B. (2005). Do you know I have Asperger's syndrome? Risks of a non-obvious disability. *Health, Risk & Society*, 7 (1), pp. 73–83.

Professional Standards Authority (PSA) for Health and Social Care (2020). *In-Year Review of Society of Homeopaths*. [online] Available at: www.professionalstandards.org.uk/docs/default-source/accredited-registers/panel-decisions/society-of-homeopaths-in-year-report-outcome-august-2020.pdf?sfvrsn=99b77620_5 [Accessed 26.01.2022].

Punshon, C., Skirrow, P. and Murphy, G. (2009). The not guilty verdict: Psychological reactions to a diagnosis of Asperger syndrome in adulthood. *Autism*, 13 (3), pp. 265–83.

Renty, J. and Roeyers, H. (2006). Quality of life in high-functioning adults with autism spectrum disorder. *Autism*, 10 (5), pp. 511–24.

Rossignol, D. and Frye, R. (2011). A review of research trends in physiological abnormalities in autism spectrum disorders: Immune dysregulation, inflammation, oxidative stress, mitochondrial dysfunction and environmental toxicant exposures. *Mol Psychiatry*, 17, pp. 389–401.

Rossignol, D. A., Bradstreet, J. J., Van Dyke, K., Schneider, C., Freedenfeld, S. H., O'Hara, N., Cave, S., Buckley, J. A., Mumper, E. A. and Frye, R. E. (2012). Hyperbaric oxygen treatment in autism spectrum disorders. *Med Gas Res*, 2 (1), 16.

Rowe, A. (2013). *The Girl with the Curly Hair: Asperger's and me*. London: Lonely Mind Books.

Schuck, R. K., Flores, R. E. and Fung, L. K. (2019). Brief report: Sex/gender differences in symptomology and camouflaging in adults with autism spectrum disorder. *J Autism Dev Disord*, 49 (6), pp. 2597–604.

Smith, C. (2019). *Girls and Autism: Educational, family and personal perspectives*. Edited by B. Carpenter, F. Happé and J. Egerton. London: Taylor and Francis.

Stagg, S. D. and Belcher, H. (2019). Living with autism without knowing: Receiving a diagnosis in later life. *Health Psychol Behav Med*, 7 (1), pp. 348–61.

Taylor, S. E. (1983). Adjustment to threatening events: A theory of cognitive adaptation. *American Psychologist*, 38 (11), pp. 1161–73.

The Westminster Commission for Autism (2018). *A spectrum of harmful interventions*. [online] Available at: https://westminsterautismcommission.files.wordpress.com/2018/03/a-spectrum-of-harmful-interventions-web-version.pdf [Accessed 12.11.2021].

Wen, W. and Wen, S. W. (2014). Expanding upon the 'extreme male brain' theory of autism as a common link between other major risk factors: A hypothesis. *Medical Hypotheses*, 82 (5).

Werling, D. M. and Geschwind, D. H. (2013). Sex differences in autism spectrum disorders. *Curr Opin Neurol*, 26 (2) pp. 46–53.

Xiong, T., Chen, H., Luo, R. and Mu, D. (2016). Hyperbaric oxygen therapy for people with autism spectrum disorder (ASD). *The Cochrane Database of Systematic Reviews*, 10 (10).

Young, H., Oreve, M. J. and Speranza, M. (2018). Clinical characteristics and problems diagnosing autism spectrum disorder in girls. *Arch Pediatr*, 25 (6), pp. 399–403.

FOUR

The importance, experience and challenges associated with diagnosis

Introduction

One of the factors associated with the increase in the numbers of individuals with autism is the view that more people are presenting themselves, or being presented by families, for diagnosis. It is generally considered that autism cannot be reliably diagnosed before the age of 2 years, but parents often report subtle differences from typical developmental milestones during the first year of life, such as delays in sitting up or walking (Chawarska et al., 2007), or say that their child did not enjoy cuddles, or was difficult to feed or to comfort (Young et al., 2003). At the other end of the age range, is the impact that late diagnosis may have upon adults.

———————————— Learning objectives ————————————

This chapter will:

- Introduce you to the importance, experience and challenges associated with diagnosis of autism in relation to children and adults
- Invite you to evaluate the use of DSM-5 and ICD-11 as the key diagnostic classification systems
- Introduce you to a range of tools used in the diagnosis of autism
- Invite you to consider the impact a diagnosis of autism may have on siblings

─────────────────────────── Key terms ───────────────────────────

DSM-5, ICD-11, diagnosis, ADOS (Autism Diagnostic Observation Schedule), DISCO (Diagnostic Interview for Social and Communication Disorders), ADI-R (Autism Diagnostic Interview - Revised), 3Di (Developmental, Dimensional and Diagnostic Interview), children, siblings, adults

─────────────────────────── Pause for reflection ───────────────────────────

• What do you think are the key challenges which follow a diagnosis autism for parents of young children?
• What are the implications of diagnosis upon services such as Health and Social Care?

DSM-5 and ICD-11

Autism Spectrum Disorder (ASD) is classified in two key diagnostic classification systems: the International Classification of Diseases (ICD-11) (World Health Organization, 2019) and the Diagnostic and Statistical Manual of Mental Disorders (DSM-5) (APA, 2013). Under both, it is characterised by deficits within social communication, additionally, repetitive and restrictive activities/interests, both suggesting a dyad of impairment. However, the previous ICD (10) acknowledged a triad of impairment by separating social interaction and communication into two characteristics, this was also evident in previous DSM classification. The DSM-5 provides a single diagnosis of ASD, the ICD-11 takes a similar approach but sub-diagnoses autism with or without an intellectual disability. Pina-Camacho et al. (2011) support the idea of a dyad of impairment and conducted a systematic review of 208 studies looking into functional and diffusion tensor imaging and concluded that evidence partially supports the dyad of impairment of social communication and behaviour; however, they highlight that neuroimaging data suggest that pragmatic language deficits should be mentioned explicitly in the criteria for social communication.

The ICD-11 updates the diagnostic criteria for autism and is now more in line the DSM-5 (Diagnostic and Statistical Manual of Mental Disorders) published in 2013 by the American Psychiatric Association. This is to say that it includes Asperger syndrome, Childhood Disintegrative Disorder, and certain other generalised developmental disorders, within the category of 'Autism'. With regard to the described characteristics of autism, the ICD-11 also includes the same two categories as the DSM-5: difficulties in interaction and social communication on the one hand, and restricted interests and repetitive behaviours on the other. It thus removes a third characteristic listed in the previous edition of the ICD, related to language problems. Both classifications also point to the importance of examining unusual sensory sensitivities, which is common among people on the autism spectrum.

While both classifications are similar there are some differences between them – the functional impairment of a person's illness are a compulsory element of the DSM-5 criteria; however, this is not the case in the ICD-11. According to Chaste and Leboyer (2012), the revised DSM-5 classification system saw a move from the triad of impairments which identified difficulties in social communication and interaction with restrictive stereotypical behaviour and interests to a single extensive spectrum disorder, containing a dyad of impairments, social communication and interaction and restricted and repetitive behaviours. However, Clarke et al. (2017) evidence criticism from parents and researchers, concerned that the new criteria will impact on the services received for people diagnosed prior to the new DSM-5.

Both categorise social communication and interaction by social-emotional reciprocity, nonverbal communicative behaviours and developing and maintaining relationships, perhaps disregarding commonly occurring language difficulties. It could also be suggested that diagnosis is subjective to psychologists' views and influenced by societal constructions, as eye contact controversially stems from these expectations. Interestingly, ICD-11 recognises that these characteristics may not occur until social demands increase later in life (WHO, 2019), whereas DSM-5 demands for difficulties in social communication to be present in early development (APA, 2013). Both diagnostic and classification systems indicate an importance of examining unusual sensory difficulties, with a focus on inflexible adherence to routine, fixated interests of abnormal intensity and hypersensitivity to the environment.

However, ICD-11 highlights less the type of play that a child takes part in, but rather emphasises whether children follow or impose strict rules of play. It also provides detailed guidelines for distinguishing between autism with and without an intellectual disability. The DSM-5, for its part, only states that autism and intellectual disability can occur simultaneously. With regard to autism during childhood, ICD-11 places less emphasis on the type of play that children partake in, since this may vary depending on the country or culture. Instead, it focuses more on whether children follow or impose strict rules when they play, a behaviour that can be perceived in any culture and is a common characteristic among autistic people.

Severity levels and DSM-5

A DSM-5 autism spectrum disorder diagnosis includes a support level requirement:

- Level 1 – children need support.
- Level 2 – children need substantial support.
- Level 3 – children need very substantial support.

These levels reflect the fact that some people have autism characteristics that only mildly affect their everyday lives, while others have characteristics that severely affect their everyday lives. The diagnosis indicates support levels for each area of difficulty.

This means that children might have different support levels for their social-communication skills compared to their restricted, repetitive and/or sensory behaviours. Or they might have the same support level for both. However, these levels should not be used to decide whether a child is eligible for services (Raising Children Network Australia, 2021). Yet, Weitlauf et al. (2014) argue that quantitative methods or practice recommendations for differentiating between levels remain undetermined, which leaves the field vulnerable to potential discrepancies between severity categorisations that may have inadvertent service implications.

According to DSM-5 diagnostic criteria (APA, 2013), there are three severity levels of autism which relate to Social Communication and Restricted and Repetitive Behaviours. Level 1 is currently the lowest classification. Those on this level will require some support to help with issues like inhibited social interaction and communication along with problems of organisation, planning skills and inflexible behaviour. At Level 2, individuals require substantial support and have marked problems with verbal and nonverbal communication skills and social impairments, alongside having very restricted and repetitive behaviours and interests. Level 3 is the most severe end of the spectrum, requiring very substantial support. There will be very limited social interactions, verbal and nonverbal skills, alongside inflexible behaviour and difficulty coping with change. Signs associated with both Level 1 and Level 2 are still present but are far more severe.

Pause for reflection

- Both DSM-5 and ICD-11 are more closely aligned than previously; what do you think are the implications of this for individuals who have had a previous diagnosis, for example of Asperger syndrome?

Early signs and diagnosis

In some children, autism symptoms are evident in the first few months of life. Other children don't display symptoms until the age of two. Mild symptoms can be difficult to spot and may be mistaken for a shy temperament or the 'terrible twos'. Parents of autistic children will report first having concerns about their child's development as early as 12–18 months of age and some clinicians can diagnose autism as early as 14 months (Guinchat et al., 2012); however, diagnosis typically occurs later in Europe (3.5 years), the USA (4 years), and Canada (6 years). Early diagnosis and treatment have been linked to greater reduction in the core symptoms of autism, higher likelihood of receiving behavioural therapy, and a reduction in the use of psychotropic medication (Zuckerman et al., 2017). Rising awareness among parents and professionals regarding the early signs of autism, as well as ongoing monitoring of infants who, due to genetic liability, are at risk for developing the disorder, has led in recent years to a rapid increase in the number of very young children referred for a diagnostic evaluation with parents and professionals noting first concerns in the second year of life (Ozonoff et al., 2005). The NHS (2019a) suggest that signs of autism in young children include:

- not responding to their name;
- avoiding eye contact;
- not smiling when you smile at them;
- getting very upset if they do not like a certain taste, smell or sound;
- repetitive movements, such as flapping their hands, flicking their fingers or rocking their body;
- not talking as much as other children.

Studies report that the most common disorders associated with autism are language problems (78 per cent) and intellectual disability (49 per cent) (Höglund Carlsson et al., 2013). Early detection and diagnosis of autism are important because of the implications for access to therapeutic care. When diagnosing younger children, assessment of cognitive and language ability is essential to contextualise the emerging autistic symptoms in the global profile of development, as many of the interaction problems that may arise will be influenced by a child's language level and mental age. It is believed that cognitive level and early intervention are the most significant variables affecting outcomes for autistic children (Harris and Handleman, 2000). The early identification and diagnosis of autism continues to rely on parental report and clinical observations of key behavioural markers to identify children at high likelihood for autism in infancy and toddlerhood. Early behavioural markers of autism can be reliably observed and measured during the second year of life (Landa et al., 2013). The most frequently identified differences have been found in reduced, infrequent, or inconsistent use of eye contact, response to name, imitation, social smiling, gestures, pretend play, and 'joint attention' skills such as pointing to, and showing, objects to share interest, and following gaze and pointers among autistic children when compared with typically developing children.

These social-communication markers of autism have formed the basis of many screening and developmental surveillance tools for the early identification of children at 'higher-likelihood' of developing autism. However, parental reports and screening at one age only have adversely impacted on the accuracy and sensitivity of these tools. Barbaro and Dissanayake (2009) suggest that it is important to monitor behaviour repeatedly over time, thereby increasing the opportunity to identify early manifestations of ASD and facilitating the charting of subtle behavioural changes that occur in the development of infants and toddlers. Øien et al. (2018) state that there is a need to enhance the understanding of early markers of autism in boys and girls, as well as factors affecting parental report on early delays and abnormalities, to improve the sensitivity of screening instruments.

Case study

Two friends, Jo and Steph, who had not seen each other for a while, were chatting about Jo's 3-year-old son, Maitland. This is the conversation:

'He was developing and showing some milestones that are typical up to about 12 months. Maybe six months later, he started to lose the ability to do some of those things. He started to speak some words when he was one and a half, but when he reached his third birthday, he didn't speak at all. When he was younger, he wasn't interacting, there was a real lack of eye contact. He has three other cousins around the same age. He'd be sitting with his cousins, a group of little two-year-olds and they'd be playing with these certain toys together and Maitland will move away, not wanting anything to do with these other kids.'

- What suggestions and next steps would you suggest that Jo could take?
- Research the typical key milestones associated with the skills identified in the conversation and suggest how these may be later or missed in an autistic child.

Diagnostic tools

Diagnosis of autism is still based upon the presence of characteristically atypical patterns of behaviour during early development. Enduring difficulties in social relationships and social communication, or the presence of stereotyped behaviour, restricted interests and/or resistance to change should alert the clinician to the possible presence of autism. There are a number of tools which are used to diagnose individuals who might be autistic. They usually rely on two main sources of information: descriptions of the person's development and behaviour collected via an interview and direct observation of that behaviour. Diagnostic manuals such as ICD-11 (WHO, 2019) and DSM-5 (APA, 2013) set out the criteria for autism to be diagnosed. These create the foundation for tools such as the DISCO (Diagnostic Interview for Social and Communication Disorders), the ADI-R (Autism Diagnostic Interview - Revised), the ADOS (Autism Diagnostic Observation Schedule) and 3Di (Developmental, Dimensional and Diagnostic Interview).

ADOS (Autism Diagnostic Observation Schedule)

The Autism Diagnostic Observation Schedule (ADOS) is an observation measure designed to assess reciprocal social interaction and communication, play, and use of imagination (Lord et al., 2000). The ADOS attempts to set a 'social world' in which behaviours associated with ASD can be observed via play, tasks and conversation. The ADOS can be used to assist with educational planning and was originally developed to be used in conjunction with the Autism Diagnostic Interview (ADI). This combination of instruments has been deemed the 'gold standard' for the assessment of ASD (Filipek et al., 2000).

There are four 'modules', one of which is administered depending on the individual's verbal ability. Module 1 is used for children who are preverbal or have single-word language. Module 2 is appropriate for individuals with phrase speech abilities. Module 3 is used for children and adolescents who are verbally fluent. Verbally fluent adolescents and adults would be assessed with Module 4. Lord et al. (2000) state that results indicate substantial interrater and test-retest reliability for individual items, excellent interrater reliability within domains and excellent internal consistency. ADOS can be used to evaluate almost anyone suspected of having autism, from as young as 12 months old with no language to verbally fluent adults. It generates accurate assessments of autism and development disorders across all ages, language skills, cultural backgrounds and developmental levels. It is a standardised diagnostic assessment of social, imagination and communication skills of individuals who may have autism spectrum disorders. The assessment uses planned social situations to trigger target responses and interpersonal interactions. These communication opportunities are designed to elicit a wide range of verbal, physical, social and imaginative interchanges.

DISCO (Diagnostic Interview for Social and Communication Disorders)

The Diagnostic Interview for Social and Communication Disorders (DISCO) is a semi-structured interview designed to assess impairments in the areas of social interaction, social communication and social imagination, and repetitive behaviours associated with autism. It is a schedule for the diagnosis of autistic spectrum and related disorders and assessment of individual needs. It enables information to be recorded systematically for a wide range of behaviours and developmental skills and is suitable for use with all ages and levels of ability. In addition to helping the clinician to obtain a profile of everyone's pattern of development and behaviour, it also enables identification of specific features found in autistic spectrum disorders that are relevant for use with established diagnostic systems (Wing et al., 2000).

DISCO was developed for use at the Centre for Social and Communication Disorders (now renamed as the Lorna Wing Centres), by Dr Lorna Wing and Dr Judith Gould, as both a clinical and a research instrument for use with children, young people and adults of any age. Its special value is that it collects information using a dimensional approach and concerning all aspects of each individual's skills, challenges and untypical behaviours, not just the features of autism spectrum disorder. Where possible, information concerning the person's history in infancy and childhood is collected from an informant who has known the person from birth. However, when for an adult there is no informant available to give an early history, the items of the schedule can be completed for current skills, challenges and untypical behaviour. When adults have very good recall of their own lived experience as a child or young person, this can provide useful insights into their earlier development and helps inform the interviewer.

The DISCO takes a dimensional approach and obtains a profile of development and behaviour, as well as identifying specific features associated with autism.

Information about developmental history and current functioning is obtained. The interview takes between two and three hours to complete. The questions are flexible so can be adapted depending on the individual's level of functioning, prior information, and cultural background. That the DISCO is not associated with diagnostic systems ensures that it will still be relevant as changes get made to the DSM and ICD systems and that it is a reliable instrument for diagnosis when sources of information are used from the whole interview. It is particularly effective for diagnosing disorders of the broader autistic spectrum (Leekam et al., 2002).

ADI-R (Autism Diagnostic Interview - Revised)

The ADI-R is a clinical diagnostic instrument for assessing autism in children and adults and is one of the gold standard clinical diagnostic instruments for assessing autism (Lord et al., 1994). It is a semi-structured interview designed to assess the three core aspects of autism: social, communication, and restricted behaviours or interests. The ADI-R is designed for individuals aged 18 months and older and consists of 93 items covering areas of family background, developmental history, language, communication, social development, interests, and general behaviour (Rutter et al., 2003). As the procedure is standardised it needs to be followed carefully, and the interviewer records and codes responses based on descriptions of behaviours by the caregiver.

The ADI-R typically takes 1–2 hours and focuses on the child's current behaviour or behaviour at a certain point in the areas of reciprocal social interaction, communication and language, and patterns of behaviour. The interview is divided into five sections: opening questions; communication questions; social development and play questions; repetitive and restricted behaviour questions; and questions about general behaviour problems. The ADI-R is a revised version of the original ADI and the information obtained can be used in a diagnostic algorithm for autism as described in both the ICD-10 and DSM-IV manuals. This tool focuses on behaviour in three main areas: qualities of reciprocal social interaction; communication and language; and restricted and repetitive, stereotyped interests and behaviours.

3Di (Developmental, Dimensional and Diagnostic Interview)

The Developmental, Dimensional and Diagnostic Interview (3Di) (Skuse et al., 2004) is a standardised, computer-based diagnostic interview in which individual symptoms can be scored in terms of their severity and frequency from information provided by parents and teachers of children with suspected autism. It is a parental interview which can be used in both clinical and non-clinical samples. The interview consists of 183 items, and covers areas of demographics, family, developmental history and motor skills. There are 266 questions that are concerned with disorders on the autism spectrum, and 291 questions that relate to mental state relevant to other diagnoses. The questions need to be asked in the way that they are written, and the authors have attempted to make them sound as natural as possible. It is possible to abbreviate the questionnaire if a specific diagnosis is suspected or if certain modules are not relevant (e.g. verbal questions for a nonverbal individual). The full interview takes 90 minutes to administer. The authors have developed a 'pre interview package' for parents to complete in advance and this information can be entered into the computer. The child can then be assessed using an abbreviated interview which takes 45 minutes to complete. It provides an efficient and accurate means of assessing, in dimensional terms, the presence of autistic symptoms in both clinical and normal populations (Skuse et al., 2004).

Exercise

Autism spectrum disorder in adults: diagnosis and management.

NICE (2016) clinical guidelines advise the NHS on caring for people with specific conditions or diseases and the treatments they should receive. The information applies to people using the NHS in England and Wales. They set out the advice about diagnosing, supporting and caring for adults with autism that is set out in NICE clinical guideline 142. It can be accessed via:

www.nice.org.uk/guidance/cg142

Read the sections on the AQ-10 test and the recognition, referral, diagnosis and management of adults on the autism spectrum (5.4 Assessment and Diagnosis of Autism in Adults).

- What are the key findings from the research?
- How does the assessment and diagnosis of autism in adults and children differ?

The impact of diagnosis on siblings

Much has been written about the impact of a diagnosis on families, but research into the impact reveals both positive and negative effects of growing up with an autistic brother or sister. For example, they have been shown to exhibit higher levels of internalising and externalising disorders, with Ross and Cuskelly (2006) finding that aggressive behaviour was the most reported interaction problem and anger was the usual response. Petalas et al. (2009) found a general acceptance of the autistic siblings (e.g. feelings of pride and appreciation for siblings), identification (to varying extents) of positive aspects of having autistic brothers or sisters, social isolation, the need to change their behaviour to cope with siblings' idiosyncratic behaviours, reduced recreational time with families, and deprivation of social support from a variety of sources.

There are published mixed reports on sibling cohesion. Orsmond and Seltzer (2007) found that during childhood and adolescence, siblings described both positive and negative aspects of their sibling relationship and suggest that lack of

closeness in the sibling relationship and social and emotional difficulties may continue. Angell et al. (2012) identified the positive effects of growing up with siblings
with disabilities, including high family cohesion and less sibling rivalry and those
interviewees told them that they infrequently quarrelled with their autistic siblings,
that they enjoyed mutual activities, and that they were friends with their siblings.
However, there were also comments focused on their embarrassment or frustration
with their siblings' aggressive or socially inappropriate behaviour. Siblings of autistic children who themselves do not have autism face unique stressors, including
perceived and actual responsibility over the welfare of their sibling (Ferraioli and
Harris, 2009).

Watson et al. (2021) undertook a systematic review of the experience of being a
sibling of a child with an autism spectrum disorder. They suggest that it is important
to challenge the 'doom and gloom' assumption. They reported that the review found
that siblings described the positive influence having an autistic sibling had on their
personal development, including their desire to promote the acceptance of autistic
people in wider society. Also, similarly, interactions with their autistic sibling
allowed for the development of pride and appreciation of their unique personality
characteristics. However, some developed coping strategies such as 'giving in' to
their sibling, keeping things to themselves in order not to burden others and self-
isolating to keep out of harm's way. Some of the challenges within sibling pairs
when one child has autism are likely attributable to core features. Weaknesses in
social interaction impact not only interactions with peers, but also relationships at
home with family. For example, impaired verbal and nonverbal communication and
difficulty maintaining friendships are inherent to autism (APA, 2013), and these difficulties persist into adolescence and adulthood. These social difficulties can affect
the sibling pair through reduced reciprocity and communication over shared interests. For example, Bauminger and Kasari (2000) found that autistic children were
both lonelier and had less complete understanding of loneliness. Also, where they
did have a friend, the quality of their friendship was poorer in terms of companionship, security and help.

Bronfenbrenner's (1977) ecological systems model posits child development is
influenced through microsystems (e.g. direct interactions between the child and
their family members and teacher) and the mesosystem (e.g. interactions between
the child's microsystem, such as sibling's interactions with the child's teacher).
Applying the ecological systems model to sibling research within autism indicates
that having a family member with autism not only directly impacts the sibling, but
also that connections between the sibling and other members within the system,
such as parents or teachers who interact with both the sibling and brother or sister,
also can impact the sibling relationship. Siblings of autistic children are likely to
learn about symptoms through the adults in their lives who also interact with their
autistic brother or sister and from their parents (Macedo Costa and Pereira, 2019).
Chapter 2 also covers aspects of family interactions.

———————————— Key research in the field ————————————

Mossa, P., Eirinakia, V., Savagea, S. and Howlin, P. (2019). Growing older with autism – The experiences of adult siblings of individuals with autism. *Research in Autism Spectrum Disorders*, 63, pp. 42–51.

Objective

Most studies of siblings of individuals with autism have involved children or adolescents. In this study the researchers explored the personal experiences of adults in middle adulthood who were raised with a sibling with autism. At the time of the interview, the mean age of participants was 40 years; that of their autism siblings was 39 years.

Method

As part of a larger scale adult sibling study, 56 individuals (37 females, 19 males; mean age 40 years) were asked about their experiences of growing up with a sibling with autism and about their worries for the future.

Findings

Most participants (77 per cent) described positive benefits, often related to the impact on their own life or personality (e.g. making them more tolerant or caring) and to the positive characteristics of their sibling with autism. Only 14 per cent could describe no positive aspects. The principal problems described were related to coping with behavioural difficulties (39 per cent) and disruption to family relationships (32 per cent) or social life (23 per cent). There was no association between the level of negative descriptions and individual sibling characteristics, participants' social functioning or mental health. The main concerns for the future, expressed by the majority of participants, focused on problems of finding appropriate care (77 per cent) and the potential emotional impact on the autism siblings of loss of parents.

Conclusion

Most participants described a mix of positive and negative experiences, but current concerns focused predominantly on future long-term care. Many adult siblings will become increasingly responsible for ensuring the welfare of the individual with autism. Medical and other services need to recognise the importance of this role, and the need actively to involve siblings in care planning and decision-making.

———————————— Pause for reflection ————————————

- What do you think are the benefits of being diagnosed with autism as an adult?
- Are there any issues that the person may face with respect to family, social life and employment?

Diagnosis in adults

The NHS (2019b) state that common signs of autism in adults include:

- finding it hard to understand what others are thinking or feeling;
- getting very anxious about social situations;
- finding it hard to make friends or preferring to be on your own;
- seeming blunt, rude, or not interested in others without meaning to;
- finding it hard to say how you feel;
- taking things very literally – for example, you may not understand sarcasm or phrases like 'break a leg';
- having the same routine every day and getting very anxious if it changes.

NICE guidelines for autism (NICE, 2012) diagnosis in adulthood is reached on a consensus of expert opinion made by observations from multidisciplinary assessments, including detailed developmental history taking (if available), current behavioural factors, and cognitive abilities. Using the ADOS-2 module four (for adult populations), they suggest that comprehensive (diagnostic, needs and risks) assessment of suspected autism should be undertaken by professionals who are trained and competent, be team-based and draw on a range of professions and skills and where possible involve a family member, partner, carer or other informant or use documentary evidence (such as school reports) of current and past behaviour and early development. Difficulties in social interaction and communication and the presence of stereotypical behaviour (resistance to change or restricted interests) that have been present in childhood and continuing into adulthood, as well as behavioural problems functioning at home, in education or in employment along with past and current physical and mental disorders should be examined.

Being diagnosed as autistic in adulthood is not straightforward, with autistic adults in the UK reporting an average diagnostic delay of just over 5 years, from the point which they first considered they may be autistic until receiving an official autism diagnosis. Jones et al. (2014) found that diagnostic practices, and the time taken to diagnose autism in adults, vary widely across the UK. However, adults have also reported 'unsatisfactory' experiences of the diagnostic process, often feeling misunderstood, ignored and even dismissed by health professionals. For example, Bargiela et al. (2016) found that the knowledge and assumptions of teachers, GPs, mental healthcare workers and other professionals contribute to the diagnostic bias against autistic females. While the diagnostic process and its immediate aftermath are often perceived to be an 'emotional rollercoaster', many adults report the ways their lives have changed for the better since receiving a diagnosis and formally identifying as autistic and a sense of belonging as they engage with others in the autistic community. Stagg and Belcher (2019) interviewed nine adults over the age of 50 who had recently been diagnosed with autism, and thematic analysis was used to analyse the transcripts. Results showed that the participants had received treatment for anxiety and depression. They reported autistic behaviours in their childhood and growing up they felt isolated and alien, although receiving a diagnosis was seen as a positive step and allowed for a reconfiguration of self and an appreciation of individual needs.

Case study

Peter is 21 years old and has just started at university. He had difficulties when he started to study a previous course. He had attended the Induction but often missed lectures and seminars. He thought that following a course with exams would be, as he put it, 'Right up my street'. However, in the first-year exams, he walked out and failed to attend an appointment with Wellbeing.

He struggled to make friends and his hobby was collecting sci-fi comics. When he eventually discussed his feelings and behaviours it transpired that he had difficulties understanding the process of making and keeping lecture times, making use of study time and communicating with academic staff and other students.

Peter has evidence of significant anxiety and low mood and recognised that he had lifelong difficulties with social situations. After receiving a diagnosis of autism, he felt that it helped him to make sense of his life, including his university studies. The diagnosis will allow reasonable adjustments to be put in place, which hopefully will enable him to complete his degree and get a job.

- What might have led Peter to seek a diagnosis later in life?
- What reasonable adjustments could be put in place to support his academic and social life while at university?

Research into undiagnosed older adults is essential as many individuals who eventually go on to receive a diagnosis of autism are already being treated for social problems, anxiety and mood disturbances. Geurts and Jansen (2012) found that the pathways to an adulthood autism diagnosis are very heterogeneous. In a retrospective study, they found that men had contacted a mental health care clinic slightly earlier than women. The main referral reasons were social problems, feelings of anxiety and mood disturbances and the most common earlier diagnoses were anxiety and mood disorders or psychosis-related disorders. Mental health concerns are cited as a primary reason for adults eventually receiving a diagnosis and Jones et al. (2014) found that adult respondents displayed above average levels of depressed mood and anxiety, with greater support being requested in this area. Additionally, adults face isolation and poor employment prospects, and health and educational services for autistic adults remain underdeveloped. Howlin and Moss (2012) reviewed studies of outcome in adulthood and found that many autistic people are significantly disadvantaged regarding employment, social relationships, physical and mental health, and quality of life. Murphy et al. (2016) state that research is required to better understand the needs of autistic adults including health, aging and service development.

Two scoping reviews, Thompson-Hodgetts et al. (2020) and Huang et al. (2020), found that receiving an autism diagnosis has a significant emotional impact on adults. Disclosure was a complex process requiring careful consideration of individual risks and benefits in different situations. Two-thirds of employed participants disclosed their diagnosis at work, but almost half of participants in education did not disclose to their university or vocational college. Also, deciding to disclose a diagnosis of autism to others can be a major decision and while some perceive primarily positive outcomes of disclosure, others often experience negative outcomes and stigma from disclosure. Some perceive that disclosure has positive effects on social acceptance and perceptions of disability for people with autism, especially when explanatory information about autism was provided with the autism label, while others indicated reluctance to disclose their diagnosis due to perceived negative outcomes and stigma. Also, accessibility and processes were inconsistent, and formal support services are lacking. Murphy et al. (2016) state that although there has been a considerable increase in research over the last 20 years, much remains to be done in health services research for autistic people. Research is required to determine a better understanding of the needs of adults including health, aging, service development, transition, treatment options across the lifespan, sex differences, and the views of autistic adults.

Taylor's (1983) cognitive adaptation model suggests that individuals faced with life-changing information need to re-evaluate their sense of self and their possible futures. This re-evaluation involves three mechanisms: meaning making, taking control and self-esteem building. The model suggests that individuals need to examine the causes of the life-changing event and consider how this change alters their current meaning system. They need to re-evaluate and gain control over their current circumstances and build self-esteem (Stagg and Belcher, 2019). Among autistic adults, strong post-diagnostic support has been shown to improve quality of life with Renty and Roeyers (2006) identifying that support characteristics were related to quality of life in adults, whereas disability characteristics were not.

Delayed diagnosis into adulthood is common, and self-diagnosis is a growing phenomenon. Fear of not being believed by professionals was identified as the most frequently occurring and most severe barrier (Lewis, 2017). Some of these individuals, described as the 'lost generation', were previously excluded from a diagnosis of classic autism. Making a first diagnosis of autism spectrum conditions in adults can be challenging for practical reasons, developmental reasons and clinical reasons (Lai and Baron-Cohen, 2015). McDonald (2020) used an online survey that included demographic questions and measures for stigma, self-concept, quality of life and wellbeing; she found that self-diagnosed participants were more likely to be older, women, or employed and less likely to be students, or prefer the term 'autism' rather than those with an autism diagnosis. The groups were remarkably similar in reported stigma, self-esteem, and lower quality of life than the general population. The self-diagnosed group were experiencing challenges like adults with an autism diagnosis on these factors and this group matched the suggested profile for the 'lost generation' of autistic individuals who were not diagnosed with autism. Both groups appear to struggle with employment, stigma and quality of life.

Exercise

In this chapter, we have covered the importance, experience and challenges associated with diagnosis of autism on children, siblings and adults. Families are another key group who may be impacted by a diagnosis of an individual member. Local authorities in England must publish information about the provision they expect to be available in their area for children and young people from 0 to 25 who have special educational needs. This is known as the local offer.

www.nhs.uk/conditions/autism/autism-and-everyday-life/help-for-families/

- Research the local offer for autistic children, young people and their families from your local authority.
- Compare this with the advice given by the NHS.

Key points

- The experience and impact of a diagnosis of autism has far-reaching consequences on the lives of children, young people and adults
- DSM-5 and ICD-11 are the key diagnostic classification systems
- There are a range of tools utilised in the diagnosis of autism in children and adults
- It is important to understand the individual reasons behind seeking a diagnosis of autism
- There are clear guidelines which should be followed when seeking a diagnosis and subsequent access to support

Questions to consider

- Why do you think it is important to recognise the consequence of diagnosis and the impact it may have on the individual and their family?
- Is it possible to objectively weigh the advantages and disadvantages of diagnosing autism?
- Why is it important to be able to identify the key indicators of autism at different stages in life?

Further reading

Crawford, M. J. and Weber, B. (2016). *Autism Intervention Every Day!: Embedding activities in daily routines for young children and their families.* Baltimore: Paul H. Brookes Publishing.

Children with autism often don't get a diagnosis in their first few years of life – but if a very young child is exhibiting red flags, what should professionals and parents do in the meantime? This book

(Continued)

has accessible, real-world solutions for use with children birth to three, with or without an autism diagnosis. This practical guide is packed with simple, highly effective suggestions for strengthening critical skills during daily routines, from dressing in the morning to getting ready for bed. Early interventionists and other professionals will learn how to coach families in weaving these activities into everyday life with their child, so that intervention continues long after the professional goes home.

Rudelli, N., Straccia, C. and Petitpierre, G. (2021). Fathers of children with autism spectrum disorder: Their perceptions of paternal role a predictor of caregiving satisfaction, self-efficacy and burden. *Research in Autism Spectrum Disorders*, 83.

The positive effect of a father's involvement in children's upbringing is now recognised. However, research on fathers raising children with autism is still scarce. This study examines the relationship between the perception fathers of autistic children have of the importance of their role in the development of their children and the feelings (self-efficacy, caregiving burden, satisfaction) they express about their parenting experience. The results from hierarchical multiple regression analyses show that the importance that fathers attach to the paternal role predicts positively their caregiving satisfaction and their feeling of self-efficacy. The children's challenging behaviours predict positively the caregiving burden whereas the assessment of social support predicts it negatively.

Towle, P. (2013). *The Early Identification of Autism Spectrum Disorders: A visual guide*. London: Jessica Kingsley.

Identifying autism as early as possible can have a significant, positive impact on the child's journey to adaptation and independence. Yet too few diagnoses take place at an early, developmentally crucial stage. This unique visual guide aims to equip readers with the skills to recognise ASD in very young children. The book provides a systematic framework for understanding the complex nature of ASD. From social interaction to communication to restricted and repetitive behaviours, each chapter focuses on key symptoms and uses photographs to illustrate and enhance understanding of presenting or absent behaviours.

References

American Psychiatric Association (2013). *Diagnostic and Statistical Manual of Mental Disorders* (5th edition). Washington, DC: American Psychiatric Publishing.

Angell, M. E., Meadan, H. and Stoner, J. B. (2012). Experiences of siblings of individuals with autism spectrum disorders. *Autism Res Treat*, 1 (11).

Barbaro, J. and Dissanayake, C. (2009). Autism spectrum disorders in infancy and toddlerhood: A review of the evidence on early signs, early identification tools, and early diagnosis. *J Dev Behav Pediatr*, 30 (5), pp. 447–59.

Bargiela, S., Steward, R. and Mandy, W. (2016). The experiences of late-diagnosed women with autism spectrum conditions: An investigation of the female autism phenotype. *J Autism Dev Disord*, 46 (10), pp. 3281–94.

Bauminger, N. and Kasari, C. (2000). Loneliness and friendship in high-functioning children with autism. *Child Development*, 71 (2), pp. 447–56.

Bronfenbrenner, U. (1977). Towards an experimental ecology of human development. *American Psychologist*, 32 (7), pp. 513–31.

Chaste, P. and Leboyer M. (2012). Autism risk factors: Genes, environment, and gene-environment interactions. *Dialogues Clin Neurosci*, 14 (3), pp. 281–92.

Chawarska, K., Paul, R., Klin, A., Hannigen, S., Dichtel, L. E. and Volkmar, F. (2007). Parental recognition of developmental problems in toddlers with autism spectrum disorders. *J Autism Dev Disord*, 37 (1), pp. 62–72.

Clarke, L. A., Cuthbert, B., Lewis-Fernández, R., Narrow, W. E. and Reed, G. M. (2017). Three approaches to understanding and classifying mental disorder: ICD-11, DSM-5, and the National Institute of Mental Health's Research Domain Criteria (RDoC). *Psychol Sci Public Interest*, 18 (2), pp. 72–145.

Ferraioli, S. J. and Harris, S. L. (2009) The impact of autism on siblings. *Social Work in Mental Health*, 8 (1), pp. 41–53.

Filipek, P. A., Accardo, P. J., Ashwal, S., Baranek, G. T., Cook, E. H., Dawson, G., Gordon, B., Gravel, J. S., Johnson, C. P., Kallen, R. J., Levy, S. E., Minshew, N. J., Ozonoff, S., Prizant, B. M., Rapin, I., Rogers, S. J., Stone, W. L., Teplin, S. W., Tuchman, R. F. and Volkmar, F. R. (2000). Practice parameter: Screening and diagnosis of autism: Report of the Quality Standards Subcommittee of the American Academy of Neurology and the Child Neurology Society. *Neurology*, 55 (4), pp. 468–79.

Geurts, H. M. and Jansen, M. D. (2012). A retrospective chart study: The pathway to a diagnosis for adults referred for ASD assessment. *Autism*, 16 (3), pp. 299–305.

Guinchat, V., Thorsen, P., Laurent, C., Cans, C., Bodeau, N. and Cohen, D. (2012). Pre-, peri- and neonatal risk factors for autism. *Acta Obstet Gynecol Scand*, 91 (3), pp. 287–300.

Harris, S. L. and Handleman, J. S. (2000). Age and IQ at intake as predictors of placement for young children with autism: A four-to six-year follow-up. *Journal of Autism and Developmental Disorders*, 30, pp. 137–42.

Höglund Carlsson, L., Norrelgen, F., Kjellmer, L., Westerlund, J., Gillberg, C. and Fernell, E. (2013). Coexisting disorders and problems in preschool children with autism spectrum disorders. *The Scientific World Journal*, 213979.

Howlin, P and Moss, P. (2012). Adults with autism spectrum disorders. *Can J Psychiatry*, 57(5), pp. 275–83.

Huang, Y., Arnold, S. R., Foley, K. R. and Trollor, J. N. (2020). Diagnosis of autism in adulthood: A scoping review. *Autism*, 24 (6), pp. 1311–27

Jones, L., Goddard, L., Hill, E. L., Henry, L. A. and Crane, L. (2014). Experiences of receiving a diagnosis of autism spectrum disorder: A survey of adults in the United Kingdom. *Journal of Autism and Developmental Disorders*, 44 (12), pp. 3033–44.

Lai, M. C. and Baron-Cohen, S. I. (2015). Identifying the lost generation of adults with autism spectrum conditions. *Lancet Psychiatry*, 2 (11), pp. 1013–27.

Landa, R. J., Gross, A. L., Stuart, E. A. and Faherty, A. (2013). Developmental trajectories in children with and without autism spectrum disorders: The first 3 years. *Child Dev*, 84 (2), pp. 429–42.

Leekam, S. R., Libby, S. J., Wing, L., Gould, J. and Taylor, C. (2002). The diagnostic interview for social and communication disorders: Algorithms for ICD-10 childhood autism and Wing and Gould autistic spectrum disorder. *J Child Psychol Psychiatry*, 43 (3), pp. 327–42.

Lewis, L. F. (2017). A mixed methods study of barriers to formal diagnosis of autism spectrum disorder in adults. *J Autism Dev Disord*, 47 (8), pp. 2410–24.

Lord, C., Risi, S., Lambrecht, L., Cook, E. H. Jr., Leventhal, B. L., DiLavore, P. C., Pickles, A. and Rutter, M. (2000). The autism diagnostic observation schedule-generic: A standard measure of social and communication deficits associated with the spectrum of autism. *J Autism Dev Disord*, 30 (3), pp. 205–23.

Lord, C., Rutter, M. and Le Couteur, A. (1994). Autism diagnostic interview-revised: A revised version of a diagnostic interview for caregivers of individuals with possible pervasive developmental disorders. *J Autism Dev Disord*, 24 (5), pp. 659–85.

Macedo Costa, T. and Pereira, A. P. (2019). The child with autism spectrum disorder: The perceptions of siblings. *Support for Learning*, 34 (2), pp. 193–210.

McDonald, T. A. M. (2020). Autism identity and the 'lost generation': Structural validation of the autism spectrum identity scale and comparison of diagnosed and self-diagnosed adults on the autism spectrum. *Autism in Adulthood*, 2 (1).

Mossa, P., Eirinakia, V., Savagea, S. and Howlin, P. (2019) Growing older with autism – The experiences of adult siblings of individuals with autism. *Research in Autism Spectrum Disorders*, 63, pp. 42–51.

Murphy, C. M., Wilson, C. E., Robertson, D. M., Ecker, C., Daly, E. M., Hammond, N., Galanopoulos, A., Dud, I., Murphy, D. G. and McAlonan, G. M. (2016). Autism spectrum disorder in adults: Diagnosis, management, and health services development. *Neuropsychiatr Dis Treat*, 7 (12), pp. 1669–86.

National Health Service (NHS) (2019a). *Signs of autism in children*. [online] Available at: www.nhs.uk/conditions/autism/signs/children/ [Accessed 25.03.2022].

National Health Service (NHS) (2019b). *Signs of autism in adults*. [online] Available at: www.nhs.uk/conditions/autism/signs/adults/ [Accessed 25.03.2022].

National Institute for Heath and Care Excellence (NICE) (2012). *Autism Spectrum Disorder in Adults: Diagnosis and management. Clinical guideline [CGNat142] Published: 27 June 2012 Last updated: 14 June 2021*. [online] Available at: www.nice.org.uk/guidance/cg142 [Accessed 12.01.2022].

Øien, R. A., Schjølberg, S., Volkmar, F. R., Shic, F., Cicchetti, D. V., Nordahl-Hansen, A., Stenberg, N., Hornig, M., Havdahl, A., Øyen, A. S., Ventola, P., Susser, E. S., Eisemann, M. R. and Chawarska, K. (2018). Clinical features of children with autism who passed 18-month screening. *Pediatrics*, 14 (6), e20173596.

Orsmond, G. I. and Seltzer, M. M. (2007). Siblings of individuals with autism spectrum disorders across the life course. *Ment Retard Dev Disabil Res Rev*, 3 (4), pp. 313–20.

Ozonoff, S., Williams, B. J. and Landa, R. (2005). Parental report of the early development of children with regressive autism: The delays-plus-regression phenotype. *Autism*, 9, pp. 461–86.

Petalas, M. A., Hastings, R. P., Nash, S., Dowey, I. and Reilly, D. (2009). 'I like that he always shows who he is': The perceptions and experiences of siblings with a brother with autism spectrum disorder. *International Journal of Disability, Development and Education*, 56 (4), pp. 381–99.

Pina-Camacho, L., Villero, S., Fraguas, D., Boada, L., Janssen, J., Navas-Sanchez, F., Mayoral, M., Llorente, C., Arango, C. and Parellada, M. (2011). Autism spectrum disorder: Does neuroimaging support the DSM-5 proposal for a symptom dyad? A systematic review of functional magnetic resonance imaging and diffusion tensor imaging studies. *Journal of Autism and Developmental Disorders*, 42, pp. 1326–41.

Raising Children Network Australia (2021). *Autism*. [online] Available at: https://raising-children.net.au/autism [Accessed 11.11.2021].

Renty, J. O. and Roeyers, H. (2006). Quality of life in high-functioning adults with autism spectrum disorder: The predictive value of disability and support characteristics. *Autism*, 10 (5), pp. 511–24.

Ross, P. and Cuskelly, M. (2006). Adjustment, sibling problems and coping strategies of brothers and sisters of children with autistic spectrum disorder. *J Intellect Dev Disabil*, 31 (2), pp. 77–86.

Rutter, M., Le Couteur, A. and Lord, C. (2003). *ADI-R: Autism Diagnostic Interview-Revised (ADI-R)*. Los Angeles, CA: Western Psychological Services.

Skuse, D., Warrington, R., Bishop, D., Chowdhury, U., Lau, J., Mandy, W. and Place, M. (2004). The developmental, dimensional and diagnostic interview (3di): A novel computerized assessment for autism spectrum disorders. *J Am Acad Child Adolesc Psychiatry*, 43 (5), pp. 548–58.

Stagg, S. D. and Belcher, H. (2019). Living with autism without knowing: Receiving a diagnosis in later life. *Health Psychol Behav Med*, 7 (1), pp. 348–61.

Taylor, S. E. (1983). Adjustment to threatening events: A theory of cognitive adaptation. *American Psychologist*, 38 (11), pp. 1161–73.

Thompson-Hodgetts, S., Labonte, C., Mazumder, R. and Phelan, S. (2020). Helpful or harmful? A scoping review of perceptions and outcomes of autism diagnostic disclosure to others. *Research in Autism Spectrum Disorders*, 77, 101598.

Watson, L., Hanna, P. and Jones, C. J. (2021). A systematic review of the experience of being a sibling of a child with an autism spectrum disorder. *Clin Child Psychol Psychiatry*, 26 (3), pp. 734–49.

Weitlauf, A. S., Gotham, K. O., Vehorn, A. C. and Warren, Z. E. (2014). Brief report: DSM-5 'levels of support': A comment on discrepant conceptualizations of severity in ASD. *J Autism Dev Disord*, 44, pp. 471–6.

Wing, L., Leekam, S. R., Libby, S. J., Gould, J. and Larcombe, M. (2000). The diagnostic interview for social and communication disorders: Background, inter-rater reliability and clinical use. *J Child Psychol Psychiatry*, 43 (3), pp. 307–25.

World Health Organization (2019). *International Statistical Classification of Diseases and Related Health Problems* (11th edition.)

Young, R. L., Brewer, N. and Pattison, C. (2003). Parental identification of early behavioural abnormalities in children with autistic disorder. *Autism*, 7 (2), pp. 125–43.

Zuckerman, K., Lindly, O. J. and Chavez, A. E. (2017). Timeliness of autism spectrum disorder diagnosis and use of services among U.S. elementary school-aged children. *Psychiatr Serv*, 68 (1), pp. 33–40.

FIVE

Introducing and evaluating strategies when working with autistic children, young people and adults

Introduction

While there is no 'cure' for autism, there are a range of strategies, techniques and therapies that can improve the lives of people with autism. While some interventions do appear to help at least some autistic individuals, there is 'no one-size-fits-all' solution and the most appropriate approaches to use will depend on many factors. Before they are tried out, interventions should be evaluated in terms of their rationale, safety, and likely chances of success. Careful evaluation of evidence is fundamental to the framework of sound clinical practice, known as evidence-based practice. This chapter will outline four strategies commonly found in the context of education and critically examine research into their use.

─────────────── Learning objectives ───────────────

This chapter will:

- Introduce you to a range of strategies when working with autistic children and young people
- Invite you to consider how these strategies could be used with autistic adults

(Continued)

- Invite you to evaluate the results of research evidence which examine the use of these strategies
- Introduce you to the importance of evidence-based research and how it can be used critically to evaluate the effectiveness of these strategies in practice

———————————————— Key terms ————————————————

TEACCH, PECS, Social Stories™, Lego® therapy, evidence-based research and practice

———————————— Pause for reflection ————————————

- What strategies are you familiar with, or have used in your own professional practice when working with autistic children and young people?
- Why is it important that we use research evidence to evaluate practice within contexts such as education?
- How would you begin to research the effectiveness of these strategies?

As knowledge of autism has developed, an increasing range of strategies and interventions have been suggested to support autistic individuals. Surprisingly though, relatively little scientific research has been undertaken to examine whether sound evidence exists to support their use, and where such research has been undertaken, the results have often been mixed or inconclusive.

TEACCH (Treatment and Education of Autistic and related Communication Handicapped Children)

TEACCH (Treatment and Education of Autistic and related Communication Handicapped Children) is an evidence-based service, training, and research programme for individuals of all ages and skill levels with autism. It is a structured teaching approach which considers autistic behaviours and their impact on learning and aims to minimise learner difficulties by using structured and continuous interventions, environmental adaptations, and alternative-augmentative communication (Panerai et al., 2009). It is a 'whole person' approach in that it aims to support many aspects of functioning, including learning, behaviour, social and communication needs, and may be used across different settings (at home, school, in respite services and other locations) as well as across the person's lifespan. The key features of TEACCH involve planning, allowing flexible teaching to suit the needs of all learners and providing support to allow children to thrive in all environments, while focusing on a child's individual skills, interests and needs to create a child-centred plan to meet their specific needs. The structure of where, how, when, and how long supports individuals to work more independently and excel in managing their time and space (Panerai et al., 2002). Visual structures such as the use of images help to support organisation and the following of routines. It has a clear and appropriate rationale, in that it addresses the characteristic need for structure and routine in autism. Key principles include:

- emphasis on structure, including the physical structure of the person's environment and clearly defined routines;
- harnessing skills: for instance, visual skills and good memory for information
- evaluation of individual support needs on a regular basis, including use of other interventions where necessary;
- empowering parents by encouraging their full participation;
- emphasis on developing independence and generalising from learning experiences.

Harvey (2011) notes how TEACCH interventions evolved from a behaviourist approach to learning. However, it is different to behaviourism as it is based around structured learning, recognising strengths as well as difficulties, thus offering a more functional approach to rewarding behaviour, and focuses upon the reasons behind behaviours. It is also important for the practitioner to use a more child-centred approach, to ensure a child's individual skills, interests and needs are used to create a child-centred plan, thus ensuring that their specific needs are met through individualised assessments. TEACCH uses the physical environment, schedules, and organisational strategies to create structure (Mesibov et al., 2005). It is aimed to support executive functioning by supporting complex, goal-directed behaviours. Schedules and cue cards provide individuals with clear guidance and order, which allows them to learn independently while addressing transitioning and shifting attention between activities or ideas (Van Bourgondien and Coonrod, 2013).

Physical structure and organisation involve creating an environment which utilises the child's level of understanding and ability to optimise independent learning. This can be achieved in many ways: for example, arranging furniture and materials to add meaning and to ensure everything the student requires is easily accessible. Having specific areas marked out for specific activities will provide structure and the student will know what is expected of them for that activity (TEACCH, 2022). Therefore, the use of zonal organisation can break a room up into different areas, allowing children to begin to associate and understand the expectations of each zone, as some zones are dedicated to completing work, and some to play and choose (Hume and Odom, 2007). Autistic children often experience a lot of anxiety surrounding expectations and as a result of different zones, children can begin to build a routine and in turn lessen their anxieties, knowing what to expect and how to respond (Cotterill, 2019). Along with the organisation of the room, it is also important to declutter spaces and limit the number of distractions in each zone. There are many ways to do this: a simple and effective way can be to cover items/

activities with a cloth, reducing the amount of visual clutter in a zone (Martin, 2014; Zazzi and Faragher, 2018).

Clear labelling of materials, with words, images or other symbols, can provide direction and guidance about when certain materials can and cannot be used. Visual timetables create an accessible system for children to use to understand when and where they need to be in different areas; this can reduce anxiety for many autistic children as they are able to see what is next and manage their emotion based on this change, instead of dwelling on the unknown (Hume and Odom, 2007). Providing clear structure and boundaries should result in fewer verbal instructions and less confusion for the child and allows them to become more independent within the classroom (TEACCH, 2022). By providing learners with a schedule, you are giving them clear direction as to what they should expect. Not only does it provide the students with a clear understanding of what is going to happen that day, they can also help with organising and predicting daily and weekly events. By showing what to do next and where they should go, their anxiety should hopefully be reduced, and the student becomes more independent and confident transitioning between activities. The use of work systems or stations can aid by answering questions such as:

- What is the work to be done?
- What is the task?
- How much work?
- When am I finished?
- What comes next?

——————————— Research evidence ———————————

In a meta-analysis of research into TEACCH, Virues-Ortega et al. (2013) suggested that:

(a) TEACCH effects over perceptual, motor, verbal and cognitive skills may be of small magnitude;
(b) effects over adaptive behavioural repertoires including communication and activities of daily living may be within the negligible to small range;
(c) effects over social behaviour and maladaptive behaviour may be moderate to large;
(d) the evidence base currently available does not allow to identify specific characteristics of the intervention (duration, intensity and setting) and the target population (developmental age) that could be driving the magnitude of effects; and
(e) effects are, in general, replicated across age groups, although the magnitude and consistency of intervention effects are greater among school-age children and adults.

They also suggested that a name-branded intervention frequently combines a variety of elements that are not assessed separately. Namely, the brand frequently advocates for a treatment package preventing separate analyses of specific treatment components.

Panerai et al. (2002) consider the three fundamental principles of TEACCH as pro-viding an individual educational programme, environmental adaptations, and alter-native communication training. They compared an experimental group who had a specialist teacher, adapted and designated areas for different activities, precise rou-tines and communication methods tailored to everyone, with a control group. The experimental group showed statistically significant improvements in all categories such as perception, gross motor skills, hand-eye coordination, and cognitive perfor-mance. Panerai et al. (2009) used TEACCH in both residential and natural settings and found that there was significant statistical improvement in all the Vineland Adap-tive Behavior Scales (Sparrow et al., 2005) for those on the TEACCH programme, compared to those in a comparative non-specific programme. D'Elia et al. (2014) also demonstrate the benefits of using TEACCH in school and home settings. How-ever, their results suggest that using a low intensity TEACCH programme does reduce autistic symptoms and maladaptive behaviours but not as significantly as studies where the programme was not low intensity.

Sanz-Cervera et al. (2018) addressed the significant decrease in the level of stress experienced by parents and teachers working with autistic students, but more importantly they highlighted the significant improvements in developmental abili-ties and a reduction in autistic symptoms and maladaptive behaviours, regardless of whether the context of the study was a school, home or clinical setting. An improvement in verbal and nonverbal cognitive functioning, perception, social communication, and gross and fine motor skills was observed, along with a reduc-tion in repetitive or ritualised behaviours, being inflexible to change, having restricted or fixated interests, and being hyper- or hypo-sensitive to sensory input. NasoudiGharehBolagh et al. (2013), working with a group of 19 autistic students and a control group, found that TEACCH had an impact upon reducing stereotyped behaviour and communicational difficulties along with significantly increasing social communication skills and concluded that this method increases significantly interactional skills learning in autistic children. Other research findings have dem-onstrated improvements relating to social play (Francke and Geist, 2003), self-help care and perception, improved cognitive performance (Panerai et al., 1997) and aiding social adaptive functioning and developmental abilities, with Tsang et al. (2007) noting initial support for the effectiveness of using the TEACCH programme with Chinese children.

When examining evidence-based practice with structure teaching, Mesibov and Shea (2010) used the critical components of the Structured Teaching approach under the TEACCH model (physical structure; visual schedules; work systems; and task organisation [Schopler et al., 1995]). They concluded that TEACCH is an exam-ple of a programme that both reflects and contributes to the evidence base of autism interventions. Using the same criteria, Kliemann (2014) reviewed 19 articles and made evidence-based conclusions against each of the components. Based upon the review the study found that physical structure of the environment needed further research; daily schedules were not deemed to be an evidence-based practice and thus not evaluated. Independent work systems lacked the evidence base to be considered an effective or promising practice and there was a slight case for visual task organisation.

PECS (Picture Exchange Communication System)

PECS (Picture Exchange Communication System) is an evidence-based naturalistic approach, based on the principles of applied behavioural analysis, and is used to support and initiate spontaneous and functional communication. It is a pictorial augmentative communication strategy (AAC) created for children with communication difficulties (Bondy and Frost, 2001). It uses symbolic communication to teach an individual to initiate communication for a concrete outcome (Glennen and DeCoste, 1997). Autistic children and young people exchange the symbols to procure the preferred items. Each child is individually assessed to identify objects and activities that he or she finds rewarding, and a booklet or board of small pictures/photographs is compiled matching the child's preferences. The child is then guided through different stages towards the goal of making spontaneous requests for these items, one adult acting as a communication partner and a second adult as the child's physical prompter.

As the child reaches for a desired object, the physical prompter then physically guides the child to pick up a picture of the object and release it into the communication partner's hand. The physical prompter gradually reduces the prompting as the child becomes more independent in selecting pictures of what he or she wants and exchanging them for the object itself. The child is also encouraged to generalise his/her new-found communication skills to different settings and communication partners, to produce more complex communications, and eventually make comments about things they see rather than just requesting things they want.

The PECS protocol is divided into six phases:

- Phase I includes teaching an individual to request a preferred item by exchanging a single picture of that item with a communicative partner.
- In Phase II, distance and persistence is taught by increasing the distance between the individual and his/her communication partner. In this phase, the individual needs to travel to the communication book, pick up the picture of the desired item, and then move to the communication partner to exchange the picture of the desired item.
- During Phase III, the individual requests at least four desired items from the communication book. In this phase, he/she learns to discriminate between multiple pictures.
- In Phase IV, the individual uses a sentence strip with an 'I want' symbol and a picture of the desired item to learn the chaining format to create a sentence (e.g. 'I want water').

- Phase V includes teaching the individual to respond to a 'What do you want?' sentence while using the sentence strip to help him/her respond to a simple question.
- Phase VI is to teach the use of labelling or naming things. For example, the individual can respond to a question such as 'What do you see?' (Bondy and Frost, 2001).

Research evidence

Bondy and Frost (1994) found that PECS has a success rate of 59 per cent in developing independent speech. Positive increases in speech development and spontaneous communication occur following PECS training, such as in the study by Schwartz et al. (1998), who demonstrated that young children with severe communication delays and disorders can learn to use PECS quickly and efficiently and that PECS' use generalises to untrained settings and may have concomitant effects on untrained language functions. Kravits et al. (2002) found that a girl used spontaneous language including use of the icons and verbalisations across those settings in which PECS was implemented. However, Howlin et al. (2007) found an increase in use of symbols within the classroom but argue that there was no evidence of improvements in communication within other areas and that treatment effects were not maintained once active intervention ceased.

Charlop-Christy et al. (2002) used a controlled single-case study and found positive changes in nontargeted behaviours such as attention, self-initiation, reduced levels of inappropriate behaviour, aggression, and an increase in peer-play. Frea et al. (2001) also found a rapid decrease in aggressive behaviour when PECS was introduced into play activities and Ganz and Simpson (2004) reported the case of three autistic children described as having no functional speech, who made progress in the mastering of intelligible verbal utterances, expanding vocabulary and the complexity of grammar in spoken language. A meta-analysis by Ganz et al. (2012) reviewed 13 PECS intervention studies for learners with autism and intellectual disabilities and those with autism and multiple disabilities and found similar supporting evidence that PECS can improve functional communication.

Lerna et al. (2014) conducted a quantitative study to determine the long-term effects of PECS by assessing social-communicative skills in 14 nonverbal children and concluded that PECS was more beneficial for individuals with little to no functional communication skills who had autism than using conventional language training strategies. Yoder and Lieberman's (2009) quantitative study compared two social communicative interventions, PECS and Responsive Education and Prelinguistic Milieu Teaching (RPMT). The participants consisted of 36 children between the ages of 18 months and 60 months. Participants receiving the PECS intervention showed an increase in the number of picture exchanges as compared to children receiving RPMT. Flippin et al.'s (2010) meta-analysis reviewed empirical evidence on the positive impact of PECS on communication and speech outcomes but argued that it is not a well-established evidence-based intervention yet, highlighting how there were small to moderate gains in communication but small to negative gains in speech. They emphasised frequent concerns on maintaining PECS for long periods of time and concerns on generalising this in different contexts. They state that several studies indicated that PECS improved a

(Continued)

variety of communication and functional skills: speech development, social communication skills, play and so on. However, other researchers have found issues with the effectiveness of PECS.

Alsayedhassan et al. (2016) suggest that most studies have been primarily implemented by researchers. They examined the mastery of PECS training by parents and practitioners and subsequent outcomes for autistic children and young people. They reviewed 13 studies in which parents and practitioners were trained to implement PECS and to examine the communication outcomes of autistic individuals. Results show that parents and practitioners learned how to implement PECS with a high procedural integrity and maintained the skills learned. Furthermore, results demonstrate that PECS is an effective intervention to teach autistic individuals functional communication skills such as independent mands, initiations, word vocalisations, and generalisation skills. They argue that probably PECS is best used as an initial intervention to teach manding and the basic elements of what is a communicative exchange; however, it is not recommended for a long-term intervention. The effectiveness of PECS is dependent on the quality of training and the understanding of the practitioner who deploys it.

Case study

Sunita is 26 years old and has been living in her current residential home for several years. At the age of 10 Sunita was diagnosed with autism with low cognitive function and has lived in foster homes and residential institutions. The residential staff have established a predictable routine for everyday life. She carries out the same activities every day without deviation and her life is bound up with many routines and rituals. The staff are uncertain whether there is anything she really likes except from carrying out stereotypical actions such as rolling back and forth on her bed. Sunita is only able to cope with one person at a time and not at all with the other residents. She understands simple verbal explanations. She uses few words and a few 2–3-word sentences as well as some echolalia and is not able to communicate her own needs and wishes other than using inappropriate and sometimes aggressive behaviour.

- How could a PECS strategy help Sunita communicate her wishes and needs?

Social Stories™

Developed by Carol Gray (Gray and Garand, 1993), a Social Story™ is a brief story which describes a situation, skill or behaviour that a child finds challenging, and explains where and when it takes place, who is involved and what occurs and why, as well as providing the child with an appropriate response to it. Written to suit the needs of an individual child and using language well within their comprehension level, they are read prior to the target situation occurring, being read independently by the child or to them. As such, Gray believes they are most useful for children with high-functioning autism (HFA) (Gray and Garand, 1993). Gray views the format, style and wording of Social Stories™ as crucial and has prepared detailed guidelines regarding this. Initially, she stated they should contain three types of sentences: descriptive, giving information about the situation; perspective, which describe the reactions and feelings of others; and directive, which specify how the child should respond in the situation.

Gray has since revised these guidelines, including using illustrations (Gray, 1998) and introducing cooperative and affirmative sentences (Gray, 2004). Since their inception other modes of presentation have also been developed, including using videos and photographs (Thiemann and Goldstein, 2001). Thiemann and Goldstein (2001) recommend visually cued instruction to guide the social language development of young autistic children with autism as they interact with peers without disabilities and computers (Reynhout and Carter, 2009). Social Stories™ primarily seek to mediate difficulties in social imagination, such as dealing with changes to routine, but have also been used to address differences in social interaction, e.g. learning acceptable behavioural responses in each situation. Scattone et al. (2002) argue that the Social Story™ structure suits the rigid disposition of many autistic individuals.

Social Stories™ are structured in a specific way in which is objectively described the person, the ability, the situation, the social environment. It is crucial to be understood the way that the child with autism understands the social circumstance in such a social story. The purpose of Social Stories™ is to ask relevant information such as 'where' and 'when', 'who takes part', 'what exactly is' and 'why'. Social Stories™ describe in detail and with clarity social messages of a particular situation from the point of view of the child with autism and suggest appropriate responses aiming to support the child to improve their behaviour. A social story is the simplified description of a particular situation experienced by the child with autism, written through the child's eye, deriving from its experience, with the main purpose of a social story being the teaching of social rules and norms.

Research evidence

Reynhout and Carter (2009) interviewed teachers who were using Social Stories™ because they were easy to create and use; additionally, teachers believed them to be effective. Social Stories™ are also more effective when targeting inappropriate behaviours compared to teaching social skills. However, they did suggest that there were several issues with the use of them within the classroom. One factor was that the teachers had never received any form of training and they found that the guidelines were useful. However, some do implement the stories in differing ways. Additionally, all the teachers reported that they always or sometimes used other interventions such as positive reinforcement. In general, teachers appear to view Social Stories™ in a very

(Continued)

positive way, albeit constructing and implementing them in ways that differ greatly from the recommended guidelines. Teachers clearly viewed Social Stories™ as inherently attractive (Rust and Smith, 2006). Nevertheless, clinical popularity does not necessarily equate with efficacy. Most teachers perceived Social Stories™ to be effective but there was less confidence regarding maintenance and generalisation, issues that are critical for autistic children (Greenway, 2000).

In a meta-analysis of 64 single-subject research pieces, Kokina and Kern (2010) examined the use of Social Stories™ and the outcomes based on characteristics of the intervention and participant. They concluded that the effectiveness of Social Stories™ is dependent on several intervention and participant characteristics. The meta-analysis found that Social Stories™ are more effective when read immediately before a targeted situation and those that included illustrations were more effective than those that solely used written text. In a systematic review, Aldabas (2019) concluded that there were benefits in using Social Stories™ as one of the primary interventions to reduce disruptive behaviours in autistic children. The second finding is that teachers found the stories to be one of the most effective methods to teach behaviours and deal with inappropriate behaviours. The other substantial benefit is that there are no negative side effects associated with the Social Story™ intervention. Most research into the effectiveness of Social Stories™ has focused on autistic children, but Samuels and Stansfield (2011) examined the use of Social Stories™ with four adults with learning disabilities and social communication impairments characteristic of autism. Results found that all target behaviours showed positive change during at least one phase of the study, although data indicated a return towards baseline levels across all behaviours into the probe phase. Social Stories™ had a positive effect on improving social interaction in adults with social interaction impairments, even though this effect was short-lived.

Wong et al. (2015) conducted a comprehensive review into evidence-based practices (EBP) for autistic children and young adults. The review concluded that social narratives, of which Social Stories™ are a category, are an evidence-based strategy to support individuals. Additionally, Mayton et al. (2013) indicated Social Stories™ to be an evidence-based practice in relation to dependent variables; however, they acknowledged issues with external and internal validity across studies. They found above-standard acceptability in EBP indicators related to important aspects of dependent variables within studies and below-standard acceptability in indicators related to both internal and external validity of studies. The results from studies are promising and there is considerable empirical research carried out into Social Stories™ to date, although there is still insufficient evidence regarding which features are effective, and for whom (Davidson, 2015).

One possibility for providing support to teachers delivering interventions within naturalistic settings may be to use digital technology interfaces, such as iPads and tablets, as they are relatively inexpensive and often readily available within classrooms. Computers, video modelling and smart boards have been used in classrooms to support learners. Piloting a digitally mediated social story intervention, Smith et al. (2020) found that with the support of a new app, teachers were able to carry out interventions with a high degree of fidelity within their usual school settings. Behavioural data showed significant improvements from baseline to week 4 for all measures relating to the goals of the intervention (including a reduction in anxiety and an increase in understanding), some of which were still present at follow-up.

Stathopoulou et al. (2020) also evaluated the effects of digital Social Stories™ via an Android tablet on the social skills acquisition of students with autism and especially in their relationships with friends. They found that after a 4-week intervention period, Social Stories™ developed and delivered by school staff with the app were found to have significantly improved the behaviour, understanding and anxiety of autistic children and young people, based on teacher perception. In a review of the literature, Karal and Wolfe (2018) indicate preliminary evidence to suggest that Social Stories™ are a promising intervention to increase social interactions. The National Standards Project (NSP) provides essential information about interventions that have been shown to be effective and emphasises the necessity for evidence-based guidelines for intervention for autistic individuals (National Autism Center, 2015). They designate story-based interventions, which includes social stories, to be an emerging treatment related to social interaction and there is a need for additional and consistent research support to be rated as an established intervention.

─────────────── Case study ───────────────

Susan is 19 years of age and is currently living with her parents. She attends her local FE college where she is enrolled on a Life and Community Skills class. She is a popular member of the group and undertakes supported activities such as travel training, accessing the community and cookery classes. Both the tutor and her parents are keen to use Social Stories™ to help Susan gain more independence, yet still maintaining a routine in her life.

- How could you plan and use Social Stories™ to support Susan in one or more of the following scenarios?
  1. How to make toast.
  2. Visit to the dentist/hospital/opticians, etc.
  3. Lunchtime at college.
  4. Attending a transition interview to move onto a new course.
  5. Accessing public transport independently to get to college.

Lego® therapy

Lego® therapy is an intervention that has started to emerge in schools to help autistic children and young people in their social communication difficulties. Originally proposed by LeGoff (2004), this intervention employs the use of three key roles

'Engineer', 'Builder' and 'Supplier' to build a model together using Lego® bricks. This is facilitated by a trained adult, although child led, to allow the children a means of developing their social communication skills. It is an evidence-based approach that aims to develop social communication skills in autistic children and young people, such as sharing, turn-taking, following rules, using names and problem-solving. In practice, children work in groups of three with each participant having a distinct role to build a Lego® model collaboratively:

- Engineers use the Lego® instructions and ask the Supplier for the specific pieces of Lego® needed.
- Suppliers gives the Builder the pieces.
- Builders follow the building instructions from the Engineer to construct the model.

Exploiting a child's natural curiosity and motivation within Lego® to dictate a behavioural change is the fundamental ethos of Lego® therapy (Owens et al., 2008). It is a child-led and peer-based intervention that builds upon the child's interests in construction play to promote a willingness to collaborate and interact (LeGoff et al., 2010). The original intervention was solely aimed at autistic children and young people; however, it has also been found to benefit many children with communication and social developmental difficulties (LeGoff, 2004). Lego® therapy is delivered in 30-minute sessions, once per week, in which a triage of children jointly build Lego® models. The group first develop a name for the club, usually 'Lego® Club', alongside general session rules. The children take it in turns to fulfil specific roles and the session is facilitated by an adult, who supports the group in developing language and taking ownership of the build (LeGoff, 2004). The activity provides opportunities for children to use their joint problem solving, joint creativity, joint attention, verbal and nonverbal communication skills (LeGoff et al., 2010).

──────────────── Research evidence ────────────────

LeGoff and Sherman (2006) conducted a retrospective study of 60 children in receipt of weekly individual therapy and group sessions for at least 3 years. They compared the 3-year retrospective long-term outcomes for autistic spectrum children participating in Lego® therapy with a matched comparison sample of 57 children who received comparable non-Lego® therapy. Although both groups made significant gains, Lego® participants improved significantly more than the comparison subjects in increased social competence and reduced maladaptive behaviours.

Owens et al. (2008) suggest that autistic children may be attracted to Lego® due to Baron-Cohen's hyper-systemising theory (Baron-Cohen, 2006) (see Chapter 3). It has been suggested that they have a strong urge to systemise – to predict patterns and changes in lawful events (Baron-Cohen, 2008). Lego® therapy and the Social Use of Language Programme (SULP) were evaluated as social skills interventions for 6–11-year-olds with high-functioning autism and Asperger syndrome. Children were matched on CA, IQ and autistic symptoms before being randomly assigned to Lego® or SULP. Therapy occurred for 1 hour per week over 18 weeks. A no-intervention control group was also assessed. Results showed that the Lego® therapy group improved more than the other groups on autism specific social interaction scores (Gilliam Autism Rating Scale [GARS]; Gilliam, 2014). Maladaptive behaviour decreased significantly more in the Lego® and SULP groups compared to the control group. There was a non-significant trend for SULP and Lego® groups to improve more than the no-intervention group in communication and socialisation skills.

Pang (2010) worked with a pre-schooler named Adam with mild autistic characteristics such as language delays, behavioural problems and lack of social imagination. A series of self-developed observation checklists were used to monitor Adam's social emotional development, language development, challenging behaviours as well as fine motor skill development. After three Lego® intervention sessions, Adam increased his social interactions with peers, had more eye contact, started to share materials with his friends, expressed his interest in playing with peers, and improved his verbal communication ability. He also confirmed evidence of short-term maintenance of these behaviours after the interventions had ended.

Andras (2012) conducted a small-scale study that looked at the wider effect of ten weekly sessions of Lego® therapy on the social interaction skills of eight, autistic primary-aged children. Their behaviour was observed in the playground for a period before the sessions began, then immediately after the ten weeks of Lego® therapy and then again ten weeks after the therapy stopped. Findings show that there was more social interaction between the children after the sessions and that this effect was maintained when the therapy stopped. More recently, Levy and Dunsmuir (2020) found that Lego® therapy groups were effective at improving the social skills (as measured by duration of engagement, frequency of initiations, frequency of responses and positive social behaviours) for five out of six adolescent participants.

A scoping review explored quantitative and qualitative data on Lego® therapy from peer-reviewed journals, conference proceedings and dissertations (Lindsay et al., 2017). The researchers reported that 14 papers reported at least one improvement in social and communication skills, ASD-specific behaviours, belonging, family relationships, coping and reductions in playing alone. Common characteristics of the effective interventions included being group-based (with or without individual therapy), run by a clinician or educator in a clinic or a school, for a minimum of one hour per week for at least three to 18 hours' total intervention time. The broad nature of these characteristics makes it difficult to decipher the true effectiveness of the intervention, with further research needed to define the characteristics required for effectiveness.

Key research in the field

LeGoff, D. B. (2004). Use of Lego® as a therapeutic medium for improving social competence. *J Autism Dev Disord*, 34 (5), pp. 557–71.

Aim

The aim was to investigate how Lego® play could be used to improve social competence (SC), which was construed as reflecting three components: (1) motivation

(Continued)

to initiate social contact with peers; (2) ability to sustain interaction with peers for a period; and (3) overcoming autistic symptoms of aloofness and rigidity.

Method

Seven groups of children were chosen, with seven children in each group. Two subjects did not complete the minimum treatment duration, 12 weeks (both were in military families and left the state), so that N = 47, with five groups of seven and two groups of six. There were 34 males and 13 females, all between the ages of 6 and 16 years (mean age = 10.6, SD = 2.8). All 47 children in the study had been on a waiting list for treatment for at least three months, and 21 of these were on a waiting list for at least 6 months. The design utilised a waiting-list control group, with repeated measures, beginning with an intake assessment, prior to being placed on the waiting list.

The design was used to assess efficacy of a social skills intervention for autistic spectrum children focused on individual and group Lego® play. The intervention combined aspects of behaviour therapy, peer modelling and naturalistic communication strategies. Measures for the first two variables were based on observation of subjects in unstructured situations with peers; and the third variable was assessed using a structured rating scale, the SI subscale of the GARS. During the treatment phase of the study, the children participated in one individual therapy session (60 minutes), and one Lego® Club group session (90 minutes), per week.

Results

Results revealed significant improvement on all three measures at both 12 and 24 weeks with no evidence of gains during the waiting list period. Participants showed improvements in initiation of social contact with peers, duration of social interaction with peers, and decreased scores on a standardised measure of social impairment (GARS-SI). No gender differences were found on outcome, and age of clients was not correlated with outcome.

Conclusions

Lego® play appears to be a particularly effective medium for social skills intervention, and other researchers and clinicians are encouraged to attempt replication of this work, as well as to explore use of Lego® in other methodologies, or with different clinical populations.

Exercise

In this chapter, we have covered four of the most popular strategies to support autistic learners, but there are many more in common use, each with their own research and evidence-base, including behavioural and social skills and communication interventions.

The National Institute for Health and Care Excellence (NICE) (2016) publish *Guidance on Autism Spectrum Disorder in Adults: Diagnosis and management*. It can be viewed online at:

www.nice.org.uk/guidance/CG142/chapter/1-Guidance#interventions-for-autism-2

They also publish *Guidance on Autism Spectrum Disorder in under 19s: Support and management*. It can be viewed online at:

www.nice.org.uk/guidance/cg170

Taking examples from both documents, identify some specific interventions for the core features of autism, or interventions for challenging behaviour.

Research an example of each intervention with respect to how they could be used to support either of the groups.

Pause for reflection

- Looking back at the strategies covered in this chapter, should teachers and other professionals be guided by the research evidence as to what works, or by their own learners and service users?

Key points

- There are several strategies which are utilised daily in a wide range of settings when working with autistic children, young people and adults
- No single strategy can support all the characteristics of autism and the ones used need to be based on the needs of an individual and often alongside others
- Research evidence in support of these strategies is mixed but this does not prevent practitioners from using these with autistic learners
- Evidence-based research is a key tool in informing best practice
- Some of the strategies are long standing, but practitioners need to review these alongside the Assess, Plan, Do and Review, as well as the Quality First approach from the SEND Code of Practice (2015) (Department for Education and Department of Health, 2015)

Questions to consider

- If the research evidence in support of these strategies is mixed, what impact does this have on classroom practice, when they are used frequently in several contexts?
- These strategies are in use when working with autistic children and young people; how could they be adapted when working with adults?
- Some of these strategies such as PECS and TEACCH are comprehensive in the steps they propose; how could some of these be adapted if a teacher was looking to combine both approaches in their classroom?

Further reading

Alsayedhassan, B., Lee, J., Banda, D. R., Kim, Y. and Griffin-Shirley, N. (2021). Practitioners' perceptions of the Picture Exchange Communication System for children with autism. *Disabil Rehabil,* 43 (2), pp. 211–21.

(Continued)

This research examines the perceptions of practitioners who used the Picture Exchange Communication System via an online survey conducted with 120 practitioners using the strategy with autistic children. Using rating scales, practitioners reported their knowledge of PECS and their perceptions about the importance, benefits, and barriers of utilising the intervention. Practitioners reported they were confident when implementing PECS and considered integrating it at school to be important.

LeGoff, D. G. (2017). *How Lego®-based Therapy for Autism Works: Landing on my planet*. London: Jessica Kingsley Publishers.

Through a series of case histories of children with autism spectrum disorders (ASDs) who participated in Lego® therapy, this volume shows how and why this therapy is so effective. It provides practical guidance and inspiration for professionals working with children to improve their social interaction skills.

Mesibov, G. B., Naftel, S. and Howley, M. (2015). *Accessing the Curriculum for Learners with Autism Spectrum Disorders: Using the TEACCH programme to help inclusion*. London: Routledge.

This book provides educators with the principles and practices of Structured Teaching and how to apply these to enable learners to access the curriculum, whatever that curriculum may be. It includes examples of new technologies and a chapter on blending Structured Teaching and is suitable for use in a range of international educational contexts.

References

Aldabas, R. (2019). Effectiveness of social stories for children with autism: A comprehensive review. *Technology and Disability*, 31(1–2), pp. 1–13.

Alsayedhassan, B., Banda, D. R. and Griffin-Shirley, N. (2016). A review of Picture Exchange Communication interventions implemented by parents and practitioners. *Child & Family Behavior Therapy*, 38 (3), pp. 191–208.

Andras, M. (2012). The value of Lego therapy in promoting social skills in children with autism. *Good Autism Practice*, 13 (2), pp. 17–24.

Baron-Cohen, S. (2006). The hyper-systemizing, assortative mating theory of autism. *Prog Neuropsychopharmacol Biol Psychiatry*, 30 (5), pp. 865–72.

Baron-Cohen, S. (2008). *Autism and Asperger Syndrome*. Oxford: Oxford University Press.

Bondy, A. and Frost, L. (1994). The Picture Exchange Communication System. *Focus on Autistic Behavior*, 9 (3), pp. 1–19.

Bondy, A. and Frost, L. (2001). The Picture Exchange Communication System. *Behav Modif*, 25 (5), pp. 725–44.

Charlop-Christy, M. H., Carpenter, M., Le, L., LeBlanc, L. A. and Kellet, K. (2002). Using the picture exchange communication system (PECS) with children with autism: Assessment of PECS acquisition, speech, social-communicative behavior, and problem behavior. *J Appl Behav Anal*, 35 (3), pp. 213–31.

Cotterill, T. (2019). *Principles and Practices of Working with Pupils with Special Educational Needs and Disability: A Student Guide*. London: Routledge.

Davidson, A. (2015). The effectiveness of strategies that promote the inclusion of children with autism in mainstream classrooms. *The STeP Journal Student Teacher Perspectives*, 2 (3), pp. 88–106.

D'Elia, L., Valeri, G., Sonnino, F., Fontana, I., Mammone, A. and Vicari, S. A. (2014). Longitudinal study of the TEACCH program in different settings: The potential benefits of low intensity intervention in preschool children with autism spectrum disorder. *J Autism Dev Disord*, 44 (3), pp. 615–26.

Department for Education and Department of Health (2015). *Special Educational Needs and Disability Code of Practice: 0 to 25 years*. [online] Available at: www.gov.uk/government/publications/send-code-of-practice-0-to-25 [Accessed 25.06.2021].

Flippin, M., Reszka, S. and Watson, L. (2010). Effectiveness of the Picture Exchange Communication System (PECS) on communication and speech for children with autism spectrum disorders: A meta-analysis. *American Journal of Speech-Language Pathology/American Speech-Language-Hearing Association*, 19, pp. 178–95.

Francke, J. and Geist, E. (2003). The effects of teaching play strategies on social interaction for a child with autism: A case study. *Journal of Research in Childhood Education*, 18 (2), pp. 125–40.

Frea, W. D., Arnold, C. L. and Vittimberga, G. L. (2001). A demonstration of the effects of augmentative communication on the extreme aggressive behavior of a child with autism within an integrated preschool setting. *Journal of Positive Behavior Interventions*, 3 (4), pp. 194–8.

Ganz, J. B. and Simpson, R. L. (2004). Effects on communicative requesting and speech development of the Picture Exchange Communication System in children with characteristics of autism. *J Autism Dev Disord*, 34 (4), pp. 395–409.

Ganz, J. B., Davis, J. L., Lund, E. M., Goodwyn, F. D. and Simpson, R. L. (2012). Meta-analysis of PECS with individuals with ASD: Investigation of targeted versus non-targeted outcomes, participant characteristics, and implementation phase. *Res Dev Disabil*, 33 (2), pp. 406–18.

Gilliam, J. E. (2014). Gilliam Autism Rating Scale (3rd Edition) (GARS-3). Austin, TX: Pro-Ed

Glennen, S. L. and DeCoste, D. C. (1997). *The Handbook of Augmentative and Alternative Communication*. San Diego, CA: Singular.

Gray, C. (1998). Social Stories 101. *The Morning News*, 10 (1), pp. 2–6. Michigan: Jenison Public Schools.

Gray, C. A. (2004). Social Stories 10.0: The new defining criteria and guidelines. *Jenison Autism Journal*, 15 (4), pp. 2–21.

Gray, C. and Garand, J. (1993). Social Stories: Improving responses of students with autism with accurate social information. *Focus on Autistic Behavior*, 8, pp. 1–10.

Greenway, C. (2000). Autism and Asperger syndrome: Strategies to promote prosocial behaviours. *Educational Psychology in Practice*, 16, pp. 469–86.

Harvey, J. A. (2011). *What's so Special about Special? Improving inclusion for children with autism in mainstream schools*. [online] Available at: https://etheses.bham.ac.uk/id/eprint/3287/1/Harvey_12_Applied_Vol1.pdf [Accessed 01.02.2022].

Howlin, P., Gordon, R. K., Pasco, G., Wade, A. and Charman, T. (2007). The effectiveness of Picture Exchange Communication System (PECS) training for teachers of children with autism: A pragmatic, group randomised controlled trial. *Journal of Child Psychology and Psychiatry*, 48 (5), pp. 473–81.

Hume, K. and Odom, S. (2007). Effects of an individual work system on the independent functioning of students with autism. *Journal of Autism and Developmental Disorders*, 37, pp. 1166–80.

Karal, M. A. and Wolfe, P. S. (2018). Social story effectiveness on social interaction for students with autism: A review of the literature. *Education and Training in Autism and Developmental Disabilities*, 53 (1), pp. 44–58.

Kliemann, K. (2014). A synthesis of literature examining the structured teaching components of the TEACCH model employing the use of a visual conceptual model. *The Journal of Special Education Apprenticeship*, 3 (2), 3

Kokina, A. and Kern, L. (2010). Social Story interventions for students with autism spectrum disorders: A meta-analysis. *J Autism Dev Disord*, 40 (7), pp. 812–26.

Kravits, T. R., Kamps, D. M., Kemmerer, K. and Potucek, J. (2002). Brief report: Increasing communication skills for an elementary-aged student with autism using the Picture Exchange Communication System. *J Autism Dev Disord*, 32 (3), pp. 225–30.

LeGoff, D. B. (2004). Use of Lego® as a therapeutic medium for improving social competence. *J Autism Dev Disord*, 34 (5), pp. 557–71.

LeGoff, D. B. and Sherman, M. (2006). Long-term outcome of social skills intervention based on interactive LEGO play. *Autism*, 10 (4), pp. 317–29.

LeGoff, D. B., Krauss, G. W. and Levin, S. A. (2010). LEGO®-based play therapy for autistic spectrum children. In A. A. Drewes and C. E. Schaefer (Eds), *School-based Play Therapy*. New York: John Wiley and Sons Inc, pp. 221–235.

Lerna, A., Esposito, D., Conson, M. and Massagli, A. (2014). Long-term effects of PECS on social-communicative skills of children with autism spectrum disorders: A follow-up study. *International Journal of Language and Communication Disorders*, 49 (4), pp. 478–85.

Levy, J. and Dunsmuir, S. (2020). LEGO®-based therapy: Building social skills for adolescents with an autism spectrum disorder. *J Educ Child Psychol*, 37 (1), pp. 58–83.

Lindsay, S., Hounsell, K. G. and Cassiani, C. (2017). A scoping review of the role of LEGO® therapy for improving inclusion and social skills among children and youth with autism. *Disabil Health J*, 10 (2), pp. 173–82.

Martin, C. S. (2014). Exploring the impact of the design of the physical classroom environment on young children with autism spectrum disorder (ASD). *Journal of Research in Special Educational Needs*, 16 (4), pp. 280–98.

Mayton, M. R., Menendez, A. L., Wheeler, J. J., Carter, S. L. and Chitiyo, M. (2013). An analysis of Social Stories research using an evidence-based practice model. *Journal of Research in Special Educational Needs*, 13 (3), pp. 208–17.

Mesibov, G. B. and Shea, V. (2010). The TEACCH Program in the Era of Evidence-Based Practice. *Journal of Autism Developmental Disorders*, 40 (5), pp. 570–79.

Mesibov, G. B., Shea, V. and Schopler, E. (2005). *The TEACCH Approach to Autism Spectrum Disorders*. New York: Kluwer.

NasoudiGharehBolagh, R., Zahednezhad, H. and VosoughiIlkhchi, S. (2013). The effectiveness of treatment-education methods in children with autism disorders. *Procedia – Social and Behavioral Sciences*, 84, pp. 1679–83.

National Autism Center (2015). *National Standards Project*. [online] Available at: https://nationalautismcenter.org/national-standards-project/ [Accessed 23.01.2022].

Owens, G., Granader, Y., Humphrey, A. and Baron-Cohen, S. (2008). LEGO therapy and the social use of language programme: An evaluation of two social skills interventions for children with high functioning autism and Asperger Syndrome. *J Autism Dev Disord*, 38 (10), pp. 1944–57.

Panerai, S., Ferrante, L. and Caputo, V. (1997). The TEACCH strategy in mentally retarded children with autism: A multidimensional assessment. Pilot study. Treatment and Education of Autistic and Communication Handicapped children. *J Autism Dev Disord*, 27 (3), pp. 345–7.

Panerai, S., Ferrante, L. and Zingale, M. (2002). Benefits of the Treatment and Education of Autistic and Communication Handicapped Children (TEACCH) programme as compared with a non-specific approach. *Journal of Intellectual Disability Research*, 46 (4), pp. 318–27.

Panerai, S., Zingale, M., Trubia, G., Finocchiaro, M., Zuccarello, R., Ferri, R. and Elia, M. (2009). Special education versus inclusive education: The role of the TEACCH program. *J Autism Dev Disord*, 39 (6), pp. 874–82.

Pang, Y. (2010). Lego games help young children with autism develop social skills. *International Journal of Education*, 2 (2), pp. 1–9.

Reynhout, G. and Carter, M. (2009). The use of social stories by teachers and their perceived efficacy. *Research in Autism Spectrum Disorders*, 3 (1), pp. 232–51.

Rust, J. and Smith, J. (2006). How should the effectiveness of social stories to modify the behavior of child on the autistic spectrum be tested? *SAGE Publications and the National Autistic Society*, 10 (2), pp. 125–38.

Samuels, R. and Stansfield, J. (2011). The effectiveness of social stories to develop social interactions with adults with characteristics of autism spectrum disorder. *British Journal of Learning Disabilities*, 40, pp. 272–85.

Sanz-Cervera, P., Fernández-Andrés, M. I., Pastor-Cerezuela, G. and Tárraga-Mínguez, R. (2018). The Effectiveness of TEACCH intervention in autism spectrum disorder: A review study. *Papeles del Psicólogo / Psychologist Papers*, 39 (1), pp. 40–50.

Scattone, D., Wilczynski, S. M., Edwards, R. P. and Rabian, B. (2002). Decreasing disruptive behaviors of children with autism using social stories. *J Autism Dev Disord*, 32 (6), pp. 535–43.

Schopler, E., Mesibov, G. B. and Hearsey, K. (1995). Structured teaching in the TEACCH system. In E. Schopler and G. B. Mesibov (Eds), *Learning and Cognition in Autism (Current Issues in Autism)*. Boston, MA: Springer.

Schwartz, I. S., Garfinkle, A. N. and Bauer, J. (1998). The Picture Exchange Communication System: Communicative outcomes for young children with disabilities. *Topics in Early Childhood Special Education*, 18 (3), pp. 144–59.

Smith, E., Toms, P., Constantin, A., Johnson, H., Harding, E. and Brosnan, M. (2020). Piloting a digitally-mediated social story intervention for autistic children led by teachers within naturalistic school settings. *Research in Autism Spectrum Disorders*, 75.

Sparrow, S. S., Cicchetti, D. and Balla, D. A. (2005). *Vineland Adaptive Behavior Scales* (2nd Edition) (Vineland-II) [Database record]. APA PsycTests.

Stathopoulou, A., Loukeris, D., Karabatzaki, Z., Politi, E., Salapata, Y. and Drigas, A. (2020). Evaluation of mobile apps' effectiveness in children with autism social training via digital social stories. *International Journal of Interactive Mobile Technologies (iJIM)*, 14 (3), pp. 4–17.

TEACCH (2022). *TEACCH® Autism Program*. [online] Available at: https://teacch.com/ [Accessed 02.02.2022].

Thiemann, K. S. and Goldstein, H. (2001). Social stories, written text cues, and video feedback: Effects on social communication of children with autism. *Journal of Applied Behavior Analysis*, 34 (4), pp. 425–46.

Tsang, S. K., Shek, D. T., Lam, L. L., Tang, F. L. and Cheung, P. M. (2007). Brief report: Application of the TEACCH program on Chinese pre-school children with autism – Does culture make a difference? *J Autism Dev Disord*, 37 (2), pp. 390–406.

Van Bourgondien, M. E. and Coonrod, E. (2013). TEACCH: An intervention approach for children and adults with autism spectrum disorders and their families. In S. Goldstein and J. A. Naglieri (Eds), *Interventions for Autism Spectrum Disorders: Translating science into practice*. New York: Springer, pp. 75–105.

Virues-Ortega, J., Julio, F. M. and Pastor-Barriuso, R. (2013). The TEACCH program for children and adults with autism: A meta-analysis of intervention studies. *Clin Psychol Rev*, 33 (8), pp. 940–53.

Wong, C., Odom, S. L., Hume, K. A., Cox, A. W., Fettig, A., Kucharczyk, S., Brock, M. E., Plavnick, J. B., Fleury, V. P. and Schultz, T. R. (2015). Evidence-based practices for children, youth, and young adults with autism spectrum disorder: A comprehensive review. *J Autism Dev Disord*, 45 (7), pp. 1951–66.

Yoder, P. and Lieberman, R. (2009). Brief report: Randomized test of the efficacy of Picture Exchange Communication System on highly generalized picture exchanges in children with ASD. *Journal of Autism and Developmental Disorders*, 40, pp. 629–32.

Zazzi, H. and Faragher, R. (2018). 'Visual clutter' in the classroom: Voices of students with autism spectrum disorder. *International Journal of Developmental Disabilities*, 64 (3), pp. 212–24.

SIX

The role of genetics and neurobiology in the aetiology of autism

Introduction

This chapter follows on from Chapter 2 and begins with an overview of research into the importance of chromosomes and genes in the development of autism. Examining the importance of family and twin studies, it focuses upon the complexity of genetic transmission, the impact that this has on brain structure and function related to aspects of autism, including evidence from empirical research. As genetics cannot account for all the characteristics, the significance of risk and environmental factors is examined.

——————————— Learning objectives ———————————

This chapter will:

- Invite you to evaluate the research evidence to explain the role of chromosomes and genes in the aetiology of autism
- Invite you to evaluate the research evidence in understanding the impact that neurobiology has on the aetiology of autism
- Introduce you to the concept of connectivity within the brain that may explain certain aspects of autism
- Help you to consider the importance of risk factors to our understanding of autism

——————————— Key terms ———————————

Chromosomes, genes, mutations, twin studies, brain structure and function, connectivity, environment, risk factors

─────────────────────── Pause for reflection ───────────────────────

- You are asked by a parent of an autistic child, what has caused my child to become autistic?
- How would you go about finding information to help you frame a response?

───

Chromosomes, genes and autism

When autism was first described, it was hypothesised to be an environmentally caused disease. Decades of research have since revealed that autism is a highly heterogeneous and extremely complex genetic condition (Rylaarsdam and Guemez-Gamboa, 2019). Although the aetiology of autism does not reveal robust developmental markers, literature has continued to investigate its genetic and neurological factors. For example, Minshew et al. (1997) suggested that abnormalities in genetic code, differing mechanisms of brain development and cognitive, neurological factors all contribute to the behaviour syndrome that presents itself. For example, Stigler et al. (2011) report on the emergence of functional MRI techniques which led to an enhanced understanding of the neural circuitry of ASDs, demonstrating areas of dysfunctional cortical activation and atypical cortical specialisation. Carper et al. (2002) found that frontal, temporal and parietal white matter volumes, as well as frontal and temporal grey matter volumes, changed at significantly slower rates in autism patients.

Although methodologically diverse, current studies agree that at least two to four distinct autistic neuro-subtypes may exist (Hong et al., 2020). Early research (Folstein and Rutter, 1977) noted that genetic influence on autism is not due to just one gene but that there is a possibility that genetic influence on autism may be due to many genes of small effect size. Changes in over 1,000 genes have been reported to be associated with autism, but many of these associations have not been confirmed. Many common gene variations are thought to affect the risk of developing autism, but not all people with one or more of these gene variations will be affected. Individually, most of the gene variations have only a small effect. Genetic factors that have not been identified determine an individual's risk of developing this complex condition (MedlinePlus, 2021).

Satterstrom et al. (2020) identified 102 autism risk genes, expressed early in brain development; most risk genes have roles in regulation of gene expression or neuronal communication. Many of the genes found to be associated with autism are involved in the function of the chemical connections between brain neurons (synapses). In addition to genetic variations that are inherited and are present in nearly all a person's cells, recent research has also shown that de novo, or spontaneous, gene mutations can influence the risk of developing autism spectrum disorder. De novo mutations are changes in sequences of deoxyribonucleic acid (DNA) in a parent's sperm or egg cell or during fertilisation. The mutation then occurs in each cell as the fertilised egg divides. These mutations may affect single genes, or they may be changes called copy number variations (CNV), in which stretches of DNA containing multiple genes are deleted or duplicated. Autistic individuals tend to have more copy number de novo gene mutations than those without the disorder, suggesting that, for some, the risk of developing autism is not the result of mutations in individual genes but rather, spontaneous coding mutations across many genes.

A certain change in the gene sequence may make the condition very mild, so that a person doesn't have autism but has one of its symptoms instead, or a change in that sequence could make the symptoms of autism more serious. So far, the most promising leads seem to be on Chromosome 7, where genes for other language disorders are known to exist, and Chromosome 15, where genes for other developmental disorders have already been identified. Smith et al. (2020) identified a one megabase deletion in the 15q22–15q23 region in a patient with autism, developmental delay, and mild dysmorphism. Genes that map within the deletion region and genes that are interrupted or rearranged at the deletion breakpoints are candidate genes for autism.

Research with rats has modelled genetic and neurobiological development in autistic humans. For example, Ingram et al. (2000) found that rats with null mutations of HOXA1 and HOXB1, two genes critical to hindbrain development, demonstrated phenotypic features frequently seen in autistic individuals. Ingram et al. examined the cerebellar morphology of valproate-exposed rats, a drug used to treat epilepsy and bipolar disorder, and found that these rats had significantly fewer Purkinje cells and reduction in the hemispheres. The results parallel similar findings to those reported for human cases of autism. Abnormalities in anatomy and function of the cranial nerve motor nuclei have also been demonstrated in some autistic people and can be modelled in rats by exposure to valproic acid during neural tube closure.

De novo mutations, single nucleotide polymorphisms (SNPs) and copy number variations (CNVs)

Zhao et al. (2019) draw attention to how developments in genetic sequencing have led to more de novo mutations being associated with neurodevelopment, such as autism, being reported. About one-quarter of the associated genetic variants are due to de novo mutations in protein-coding genes. Brandler et al. (2018) investigated whether changes

(Continued)

in noncoding regions of the genome are associated with autism. Cheroni et al. (2020) suggest that hundreds of genes, converging at the functional level on selective biological domains such as epigenetic regulation and synaptic function, have been identified to be either causative or risk factors of autism. Autism is exceedingly heterogeneous and reflects a spectrum of genetic loads between two extremes: on the one hand, a complex and still only poorly characterised burden of low-risk variants, mostly single nucleotide polymorphisms (SNPs), and, on the other hand, many highly penetrant rare variants, often copy number variations (CNVs). Common SNPs, distributed all over the genome, have been estimated to account for at least 20 per cent of ASD liability and act additively or synergistically as risk factors, but it is reasonable to conclude that common variants affect the risk for autism, but their individual effects are modest. Gaugler et al. (2014) suggest that common variants can explain most of the heritability and estimate only 2.6 per cent of liability from rare variations. One interesting line of research is aimed at understanding timing and social timing deficits, which are fundamental in autism and may play a developmental role in its manifestation. Sleep problems are associated with this disorder, as is a reduction or loss of Purkinje cells associated with regions of the brain which coordinate fine motor movements (Wimpory et al., 2002).

The second pattern of genetic variants contributing to autism reflects the effect of rare, highly penetrant mutations or CNVs that are inherited or, more frequently, arise de novo in the germinal cells; being affected by negative selection because of their detrimental impact on reproductive fitness, their frequency in the general population remains very low. Rodin et al. (2021) implicate 46 mosaic CNV mutations arising during embryonic development as a cause of autism. Notably, the people with ASD were especially likely to have very large CNVs, with some involving 25 per cent or more of a chromosome. The CNVs spanned a median of 7.8 million bases in the ASD group, versus 0.59 million bases in controls.

See Chapter 2 for an outline of recent research into genetics.

Twin studies

Starting in the 1970s, Rutter (1978) argued that autism was, in fact, a congenital cognitive disorder caused by strong genetic factors, which marked the eventual end to theories suggesting psychological or environmental factors were primarily responsible for causing autism (Rutter and Bartak, 1971). Hallmayer et al. (2011) calculated the heritability rate for 192 pairs of twins and reported a heritability rate of 37 per cent for autism and 38 per cent for autism spectrum disorder. The heritability rate of autism was shown to be much lower than expected; this led the researchers to reconsider the notion of the heritability of autism. In Sweden, Sandin et al. (2017) conducted a study of 37,570 twin pairs, 2,642,064 full sibling pairs, 432,281 maternal half-sibling pairs, and 445,531 paternal half-sibling pairs. They found that the heritability rate for autism was 83 per cent and the heritability rate from twin studies alone was 87 per cent. These results demonstrated the greater influence of genetic factors compared to environmental factors.

Historically, early research reported that autism was an innate disorder (Bourgeron, 2016). In epidemiological twin studies, comparisons of the concordance rate between monozygotic twins (MZ) and dizygotic twins (DZ) are very important. Since MZ twins are considered to share 100 per cent of their genetic information, their concordance rate is higher compared to DZ twins, who share about 50 per cent of the genetic information. Thus, genetic factors are thought to play a major role as compared to environmental factors. There is a much higher concordance rate for autism spectrum disorder in MZ versus DZ twins (Sandin et al., 2017). Taylor et al. (2020) reviewed data from 2 twin cohorts, one born between 1982 and 2008 (n = 22,678 pairs) and the other between 1992 and 2008 (n = 15,279 pairs). Genetic factors were associated with autism and autistic traits and the relative importance of these factors was consistent over time, whereas environmental factors played a smaller role.

A meta-analysis of published twin studies supports a predominantly genetic contribution to autism, by yielding a large heritability estimate of 64–91 per cent from MZ and DZ twin pairs (Tick et al., 2016). The authors suggest that autism is due to strong genetic effects and that significant shared environmental influences are likely a statistical artefact of overinclusion of concordant DZ twins. Thaper and Rutter (2021) suggest that there are negligible shared environmental contributions and recent discoveries show that rare variants of large effect size as well as small effect common gene variants all contribute to autism risk. However, the problem is that the diagnostic concordance rate varies depending on how the affected and non-affected twins are determined. For instance, the designation for autism advocated by early researchers was significantly different from the current diagnostic criteria. Moreover, it has been reported that when using the broader autistic phenotype principle, this makes the concordance rate more variable. Twins experience shared environmental factors and non-shared environmental factors (Hallmayer et al., 2011), and it has now been reported that studies of MZ twins cannot confirm that the intrauterine state is the same. Although earlier twin studies of autism were conducted in northern Europe and the USA, subsequent studies show that autism is heritable outside of these countries. For example, Bai et al. (2019) studied cohorts from Denmark, Finland, Sweden, Israel and Western Australia and found the heritability of autism was estimated to be approximately 80 per cent, indicating that the variation in the population is mostly owing to inherited genetic influences.

In conclusion, broadly, 2.6 per cent of autism cases seem to arise from rare de novo mutations, 3 per cent from rare inherited variants, and 49 per cent from common inherited variants. However, twin studies suggest that the environment accounts for between 10 per cent and 55 per cent of the risk. Abnormalities on Chromosomes 2, 5, 7, 15 and 17, along with genes responsible for early growth and development, speech and language, as well as those linked to cerebellar growth, have been implicated in the development of autism. A key concept in understanding the role of genetics is hereditability, which Lee (2020) defines as the proportion of variation in a condition that is attributable to variation in genetics, not the proportion of a condition that is caused by genes. Heritability estimates may tell us to what extent a person's genetics predispose them to a condition, but they tell us nothing about how different environments cause those genetics to play out. He argues that, in using statistical models to estimate heritability, networks of genes interact to influence a person's odds of having autism and that genetic factors raise the odds of having autism caused by environmental exposures such as infection, air pollution or nutrition. Thus, these results do not suggest that environmental factors explain the increasing prevalence of autism.

Simplex and complex families

Autism arises in high- and low-risk families. De novo mutations contribute to a large number of autism cases, particularly with respect to low-risk simplex families. Yoon et al. (2021) estimated that de novo events contribute to 52–67 per cent of cases of autism arising from low-risk families, and 30–39 per cent of cases of all autism. The unified genetic theory for sporadic and inherited autism conjectured two risk classes of families. Highly penetrant de novo mutations contribute to most low-risk families and transmission from a carrier parent contributed to autism in most high-risk families with roughly half of autism arising from low-risk families and half from high-risk families.

An explanation that links these two types of families is that sporadic autism in the low-risk families is mainly caused by spontaneous mutation with high penetrance in males and relatively poor penetrance in females; and high-risk families are from those offspring, most often females, who carry a new causative mutation but are unaffected and, in turn, sibling and DZ concordance rates are perhaps one-tenth of MZ concordance rates, and this discrepancy, plus the suggestion of a large number of risk loci, has led many to expect that autism is attributable to complex multigenic interactions rather than simple dominant or recessive mutations.

An alternative to the multigenic interaction hypothesis is worth considering: most cases of autism are due to de novo mutation in the parental germ line, which can strike any of several critical loci. The large discrepancy in concordance rates between MZ twins and siblings can be explained thus: inherited or de novo mutation in the parental germ line affects MZ twins alike, whereas sibling and DZ concordance rates represent a mixture of modalities, sometimes inherited and sometimes de novo mutation. Most autism(s) are a result of de novo mutations, occurring first in the parental germ line. For reasons yet to be determined, female offspring are considerably more resistant to displaying the effects of such mutations than are males. Gerdts et al. (2013) found molecular findings suggest that copy number variants (CNVs) in genic regions are more common in autistic individuals compared to controls. De novo or non-inherited CNVs appear to be particular risk factors in simplex ASD families relative to multiplex families (with more than one clinical diagnosed individual).

For simplex families, a variety of relatively rare single gene mutations, each of large effect, have been associated with sporadically occurring autistic syndromes. For example, Weiss et al. (2008) identified regions of rare copy number variation in families with autism and observed an association between a microdeletion on Chromosome 16 (and the inherited reciprocal duplication) and autism. For complex families, interactive effects of multiple common susceptibility alleles (each of minor influence when operating independently) have long been hypothesised and the first common allele to be identified as a risk gene for autism is a variant of the MET gene.

Although their importance has been established in families with only one affected child (simplex families), the contribution of both de novo and inherited CNVs to autism in families with multiple affected individuals (multiplex families) is less well understood. Large autism-linked mutations tend to be inherited in families with a history of the condition but in contrast they often arise spontaneously in families with a single affected person. Studying multiplex families yields clues about autism's heritability, whereas simplex families point to spontaneous, or de novo, mutations. Large deletions or duplications of DNA tend not to occur spontaneously in multiplex families and the genetic architecture in multiplex families differs from that in simplex families (Leppa et al., 2016).

——————————————— Pause for reflection ———————————————

Research into the genetic causes and the implications that this has on neurodevelopment is valuable in understating the aetiology of autism but could be criticised as being reductionist and deterministic and does not take into consideration the 'lived experience' of autistic individuals and their families.

- How would you balance these two arguments?
- How would these factors become involved in research?

Brain structures and function in autism

Abnormalities in the genetic code may result in irregular mechanisms for brain development, leading in turn to structural and functional brain abnormalities, cognitive and neurobiological abnormalities, and symptomatic behaviours. Several brain structures have been associated with autistic symptomatology, including the cerebellum, the frontal lobes, and the temporal lobes. The cerebellum is known to regulate sequenced movement, procedural learning, emotion, thought and attention shifting (Allen and Courchesne, 2003). The cerebellum receives and integrates information from the cortex and most sensory systems, and then projects to all major motor systems, the thalamus, and some sensory cortices. The cerebellum may be involved in the ability to shift attention and develop predictive relationships, which appears to be problematic in autistic individuals (Iarocci and McDonald, 2006) and the inability to shift attention may in turn lead to deficits in joint attention, which can be considered a precursor to the development of theory of mind (Carper and Courchesne, 2000). Carper and Courchesne (2000) suggest that the cerebellum may be of particular importance in the development of autism, that the potential neurological markers for autism appear to develop quite early prenatally and may involve dysregulation of cell migration, synaptic pruning, insufficient apoptosis, and problems with myelination. Structural abnormalities in both the frontal lobe and the cerebellum have important implications for understanding the development and persistence of autism.

The frontal lobe is also central to many functions that may be implicated in autism. The prefrontal cortex is involved in executive functioning with respect to working memory, inhibition, planning, organisation, set shifting, cognitive flexibility, orienting, and disengaging attention, all of which appear to be deficient among autistic individuals (Hughes et al., 1994). Also, 40–70 per cent of individuals with autism exhibit higher order cognitive impairment, suggesting that the frontal lobe may be implicated due to its role in executive functioning (Fombonne, 2005). The frontal lobe is also one of several neural regions implicated in language. Broca's area, which mediates language production, is in the inferior prefrontal lobe. As autism is characterised by impairments in communication, ranging from a total lack of speech to difficulties with pragmatic language, this region may be involved. The functions of the temporal lobe are numerous and include audition, memory, and object perception, as well as functions that may be affected in individuals with autism. The temporal lobe is associated with receptive language, particularly because it includes Wernicke's area. The temporal lobe also appears to be involved in many of the functions that can be considered part of social cognition: joint attention, action observation and empathy. Schultz (2005) suggests that visual perceptual areas of the ventral temporal pathway are also involved in important ways in representations of the semantic attributes of people, social knowledge and social cognition. In conjunction with the amygdala, and parts of the frontal lobe, it may also mediate facial processing. Zilbovicius et al. (2006) argue that dysfunction in this region underlies the social deficits that characterise autism; for example, if individuals are unable to process faces effectively, this may underlie some of the inability to engage in social interaction.

Exercise

Chapter 7 outlines the psychological impact of genetic and neurobiological factors on autistic characteristics, in particular Theory of Mind, Executive Functioning, Central Coherence and Empathising-Systemising.

- How does the structure and function of the brain relate to these theories?

Synaptic deficits mediated by genetic factors in autism not only affect their anatomical structure, but also affect the aspects of local neuronal circuitry and the functions of brain regions. These are also related to the neuronal development and microstructural makeup of cortical folding. Differences in brain anatomy are relevant to specific clinical symptoms and features of autism and it is likely a 'neural systems' condition that is mediated by abnormalities in regionally distributed cortical networks rather than separated brain regions, with Lenroot and Yeung (2013) referring to it as a developmental disconnection syndrome. A common feature of the research into neuroanatomy is that it points to autism as a disorder of the cortex. Research has also been carried out into how neurons within the brain are connected via synapses.

─────────────── Key research in the field ───────────────

Supekar, K., de Los Angeles, C., Ryali, S., Cao, K., Ma, T. and Menon, V. (2022). Deep learning identifies robust gender differences in functional brain organization and their dissociable links to clinical symptoms in autism. *The British Journal of Psychiatry*, 220 (4), pp. 202–209.

Objective

Autism spectrum disorder affects nearly 1 in 189 females and 1 in 42 males. However, the neurobiological basis of gender differences in ASD is poorly understood and the aim of this study was to identify robust functional brain organisation markers that distinguish between autistic females and males and predict symptom severity based upon underlying biological patterns rather than overt or reported symptoms.

Method

An artificial intelligence framework that distinguished between autistic females and males with ASD and predicts the severity of clinical symptoms was used. This technology was applied to imaging data from 678 autistic children and the team was able to distinguish between boys and girls with 86 per cent accuracy. In addition, it was used to analyse 976 brain scans from typically developing boys and girls.

Findings

Among children with autism, girls had different patterns of functional connectivity to boys in several brain centres, including motor, language, and visuospatial attention systems. The largest differences between the genders were in a group of motor areas, including the primary motor cortex. Furthermore, among the girls with autism, differences in motor areas were linked to the severity of their repetitive behaviours. Autistic girls usually have fewer repetitive behaviours than boys with autism, which may contribute to delays in their diagnosis, the researchers suggest.

The team's results suggested that girls with autism whose brain patterns were more similar to those in boys with autism tended to have the most pronounced repetitive behaviors. It is not yet clear if the same pattern applies to observed differences in language centres of the brain that the study identified in boys and girls with ASD diagnoses. Language difficulties are usually more pronounced in males, the researchers pointed out.

Notably, the artificial intelligence framework could not distinguish between neurotypical females and males, suggesting that there are gender differences in the functional brain organisation in autism that differ from normative gender differences.

Conclusion

The brains of autistic females and males are functionally organised differently, contributing to their clinical symptoms in distinct ways. They inform the development of gender-specific diagnoses and treatment strategies for autism.

Connectivity in the brain

Geschwind and Levitt (2007) suggest that autism has many aetiologies and should be considered not as a single disorder but, rather, as 'autisms' and they propose a potential unifying model in which higher-order association areas of the brain that normally connect to the frontal lobe are partially disconnected during development. They put forward a theory of developmental disconnection which accommodates neurobehavioural features, development, and the heterogeneity of autism aetiology, behaviours, and cognition. A significant proportion of people with autism (approximately 20 per cent) have been found to have statistically larger and heavier brains identified by cranium measurements and structural neuroimaging. Vissers et al. (2012) reviewed findings from studies investigating functional and structural brain connectivity in high-functioning autistic individuals and found long-range cortico-cortical functional and structural connectivity, suggesting over-connectivity at a young age and under-connectivity at older ages, which may reflect impaired synaptic pruning (and therefore overgrowth) during brain development. Children and adolescents with autism have a surplus of synapses in the brain, and this excess is due to a slowdown in a normal brain 'pruning' process during development. Because synapses are the points where neurons connect and communicate with each other, the excessive synapses may have profound effects on how the brain functions. fMRI and EEG studies suggest that autistic adults have local over-connectivity in the cortex and weak functional connections between the frontal lobe and the rest of the cortex.

What all the brain findings have in common is that they point to autism as a disorder of the cortex. The cortex is the proverbial 'grey matter': the part of the brain which is largely responsible for higher brain functions, including sensation, voluntary muscle movement, thought, reasoning, and memory. In many autistic people, the brain develops too quickly, beginning at about 12 months, and by age 10, their brains are at a normal size, but 'wired' atypically. The consequences, in terms of disturbing early development, include problems within the cortex and from the cortex to other regions of the cortex in ways that compromise language and reasoning abilities. A look at how the brain processes information finds a distinct pattern in children with autism spectrum disorders. Using EEGs to track the brain's electrical crosstalk, researchers from Boston Children's Hospital (Biospace, 2013) have found a structural difference in brain connections. Compared with neurotypical children, those with autism have multiple redundant connections between neighbouring brain areas at the expense of long-distance links. They examined brain networks in terms of their capacity to transfer and process information. There were more short-range connections within different brain regions, but fewer connections linking far-flung areas. A brain network that favours short-range over long-range connections seems to be consistent with autism's classic cognitive profile – a child who excels at specific, focused tasks like memorising streets, but who cannot integrate information across different brain areas into higher-order concepts.

For example, a child with autism may not understand why a face looks angry, because his visual brain centres and emotional brain centres have less crosstalk. The brain cannot integrate these areas. It's doing a lot with the information locally, but it's not sending it out to the rest of the brain. It's a simpler, less specialised network that's more rigid, less able to respond to stimulation from the environment. Those who had autism also had the pattern of increased short-range versus long-range connections. Fahim et al. (2011) state that the autism phenotype is associated with an excess of brain volume due in part to decreased pruning during development. They speculate that this excess suggests reduced regression of neuronal processes 'pruning' in cortical and subcortical regions in AUT/FXS, which may be due to a mutation in specific genes involved in pruning and/or a lack of socio-emotional environmental experience during a critical developmental period.

In conclusion, Just et al. (2007) view autism as being a complex information processing disorder: intact or enhanced simple information processing, but poor complex/higher-order processing. fMRI and EEG studies suggest that adults with ASD have local over-connectivity in the cortex and weak functional connections between the frontal lobe and the rest of the cortex. Under-connectivity is within each hemisphere of the cortex and, thus, autism is a disorder of the association cortex. While social and communication skills may be compromised by the unique wiring in the brain, other abilities are enhanced. Autistic people have a stellar ability to use the visual parts of the right side of the brain to compensate for problems with language processing. This may be the basis for detail-orientated processing and may be a decided advantage!

------------------------------ Case study ------------------------------

Sarah is aged 16 and will start college next year, undertaking an Art and Design course. She has a profile which includes strengths in visual, rule-based and interest-based thinking. She has excellent skills in rote learning and remembering information. However, she has issues with social skills and decoding emotions through facial expression.

- How could this profile relate to connectivity within the brain?
- What advice could you give to her tutor on the new course in helping support transition and engagement on the course?

Autism is a complex disorder resulting from the combination of genetic and environmental factors and although genetic factors have shown to be accountable for the occurrence of autism, they do not fully account for all cases. Many environmental risk factors are inter-related and their identification and comparison might unveil a common scheme of alterations on a contextual as well as molecular level

(Grabrucker, 2013). It is likely that a certain combination of genes, environmental factors and possibly immunological factors influences the developmental process. Matelski and Van de Water (2016) suggest that pharmaceutical drugs, toxicants, metabolic and nutritional factors, maternal infection during pregnancy, autoantibodies to foetal brain proteins, and familial autoimmune disease have consistently been observed across multiple studies. Several environmental exposures have been identified for future study, including lead, polychlorinated biphenyls (PCBs), insecticides, automotive exhaust, hydrocarbons, and flame retardants (Shelton et al., 2012). The interaction between environmental and genetics remains a primary mechanism in autism pathophysiology, but the complex interplay of multiple genes and environmental factors makes it difficult to measure the relative contributing factors to the risk of autism.

--------------------------- Pause for reflection ---------------------------

• Why is it difficult to research environmental and risk factors in the aetiology of autism?

Environmental factors

Examining the exposure to various environmental pollutants during critical developmental periods, Pagalan et al. (2019), for example, found an association between exposure to nitric oxide (NO) and ASD but not nitrogen dioxide (NO_2), and Guo et al. (2018) stated that dioxin exposure during critical developmental periods is associated with an increased risk for developing ASD or ASD-like traits. However, in real world environments, dioxins coexist with various pollutants that bear different degrees of neurotoxicity; therefore, risk for autism may be confounded by such co-exposure to other pollutants. Grabrucker (2013) proposes a window during development in which brain pathways are more susceptible to disruption and that there are many environmental factors which can influence the development of autism, particularly lead or inorganic mercury. There is conflicting evidence on the exposure to cigarette smoking as a risk factor in pregnancy, with Wang et al. (2017) and Hadjkacem et al. (2016) highlighting that the chemicals in cigarettes can lead to foetal hypoxia and affect brain development.

However, Modabbernia et al. (2017) suggest that smoking during pregnancy does not increase the risk of the child developing autism. Sealey et al. (2016) identified that common ingredients in cosmetics and herbicides, to which almost all of us are regularly exposed, have been associated with the development of autism. Although epidemiological studies have identified numerous risk factors, none has demonstrated to be sufficient alone to account for the occurrence of autism. Cogley et al. (2021) found considerable variability among studies with regard to design, gestational age range, and risk factors investigated, as well as the age at which diagnostic assessments were completed. Matelski and Van de Water (2016) state that although advances in the recognition of exposure, changes and risk factors that contribute to autism have been made, creating relevant exposure profiles is essential to developing an understanding of how these account for the risk in developing autism.

Risk factors

One risk factor may be preterm infant birth (Cogley et al., 2021), with research showing that infants born preterm (<37 weeks' gestation) are at increased risk for cognitive, language and social-emotional development and risk of attention, social-emotional and cognitive problems in education. In a meta-analysis, Agrawal et al. (2018) found that the prevalence of autism is significantly high in the preterm population. Brumbaugh et al. (2014) hold the view that low gestational age may reflect the susceptibilities in the developing brain and reported that the increased risk may reflect maternal and perinatal characteristics that are more common for children born prematurely and may influence early brain development. Persson et al. (2020) analysed data of 3.5 million children born in Sweden, Finland and Norway between 1995 and 2015. The aim of the study was to explore the correlation between the week a child was born and the risk of autism. The results show that the children born at term (in weeks 37–42) had the lowest risk rate of 0.83, for babies born preterm in weeks 22–31, the risk rate was about 1.67, while for the babies born preterm in weeks 32–36 the risk rate was 1.08. Finally, post-term birth, in weeks 43–44, was associated with the highest risk rate observed (1.74).

Moreover, it should not just be preterm births and low gestational weight that should be considered as a risk factor for autism. Another risk factor researched has been that of parental age, with an increased parental age enhancing methylation in gametes which causes damage to the foetus's DNA (Matelski and Van de Water, 2016). This risk factor has been further supported by other studies, revealing the older the parental age, the higher the occurrence rate of autism. Lee and McGrath (2015) found paternal age to be a higher risk than the maternal age and that the increased risk of autism in the offspring of older mothers may be related to mechanisms different from those operating in older fathers. However, Larsson et al. (2005) found that there was no statistically significant association between risk of autism and weight for gestational age, parity, number of antenatal visits, parental age, or socioeconomic status. Results suggest that prenatal environmental factors and parental psychopathology are associated with the risk of autism. These factors seem to act independently.

Al-Haddad et al. (2019) suggest that certain infections during pregnancy can cause foetal brain injury, neurologic developmental abnormalities, and an increased lifelong risk for psychiatric disorders in children including those with autism, and that the scale of risk may differ by the type and severity of the maternal infection. They found an increased risk for autism if the maternal infection was severe (sepsis, pneumonia, pyelonephritis, meningitis, influenza, and chorioamnionitis) or a urinary tract infection. Hadjkacem et al. (2016) also suggested maternal infection was high (12 per cent) in parents of children with autism compared to 3.9 per cent of non-autistic children, suggesting perinatal and postnatal factors may also contribute to the onset of autism, including complication during birth causing foetal distress and lack of oxygen causing brain damage and increased risk of autism. Lyall et al. (2014) discovered that not only were maternal health and infections related to autism, but also supplementary vitamins, external pollution, and parental stresses. They reviewed 13 research papers related to smoking during pregnancy, concluding no significant relation to autism.

The stress of parents of autistic children (Kiami and Goodgold, 2017) reaches clinically significant levels, with 77 per cent of parents having significantly greater stress levels than the stress of parents with typically developing children, and Rao and Beidel (2009) found results indicate parents of children with high-functioning autism (HFA) experience significantly more parenting stress than parents of children with no psychological disorder. Autism can give rise to one of the most complex networks of family stressors and Karst and Van Hecke (2012) suggest that there is a plethora of difficulties among caregivers, including decreased parenting efficacy, increased parenting stress, and an increase in mental and physical health problems. In addition to significant financial strain and time pressures, high rates of divorce and lower overall family wellbeing highlight the burden that having an autistic child can place on families. Gray (2003) found a remarkable difference in the personal impact that mothers and fathers experienced of their child's disability. Mothers were found to be directly and considerably affected by their child's autism while fathers claimed the effect to be indirect, e.g. experiencing stress through their partners. Furthermore, mothers were more burdened with domestic responsibilities, whereas fathers focused on economic provision.

To conclude, Modabbernia et al. (2017) suggest that current evidence points to the view that several environmental factors including vaccination, maternal smoking, thimerosal exposure, and most likely assisted reproductive technologies are unrelated to risk of autism. On the other hand, advanced parental age is associated with higher risk of autism. Birth complications that are associated with trauma or ischaemia and hypoxia have also shown strong links to autism, whereas other pregnancy-related factors such as maternal obesity, maternal diabetes, and Caesarean section have shown a less strong (but significant) association with risk of autism. Research has been and is being undertaken to examine the impact of genetics on how the brain develops and functions, alongside the heritability rate in autism. Compared to genetic studies of autism, studies of environmental risk factors are in their infancy and have significant methodological limitations.

---------------------------------- Case study ----------------------------------

Jess, aged 9, is autistic. She attends a mainstream school and lives at home with her mum and dad and two brothers, both of whom are autistic. Her mum has been reading up about autism and notices some points that she would like to investigate further. They live near a main road, and she always thought that her dad showed signs of autism but was never diagnosed.

- What advice would you give her to gain more information?

---------------------------------- Key points ----------------------------------

- Research evidence seeks to explain the role of chromosomes and genes in the aetiology of autism
- The influence of genetics impacts upon the structure and functioning of the brain, including the importance of connectivity
- Autism arises in high- and low-risk families and research suggests that there are both complex and simplex families in relation to the heritability of autism
- Pre, peri, and post-natal risk factors such as maternal age, birth complications and stress have been implicated in the onset of autism
- Research studies into environmental factors such as pesticides, pollutants and cigarette smoking are in their infancy, have significant methodological limitations and yield conflicting results

---------------------------------- Questions to consider ----------------------------------

- What further research needs to be undertaken to ascertain the relationship between the factors discussed in this chapter?
- There are a range of research methods, such as questionnaires, that you could use with respect to investigating autism in families. What questions would you ask? Are there any ethical issues involved in such research?
- What techniques and procedures could be undertaken in researching the structure and functions associated with the neuro(a)typical brain?

---------------------------------- Further reading ----------------------------------

Chaste, P. and Leboyer, M. (2012). Autism risk factors: Genes, environment, and gene-environment interactions. *Dialogues in Clinical Neuroscience*, 14 (3), pp. 281–92.

The aim of this review is to summarise the key findings from genetic and epidemiological research, which show that autism is a complex disorder resulting from the combination of genetic and environmental factors. The identification of specific alleles contributing to the autism spectrum has supplied important pieces for the autism puzzle. However, many questions remain unanswered,

(Continued)

and new questions are raised by recent results. Moreover, given the amount of evidence support-ing a significant contribution of environmental factors to autism risk, it is now clear that the search for environmental factors should be reinforced.

Fahim, C., Meguid, N. A., Nashaat, N. H., Yoon, U., Mancini-Marıe, A. and Evans, A. C. (2011). The neuroanatomy of the autistic phenotype. *Research in Autism Spectrum Disorders*, 6, pp. 898–906.

The autism phenotype is associated with an excess of brain volume due in part to decreased pruning during development. This study assesses brain volume early in development to further elucidate previous findings in autism and determine whether this pattern is restricted to idiopathic autism or shared within the autistic phenotype (fragile X syndrome [FXS]). The researchers investigated brain volume in 37 participants, using the fully automated Civet pipeline anatomical magnetic resonance imaging, and 3 groups with intellectual deficiency: autism (AUT); its most associated FXS; and its most opposite.

Autism, its most associated FXS and its most opposite Williams syndrome (WS) were compared with each other and with normal controls (NC). The study found increased total and regional grey and white matter brain volume in AUT and FXS relative to WS and NC. The authors speculate that this excess suggests reduced regression of neuronal processes 'prun-ing' in cortical and subcortical regions in AUT/FXS, which may be due to a mutation in specific genes involved in pruning and/or a lack of socio-emotional environmental experience during a critical developmental period.

Modabbernia, A., Velthorst, E. and Reichenberg A. (2017). Environmental risk factors for autism: An evidence-based review of systematic reviews and meta-analyses. *Mol Autism*, 8 (1), pp. 1–16.

According to recent evidence, up to 40–50 per cent of variance in autism spectrum disorder (ASD) liability might be determined by environmental factors. The researchers conducted a review of systematic reviews and meta-analyses of environmental risk factors for ASD. They assessed each review for quality of evidence and provided a brief overview of putative mechanisms of environmental risk factors for ASD. Mechanisms of the association between environmental factors and ASD are debated but might include non-causative association (including confounding), gene-related effect, oxidative stress, inflammation, hypoxia/ischaemia, endocrine disruption, neu-rotransmitter alterations, and interference with signalling pathways.

References

Agrawal, S., Rao, S. C., Bulsara, M. K. and Patole, S. K. (2018). Prevalence of autism spectrum disorder in preterm infants: A meta-analysis. *Pediatrics*, 142 (3).

Al-Haddad, B. J. S., Jacobsson, B., Chabra, S., Modzelewska, D., Olson, E. M., Bernier, R., Enquobahrie, D. A., Hagberg, H., Östling, S., Rajagopal, L., Adams, W. K. M. and Sengpiel, V. (2019). Long-term risk of neuropsychiatric disease after exposure to infec-tion in utero. *JAMA Psychiatry*, 76 (6), pp. 594–602.

Allen, G. and Courchesne, E. (2003). Differential effects of developmental cerebellar abnormality on cognitive and motor functions in the cerebellum: An fMRI study of autism. *Am J Psychiatry*, 160 (2), pp. 262–73.

Bai, D., Yip, B. H. K., Windham, G. C., Sourander, A., Francis, R., Yoffe, R., Glasson, E., Mahjani, B., Suominen, A., Leonard, H., Gissler, M., Buxbaum, J. D., Wong, K., Schendel, D., Kodesh, A., Breshnahan, M., Levine, S. Z., Parner, E. T., Hansen, S. N., Hultman, C., Reichenberg, A. and Sandin, S. (2019). Association of genetic and environmental factors with autism in a 5-country cohort. *JAMA Psychiatry*, 76 (10), pp. 1035–43.

Biospace (2013). *'Hyperconnectivity' Seen in Brains of Children with Autism.* Stanford University Study. [online] Available at: www.biospace.com/article/around-the-web/-hyperconnectivity-seen-in-brains-of-children-with-autism-stanford-university-study-/ [Accessed 12.12.2021].

Bourgeron, T. (2016). Current knowledge on the genetics of autism and propositions for future research. *C R Biol*, 339 (7–8), pp. 300–7.

Brandler, W. M., Antaki, D., Gujral, M., Kleiber, M. L., Whitney, J., Maile, M. S., Hong, O., Chapman, T. R., Tan, S., Tandon, P., Pang, T., Tang, S. C., Vaux, K. K., Yang, Y., Harrington, E., Juul, S., Turner, D. J., Thiruvahindrapuram, B., Kaur, G., Wang, Z., Kingsmore, S. F., Gleeson, J. G., Bisson, D., Kakaradov, B., Telenti, A., Venter, J. C., Corominas, R., Toma, C., Cormand, B., Rueda, I., Guijarro, S., Messer, K. S., Nievergel, C. M., Arranz, M. J., Courchesne, E., Pierce, K., Muotri, A. R., Iakoucheva, L. M., Hervas, A., Scherer, S. W., Corsello, C. and Sebat, J. (2018). Paternally inherited cis-regulatory structural variants are associated with autism. *Science*, 360 (6386), pp. 327–31.

Brumbaugh, J. E., Hodel, A. S. and Thomas, K. M. (2014). The impact of late preterm birth on executive function at preschool age. *American Journal of Perinatology*, 31 (4), pp. 305–34.

Carper, R. A. and Courchesne, E. (2000). Inverse correlation between frontal lobe and cerebellum sizes in children with autism. *Brain: A Journal of Neurology*, 123 (4), pp. 836–44.

Carper, R. A., Moses, P., Tigue, Z. D. and Courchesne, E. (2002). Cerebral lobes in autism: Early hyperplasia and abnormal age effects. *Neuroimage*, 16 (4), pp. 1038–51.

Cheroni, C., Caporale, N. and Testa, G. (2020). Autism spectrum disorder at the crossroad between genes and environment: Contributions, convergences, and interactions in ASD developmental pathophysiology. *Mol Autism*, 11 (1), 69.

Cogley, C., O'Reilly, H., Bramham, J. and Downes, M. (2021). A systematic review of the risk factors for autism spectrum disorder in children born preterm. *Child Psychiatry Hum Dev*, 52 (5), pp. 841–55.

Fahim, C., Yong, H., Yoon, U., Chen, J., Evans, A. and Perusse, D. (2011). Neuroanatomy of childhood disruptive behavior disorders. *Aggr Behav*, 37 (4), pp. 326–37.

Folstein, S. and Rutter, M. (1977). Infantile autism: A genetic study of 21 twin pairs. *Child Psychology & Psychiatry & Allied Disciplines*, 18 (4), pp. 297–321.

Fombonne, E. (2005). Epidemiological studies of pervasive developmental disorders. In F. R. Volkmar, R. Paul, A. Klin and D. Cohen (Eds), *Handbook of Autism and Pervasive Developmental Disorders: Diagnosis, development, neurobiology, and behavior.* Hoboken, NJ: John Wiley & Sons Inc., pp. 42–69.

Gaugler, T., Klei, L., Sanders, S. J., Bodea, C. A., Goldberg, A. P., Lee, A. B., Mahajan, M., Manaa, D., Pawitan, Y., Reichert, J., Ripke, S., Sandin, S., Sklar, P., Svantesson, O., Reichenberg, A., Hultman, C. M., Devlin, B., Roeder, K. and Buxbaum, J. D. (2014). Most genetic risk for autism resides with common variation. *Nat Genet*, 46 (8), pp. 881–5.

Gerdts, J., Summers, D. W., Sasaki, Y., DiAntonio, A. and Milbrandt, J. (2013). Sarm1-mediated axon degeneration requires both SAM and TIR interactions. *J Neurosci*, 33 (33), pp. 13569–80.

Geschwind, D. H. and Levitt, P. (2007). Autism spectrum disorders: Developmental disconnection syndromes. *Curr Opin Neurobiol*, 17 (1), pp. 103–11.

Grabrucker, A. M. (2013). Environmental factors in autism. *Front Psychiatry*, 3 (118).

Gray, D. E. (2003). Gender and coping: The parents of children with high functioning autism. *Soc Sci Med*, 56 (3), pp. 631–42.

Guo, Z., Xie, H. Q., Zhang, P., Luo, Y., Xu, T., Liu, Y., Fu, H., Xu, L., Valsami-Jones, E., Boksa, P. and Zhao, B. (2018). Dioxins as potential risk factors for autism spectrum disorder. *Environ Int*, 121 (Pt 1), pp. 906–15.

Hadjkacem, I., Ayadi, H., Turki, M., Yaich, S., Khemekhem, K., Walha, A., Cherif, L., Moalla, Y. and Ghribi, F. (2016). Prenatal, perinatal and postnatal factors associated with autism spectrum disorder. *J Pediatr (Rio J)*, 92 (6), pp. 595–601.

Hallmayer, J., Cleveland, S., Torres, A., Phillips, J., Cohen, B., Torigoe, T., Miller, J., Fedele, A., Collins, J., Smith, K., Lotspeich, L., Croen, L. A., Ozonoff, S., Lajonchere, C., Grether, J. K. and Risch, N. (2011). Genetic heritability and shared environmental factors among twin pairs with autism. *Arch Gen Psychiatry*, 68 (11), pp. 1095–102.

Hong, S. J., Vogelstein, J. T., Gozzi, A., Bernhardt, B. C., Yeo, B. T., Milham, M. P. and Di Martino, A. (2020). Towards neurosubtypes in autism. *Biol Psychiatry*, 88 (1), pp. 111–28.

Hughes, C., Russell, J. and Robbins, T. W. (1994). Evidence for executive dysfunction in autism. *Neuropsychologia*, 32 (4), pp. 477–92.

Iarocci, G. and McDonald, J. (2006). Sensory integration and the perceptual experience of persons with autism. *J Autism Dev Disord*, 36 (1), pp. 77–90.

Ingram, J. L., Peckham, S. M., Tisdale, B. and Rodier, P. M. (2000). Prenatal exposure of rats to valproic acid reproduces the cerebellar anomalies associated with autism. *Neurotoxicol Teratol*, 22, pp. 319–24.

Just, M. A., Cherkassky, V. L., Keller, T. A., Kana, R. K. and Minshew, N. J. (2007). Functional and anatomical cortical underconnectivity in autism: Evidence from an FMRI study of an executive function task and corpus callosum morphometry. *Cereb Cortex*, 17 (4), pp. 951–61.

Karst, J. S. and Van Hecke, A. V. (2012). Parent and family impact of autism spectrum disorders: A review and proposed model for intervention evaluation. *Clin Child Fam Psychol Rev*, 15 (3), pp. 247–77.

Kiami, S. R. and Goodgold, S. (2017). Support needs and coping strategies as predictors of stress level among mothers of children with autism spectrum disorder. *Autism Research and Treatment*, 8685950, pp. 1–10.

Larsson, H. J., Eaton, W. W., Madsen, K. M., Vestergaard, M., Olesen, A. V., Agerbo, E., Schendel, D., Thorsen, P. and Mortensen, P. B. (2005). Risk factors for autism: Perinatal factors, parental psychiatric history, and socioeconomic status. *Am J Epidemiol*, 161 (10), pp. 916–25.

Lee, B. (2020). *Autism heritability: It probably does not mean what you think it means.* [online] Available at: www.spectrumnews.org/opinion/viewpoint/autism-heritability-it-probably-does-not-mean-what-you-think-it-means/ [Accessed 12.11.2021].

Lee, B. K. and McGrath, J. J. (2015). Advancing parental age and autism: Multifactorial pathways. *Trends Mol Med*, 21 (2), pp. 118–25.

Lenroot, R. K. and Yeung, P. K. (2013). Heterogeneity within autism spectrum disorders: What have we learned from neuroimaging studies? *Front Hum Neurosci*, 7, 733.

Leppa, V. M., Kravitz, S. N., Martin, C. L., Andrieux, J., Le Caignec, C., Martin-Coignard, D., DyBuncio, C., Sanders, S. J., Lowe, J. K., Cantor, R. M. and Geschwind, D. H. (2016). Rare inherited and de novo CNVs reveal complex contributions to ASD risk in multiplex families. *Am J Hum Genet*, 99 (3), pp. 540–54.

Lyall, K., Schmidt, R. J. and Hertz-Picciotto, I. (2014). Maternal lifestyle and environmental risk factors for autism spectrum disorders. *Int J Epidemiol*, 43 (2), pp. 443–64.

Matelski, L. and Van de Water, J. (2016). Risk factors in autism: Thinking outside the brain. *J Autoimmun*, 67, pp. 1–7.

MedlinePlus (2021). *Autism Spectrum Disorder*. [online] Available at: https://medlineplus. gov/genetics/condition/autism-spectrum-disorder/ [Accessed 12.12.2021].

Minshew, N. J., Goldstein, G. and Siegel, D. J. (1997). Neuropsychologic functioning in autism: Profile of a complex information processing disorder. *J Int Neuropsychol Soc*, 3 (4), pp. 303–16.

Modabbernia, A., Velthorst, E. and Reichenberg A. (2017). Environmental risk factors for autism: An evidence-based review of systematic reviews and meta-analyses. *Mol Autism*, 8 (1), pp. 1–16.

Pagalan, L., Bickford, C., Weikum, W., Lanphear, B., Brauer, M., Lanphear, N., Hanley, G. E., Oberlander, T. F. and Winters, M. (2019). Association of prenatal exposure to air pollution with autism spectrum disorder. *JAMA Pediatr*, 73 (1), pp. 86–92.

Persson, M., Opdahl, S., Risnes, K., Gross, R., Kajantie, E., Reichenberg, A., Gissler, M. and Sandin, S. (2020). Gestational age and the risk of autism spectrum disorder in Sweden, Finland, and Norway: A cohort study. *PLoS Med*, 17 (9), e1003207.

Rao, P. A. and Beidel, D. C. (2009). The impact of children with high-functioning autism on parental stress, sibling adjustment, and family functioning. *Behav Modif*, 33 (4), pp. 437–51.

Rodin, R. E., Dou, Y., Kwon, M., Sherman, M. A., D'Gama, A. M., Doan, R. N., Rento, L. M., Girskis, K. M., Bohrson, C. L., Kim, S. N., Nadig, A., Luquette, L. J., Gulhan, D. C.; Brain Somatic Mosaicism Network, Park, P. J. and Walsh, C. A. (2021). The landscape of somatic mutation in cerebral cortex of autistic and neurotypical individuals revealed by ultra-deep whole-genome sequencing. *Nat Neurosci*, 24 (2), pp. 176–85.

Rutter, M. (1978). Diagnosis and definition of childhood autism. *J Autism Dev Disord*, 8, pp. 139–61.

Rutter, M. and Bartak, L. (1971). Causes of infantile autism: Some considerations from recent research. *Journal of Autism & Childhood Schizophrenia*, 1 (1), pp. 20–32.

Rylaarsdam, L. E. and Guemez-Gamboa, A. (2019). Genetic causes and modifiers of autism spectrum disorder. *Frontiers in Cellular Neuroscience*, 13, 385.

Sandin, S., Lichtenstein, P., Kuja-Halkola, R., Hultman, C., Larsson, H. and Reichenberg, A. (2017). The heritability of autism spectrum disorder. *JAMA*, 318 (12), pp. 1182–4.

Satterstrom, F. K., Kosmicki, J. A., Wang, J., Breen, M. S., De Rubeis, S., An, J. Y., Peng, M., Collins, R., Grove, J., Klei, L., Stevens, C., Reichert, J., Mulhern, M. S., Artomov, M., Gerges, S., Sheppard, B., Xu, X., Bhaduri, A., Norman, U., Brand, H., Schwartz, G., Nguyen, R., Guerrero, E. E., Dias, C.; Autism Sequencing Consortium; iPSYCH-Broad Consortium, Betancur, C., Cook, E. H., Gallagher, L., Gill, M., Sutcliffe, J. S., Thurm, A., Zwick, M. E., Børglum, A. D., State, M. W., Cicek, A. E., Talkowski, M. E., Cutler, D. J., Devlin, B., Sanders, S. J., Roeder, K., Daly, M. J. and Buxbaum, J. D. (2020).

Large-scale exome sequencing study implicates both developmental and functional changes in the neurobiology of autism. *Cell*, 180 (3), pp. 568–84.

Schultz, R. T. (2005). Developmental deficits in social perception in autism: The role of the amygdala and fusiform face area. *Int J Dev Neurosci*, 23 (2–3), pp. 125–41.

Sealey, L. A., Hughes, B. W., Sriskanda, A. N., Guest, J. R., Gibson, A. D., Johnson-Williams, L., Pace, D. G. and Bagasra, O. (2016). Environmental factors in the development of autism spectrum disorders. *Environ Int*, 88, pp. 288–98.

Shelton, J. F., Hertz-Picciotto, I. and Pessah, I. N. (2012). Tipping the balance of autism risk: Potential mechanisms linking pesticides and autism. *Environ Health Perspect*, 120 (7), pp. 944–51.

Smith, M., Filipek, P. A., Wu, C., Bocian, M., Hakim, S., Modahl, C. and Spence, M. A. (2020). Analysis of a 1-megabase deletion i9n 15q22-q23 in an autistic patient: Identification of candidate genes for autism and of homologous DNA segments in 15q22-q23 and 15q11-q13. *American Journal of Medical Genetics (Neuropsychiatric Genetics)*, 96, pp. 765–70.

Stigler, K. A., McDonald, B. C., Anand, A., Saykin, A. J. and McDougle, C. J. (2011). Structural and functional magnetic resonance imaging of autism spectrum disorders. *Brain Res*, 22 (1380), pp. 146–61.

Supekar, K., de Los Angeles, C., Ryali, S., Cao, K., Ma, T. and Menon, V. (2022). Deep learning identifies robust gender differences in functional brain organization and their dissociable links to clinical symptoms in autism. *The British Journal of Psychiatry*, 15, pp. 1–8.

Taylor, M. J., Rosenqvist, M. A., Larsson, H., Gillberg, C., D'Onofrio, B. M., Lichtenstein, P. and Lundström, S. (2020). Etiology of autism spectrum disorders and autistic traits over time. *JAMA Psychiatry*, 77 (9), pp. 936–43.

Thapar, A. and Rutter, M. (2021). Genetic advances in autism. *J Autism Dev Disord*, 51 (12), pp. 4321–32.

Tick, B., Bolton, P., Happé, F., Rutter, M. and Rijsdijk, F. (2016). Heritability of autism spectrum disorders: A meta-analysis of twin studies. *J Child Psychol Psychiatry*, 57 (5), pp. 585–95.

Vissers, M. E., Cohen, M. X. and Geurts, H. M. (2012). Brain connectivity and high functioning autism: A promising path of research that needs refined models, methodological convergence, and stronger behavioral links. *Neurosci Biobehav Rev*, 36 (1), pp. 604–25.

Wang, C., Geng, H., Liu, W. and Zhang, G. (2017). Prenatal, perinatal, and postnatal factors associated with autism: A meta-analysis. *Medicine (Baltimore)*, 96 (18), e6696.

Weiss, L. A., Shen, Y., Korn, J. M., Arking, D. E., Miller, D. T., Fossdal, R., Saemundsen, E., Stefansson, H., Ferreira, M. A., Green, T., Platt, O. S., Ruderfer, D. M., Walsh, C. A., Altshuler, D., Chakravarti, A., Tanzi, R. E., Stefansson, K., Santangelo, S. L., Gusella, J. F., Sklar, P., Wu, B. L., Daly, M. J.; Autism Consortium (2008). Association between microdeletion and microduplication at 16p11.2 and autism. *N Engl J Med*, 358 (7), pp. 667–75.

Wimpory, D., Nicholas, B. and Nash, S. (2002). Social timing, clock genes and autism: A new hypothesis. *J Intellect Disabil Res*, 46, pp. 352–8.

Yoon, S., Munoz, A., Yamrom, B., Lee, Y., Andrews, P., Marks, S., Wang, Z., Reeves, C., Winterkorn, L., Krieger, A. M., Buja, A., Pradhan, K., Ronemus, M., Baldwin, K. K.,

Levy, D., Wigler, M. and Iossifov, I. (2021). Rates of contributory de novo mutation in high and low-risk autism families. *Commun Biol*, 4, 1026.

Zhao, H., Wang, Q., Yan, T., Zhang, Y., Xu, H. J., Yu, H. P., Tu, Z., Guo, X., Jiang, Y. H., Li, X. J., Zhou, H. and Zhang, Y. Q. (2019). Maternal valproic acid exposure leads to neurogenesis defects and autism-like behaviors in non-human primates. *Transl Psychiatry*, 9 (267), pp. 1–13.

Zilbovicius, M., Meresse, I., Chabane, N., Brunelle, F., Samson, Y. and Boddaert, N. (2006). Autism, the superior temporal sulcus and social perception. *Trends Neurosci*, 29 (7), pp. 359–66.

SEVEN

Psychological theories of autism

Introduction

Psychological theories of autism seek to explain the characteristic behaviour and thinking style in terms of underlying psychological processes, that is, how autistic people process information about other people and the environment. Historically, in the interests of parsimony, researchers focused their efforts on isolating a single primary cognitive deficit that could provide a unifying explanation for the constellation of symptoms that are unlikely to co-occur by chance (Morton and Frith, 1995). Each of the psychological theories outlined in this chapter is based on research and offers possible insights into the cognitive processes and experiences of autistic individuals. On balance, Rao et al. (2016) suggest that each considered theory explains some aspects of autism, but it is in combination that their explanatory power increases. The issue for several researchers is that the focus of many of these theories are embedded in a neurobiological approach to our understanding of autism. They argue that we should consider the dominant view of autism as a fixed, neurological deficit, instead of focusing on autism as an identity. Alongside this deficit model, is the need to reassess autism with a focus on a range of strengths and abilities.

────────────── Learning objectives ──────────────

This chapter will:

- Introduce you to several well-researched theories associated with cognitive explanations of autistic characteristics, including Theory of Mind, Executive Functioning, Central Coherence, the Enhanced Perceptual Functioning model, and Empathising-Systemising
- Invite you to evaluate empirical research on the role of psychology in autism
- Introduce you to the area of Critical Autism Research in relation to the widely held belief of the neurological basis of autism
- Invite you to consider the view that research into autism needs to include the view of autistic individuals as researchers

———————————————— Key terms ————————————————

Theory of Mind, Executive Functioning, Central Coherence, Empathising-Systemising, Critical Autism Research, looping, Pathological Demand Avoidance (PDA)

———————————————— Pause for reflection ————————————————

- What do you think is the relationship between neurobiology and psychological factors in autism?
- Why is an understanding of the psychological theories of autism important to practitioners working with autistic learners in a range of contexts?

Theory of Mind

Premack first coined the term Theory of Mind (ToM) in the 1970s, referring to the ability to impute mental states to self and others, including desires, knowledge, beliefs, and intentions, to predict behaviour (Premack and Woodruff, 1978). To display flexible and explicit ToM, it was acknowledged that children must have the capacity to construct different abstract representations of reality, and to navigate between them to distinguish their mental states from those of others using various cues, therefore acting as 'theorists' (Wimmer and Perner, 1983). Children who have good ToM show greater markers of social adaptation, better communication skills and better-quality social relationships, among other features. ToM has been a central feature of research into autism for several years. It is essentially the ability to put oneself in another's shoes: to take their cognitive, emotional, and visual perspective. Warrier and Baron-Cohen (2018) suggest that ToM deficits were caused by a defective innate cognitive mechanism, making it impossible to envision what goes on in other minds. The roots of the theory lie in infants' strong interest in people, evident in their attention to human faces and ability to respond to expressions within the first few months of life. These early studies indicated profound innate difficulties relating to other people (Rao et al., 2016). It was suggested by Baron-Cohen et al. (1985) that autistic individuals lack a ToM; this means that they struggle to form an understanding of mental states, including other people's thoughts and feelings.

Impaired ToM can affect social communication in several ways including:

- not realising what someone really means;
- not realising the effect that they have on others' feelings;
- not realising there are social hierarchies and rules of deference;
- not understanding that others might have different knowledge from themselves.

ToM tasks are still widely used to measure the ability to attribute mental states to others and the association with other aspects of social-communicative functioning The most widely used test is the unexpected transfer test of false belief, which was devised by Wimmer and Perner (1983). Typically, children are presented with a short scenario depicting a contradiction between reality and a character's belief. For example, in the change of location paradigm referred to as the Sally and Ann task, two dolls, Sally and Ann, are presented to a child. Sally places her marble in a basket, and then leaves the scene. Ann takes the marble out of the basket and puts it in a box. When Sally comes back, the child is asked where she would search for the marble. To succeed in this task, children must answer, 'in the basket', even though they know that the marble is really in the box. This type of scenario enables experimenters to determine a child's ability to understand that a person's mental state is not a simple reflection of reality.

Baron-Cohen et al. (1985) found that 80 per cent of children with autism failed the task, which supported their conclusion that children with autism may have a deficit in ToM. Even if they could pass the first task, they could not pass the second (Rajendran and Mitchell, 2007). Frith and Happé (1994) state that the idea of people with autism being characterised as enduring from a type of 'mindblindness' or lack of ToM has helped with the study of child development.

However, some authors argue that ToM-based tasks do not fully represent the abilities of autistic people because all tasks are centred around mental states derived from non-autistic people (Davis and Crompton, 2021). Bowler (1992) challenged results from these tasks and found that 73 per cent of individuals with Asperger syndrome passed the second false belief task in his study. Livingston et al. (2019) argue that there are limitations to the 'classical' ToM task, such as the Sally–Ann false belief task, or the Strange Stories task, with Gernsbacher and Yergeau (2019) suggesting that the various tasks rely heavily on spoken language. Nevertheless, Rajendran and Mitchell (2007) analysed studies into the idea of ToM and concluded that although studies into the concept are declining, the idea that autistic individuals have difficulties in understanding their mind and others is undeniable. Additionally, they acknowledge although the ToM concept can explain some cognitive differences seen in autism, it cannot be used to explain the whole autistic profile. Rao et al. (2016) conclude that ToM can explain social deficits in individuals with autism; however, they highlight that the deficits are not specific to autism and do not account for the repetitive and restrictive behaviours.

———————————————— Pause for reflection ————————————————

- There are several terms allied to Theory of Mind, including mindblindness, mentalising, mindreading, and perspective taking. How do you think these terms are related?

Central Coherence

Central Coherence (CC) is the ability to integrate pieces of information into a whole (Happé and Frith, 1996). With very weak Central Coherence, an autistic individual focuses on details without attending to the central meaning. Strong Central Coherence enables someone to comprehend and remember the gist of a conversation, story, or situation and to integrate multiple cues to get a sense of the whole. The normal operation of Central Coherence compels human beings to give priority to understanding meaning, to make 'sense' from perceiving connections and meaningful links, even from meaningless materials (Aljunied and Frederickson, 2013). In autistic children, this capacity for coherence is diminished, thus, their ability to process information is affected in that ideas and thoughts are 'detached' from context and lack meaningful connectedness with one another. This results in a unique cognitive profile of individuals with autism where they show a bias towards processing local, detailed information and a corresponding weakness in extracting global form or meaning.

The current working model of Central Coherence (Booth and Happé, 2010) is that a continuum of cognitive style may exist in the general population, from strong coherence (tendency to miss details and concentrate on gist) to weak coherence or detail focus (good proofreading and memory for details and verbatim information). On this conceptualisation, autistic people lie at the extreme detail-focused end of the normal continuum. Weak Central Coherence can impact cognition in several ways:

- If every detail is important, changes to the environment might be overwhelming.
- If every detail is important, a change may result in something that has to be learned new, rather than being understood as something that is essentially similar. Generalising is difficult.
- Challenges to integrating multiple stimuli might lead to difficulty noticing and responding to others' emotions.
- Challenges attending to and integrating a range of types of cues, rather than the 'whole' of a social scene, might lead to misinterpretation. Faulty conclusions may lead to inappropriate solutions.
- However, being able to attend to details that most of us overlook can also be a gift. It can lead to important new understandings (Baron-Cohen et al., 2009).

Weak Central Coherence (WCC) is most often demonstrated using visuo-spatial tasks such as the embedded figures test. This involves finding small shapes within larger shapes, and strong performance is thought to demonstrate an ability to ignore the latter. The initial measures of Central Coherence were based on a test developed for assessing field dependence/independence, namely the embedded figures test (Witkin et al., 1971). In the landmark study by Shah and Frith (1983), the Children's

Embedded Figures Test (CEFT) was used, which involves detecting a hidden figure (e.g. a house) within a larger meaningful drawing (e.g. a rocking horse). They found that autistic children were significantly superior in the task, which requires field-independent perceptual skills. The strong field independence is seen to reflect a diminished Central Coherence. This is the key implication of the Central Coherence theory – those autistic individuals have a unique profile of perceptual and cognitive abilities in which superiority in processing local, detail-level information is contrasted with inferiority in processing global and contextual information. WCC can account for several well-established deficits in autism, such as 'hyperfocusing', a tendency towards stimulus over-selectivity (Lovaas et al., 1979). Numerous studies have found that autistic individuals are comparatively good at the embedded figures test, and tasks requiring similar abilities such as block design, and this may indicate WCC (Happé and Frith, 2006).

Most people tend to globally process information in context and for meaning, though often at the cost of attending to or remembering local details (Loth et al., 2011). Frith and Happé (1994) proposed that in autism, the drive for coherence might be weaker than normal, theoretically named as 'Weak Central Coherence'. That is, individuals process things in a focused-detail or fragmentary way, processing the integral parts, rather than the global whole. Rajendran and Mitchell (2007) state Weak Central Coherence is a domain general process; a key strength is that it explains some of the non-social as well as social features of autism, such as acute attention to detail that ranges from thoroughness to obsession. Frith and Happé (1994) imply that it is advantageous where autistic people are good at tasks that focus on attention to local information. Conversely, Loth et al. (2011) argue that detail focusing can interfere with social functioning, specifically cognitive processes such as schematisation which modulates social understanding and hierarchical organisation, overall reducing generalisation.

The Enhanced Perceptual Functioning model

Another debate concerns how we conceptualise CC, as reduced integration or an enhanced ability to focus on local detail. Chamberlain et al. (2013) suggest that local processing biases associated with drawing appear to arise from an enhancement of local processing alongside successful filtering of global information, rather than a reduction in global processing. Happé and Frith's (2006) review of over 50 empirical studies of coherence suggested robust findings of local bias in autism, with mixed findings regarding weak global processing. Local bias appeared not to be a mere side-effect of executive dysfunction and may be independent of theory of mind deficits. Integration involves combining local and global information. For example, to determine the pronunciation of a homograph (e.g. bow = bəʊ / baʊ) (Happé, 1997), we must identify the possible pronunciations of the word (local information) and use context (global information) to choose the right one. Reduced integration might be regarded as an impairment, as it is difficult to imagine a task where it might confer advantages. Conversely, WCC could be conceptualised as an enhanced ability to focus on detail at the expense of the whole. This kind of ability could be regarded as a strength as it allows us to perform better at tasks such as the embedded figures test. The main objection to the theory of WCC has been that it does not help us understand underlying psychological mechanisms responsible for the impairments in abstract reasoning and, as such, does not provide the full account of such deficits (Radenovic, 2010).

The Enhanced Perceptual Functioning (EPF) model was originally proposed by Mottron and Burack (2001) as a framework within which the perceptual character-istics of autistic persons could be understood. This model was proposed as an alternative to WCC and suggests that patterns of perceptual processing among per-sons with savant syndromes, blindness, visual agnosia, and frontotemporal dementia are examined as models of a vertical imbalance that may be a source of enhanced abilities in general, and among autistic individuals. Previous studies found normal or even superior performance of autistic patients on visuo-spatial tasks requiring local search, like the embedded figures test. One interpretation of this is WCC, in which individuals may show a reduced general ability to process information in its context and may therefore tend to favour local over global aspects of information processing. An alternative view is that the local processing advantage may result from a relative amplification of early perceptual processes which boosts processing of local stimulus properties but does not affect processing of global context. The model proposes that an over-functioning of lower-level perceptual mechanisms dur-ing the completion of perceptual and cognitive tasks leads to the enhanced extraction of elementary visual and auditory information, thus the over-functioning of brain regions typically involved in primary perceptual functions may explain the autistic perceptual endophenotype (Mottron et al., 2006).

Exercise

The Sally–Ann false belief task is often used to demonstrate an understanding of Theory of Mind.
   The task can be viewed at:
   https://www.open.edu/openlearn/ocw/mod/oucontent/view.php?id=67018&section=1.3

- Carry out Activity 1 and answer the questions which follow.
- Watch the videoclip of Baron-Cohen carrying out the false belief task with children. What supporting evidence does he provide?

Watch the videoclip Autism and Talent with Francesca Happé
   https://www.youtube.com/watch?v=APa_0WiiUok

- What are the key points she is making in relation to autism and talent and the theories discussed in this chapter?

Executive Functioning

Executive functions depend on an extensive brain circuit, involving cortical and subcortical areas such as the prefrontal cortex, the supplementary motor area, the parietal lobe, the basal ganglia and the thalamus (Ardila, 2019). Executive Functions (EF) refer to higher-order cognitive processes such as the ability to adapt behaviour to a changing situation, to plan and organise future behaviour, and to think abstractly. It is an umbrella term for functions such as planning, working memory, impulse control, inhibition, and shifting set, as well as for the initiation and monitoring of action (Hill, 2004). Happé and Frith (1996) suggest that there is some overlap in EF, ToM and CC. Executive Dysfunction is defined as impairments is socio-communication and stereotypical behaviours and which encompasses a wide set of higher-order processes such as working memory, cognitive flexibility, inhibition, both behavioural and emotional control, initiation, and planning (Diamond, 2013). Thought to be essential to goal-oriented behaviour, executive functions are closely related to other cognitive processes such as working memory and attention and are also important in affective processing and behaviour.

Executive Functioning difficulties may manifest in everyday life as:

- difficulty planning and organising;
- difficulty concentrating, dividing attention, or shifting attention from one activity to another;
- impulse control problems – knowing how to start and stop behaviours;
- difficulty adapting to new situations;
- difficulty getting started with a task or conversation;
- difficulty reflecting on past experiences and adapting what's worked and didn't work;
- difficulty predicting ahead and planning to achieve a desired outcome or avoid a pitfall.

Baddeley (1996) suggests that EF can be explained by a unitary 'central executive', whereas others suggest a range of individual but associated processes which operate in parallel without an overarching control system (Goldman-Rakic, 1995). Lopez et al. (2005) found cognitive flexibility, working memory and inhibition, but not fluency and planning, were strongly associated with stereotyped and repetitive behaviours in autistic adults. Neuroimaging studies lend support to the idea that Executive Function difficulties can be seen as central to autism (Gilbert et al., 2008) and may relate to findings of structural and functional differences in the prefrontal cortex (PFC). Executive functioning has been found to be impaired across several psychiatric and developmental disorders such as schizophrenia, bipolar disorder, depression, addiction, obsessive-compulsive disorder, anxiety and ADHD (Goodkind et al., 2015).

A recent meta-analysis of 16 magnetic resonance imaging (MRI) studies of EF in autistic individuals found that a wider network of EF regions is not activated (May and Kana, 2020). They reported that while parts of the brain's EF network are activated in both autistic and control participants, the autistic group does not activate a wider network of EF regions such as the parietal cortex. This may be due to poor EF network connectivity, or a constrained EF network in autistic individuals.

Hill (2004) makes the explicit link to frontal lobe failure in neuropsychological patients which can impair executive function. Craig et al. (2016) reviewed 26 studies that examined Executive Function comparing ASD and/or ADHD children and found that Executive Dysfunction has been shown to be a promising endophenotype in neurodevelopmental disorders such as autism spectrum disorder (ASD) and attention-deficit/hyperactivity disorder (ADHD). The ASD + ADHD group appears to share impairment in both flexibility and planning with the ASD group, while it shares the response inhibition deficit with the ADHD group. Conversely, deficit in attention, working memory, preparatory processes, fluency, and concept formation does not appear to be distinctive in discriminating from ASD, ADHD, or ASD + ADHD. Based on a neurocognitive endophenotype, they suggested that the common co-occurrence of Executive Function deficits seems to reflect an additive comorbidity, rather than a separate condition with distinct impairments.

However, Alsaedi et al. (2020) suggest that research reporting Executive Dysfunction to be a causal factor in autism remains controversial. An accumulation of evidence has indicated that deficits in the executive functions should be considered central deficits in those with autism, since such deficits are exhibited by individuals regardless of their age and functional level.

Rao et al. (2016) suggest that the main theories seem to explain some aspects of autism, but it is in combination that their explanatory power seems to increase. Language abilities and Executive Functioning are necessary for Theory of Mind development, which in turn is required for narrative abilities to enable spontaneous conversation. Central Coherence in turn is necessary to understand the bigger picture, but no single deficit may explain all the core characteristics of autism.

———————————————— Pause for reflection ————————————————

- What do terms such as Executive Dysfunction and Weak Central Coherence say about the deficit approach that surrounds discourses in autism?

———————————————— Case study ————————————————

Frankie is aged 11 and gets on well with his mum, he loves his little brother and says he really likes learning. Frankie was always described as being on the go, 'a cross between a butterfly and a bull in a china shop' was the way his grandmother described him. However, as Frankie grew up it became apparent that things were not the same for him as other children. He enjoys Art lessons, when he can copy famous paintings and excels at spot the difference games with other children. However, his teachers have noticed that he often forgets to do homework and his mum has said that she must encourage him to start the questions he needs to research. In class, he is distracted and has an issue with listening to and following multi-step instructions, including understanding positions and roles when playing football. Happy to work by himself on tasks, he finds it difficult to be part of a group and other children often tell the teacher that he does not listen to their point of view, often appears rude and he himself says that he finds it difficult to keep friends.

- How do these characteristics relate to the theories covered in this chapter?
- Research some strategies which you think a teacher or teaching assistant could use with Frankie to support some of the described issues.

Empathising-Systemising (E-S) theory

Wen and Wen (2014) and Krahn and Fenton (2012) both discuss Baron-Cohen's (2003) principle which suggests autism is associated with the extreme male brain theory (EMB). This is discussed further in Chapter 3. Wen and Wen (2014) examine evidence of a link between excess prenatal levels of testosterone and autism and state both males and females display stereotypically male behaviours and suggest that autistic individuals demonstrate greater ability with systemising, which is seen as a male trait, than empathising, which is considered a female characteristic. They also suggest that excessive prenatal androgens have a pathological effect on neurotypical traits, which results in more males being diagnosed with autism. Baron-Cohen's Empathising-Systemising (E-S) theory suggests that core features of autism can be explained by a deficit in empathising or systemising. He claims that these are two key dimensions in defining the male and female brain, with the male brain as those individuals who systemise significantly more than in the female brain (Baron-Cohen, 2002). Empathy is the ability to distinguish another person's mental state and to respond with an appropriate emotion, whereas systemising is defined as the drive to build or analyse rule-based systems that follow rules to predict how that system will behave (Greenberg et al., 2018). Autism risk and expression are associated with brain 'masculinisation', due to exposure of prenatal testosterone. This in turn drives altered expression of sex-differential phenotypes, especially those related to systemising and empathising (Crespi et al., 2019). Baron-Cohen (2002) estimated that girls tend to be more nurturing, chatty, and humane while boys tend to engage and compete more in open aggressive behaviours (Krahn and Fenton, 2012). The hormonal link between physical aggression (an anti-social trait) and testosterone was established through studies involving animals.

The theory also suggests the deficits in empathising could account for social and communication abnormalities diagnosed in autism and could possibly account for difficulties in Theory of Mind, specifically the ability to understand others' mental states (Craig et al., 2019). From questionnaire responses, Baron-Cohen reported that autistic respondents tended to score high on systemising and low on empathising, whereas few of the typically developed respondents tested showed the same pattern (Baron-Cohen et al., 2014). According to this profile, autistic people have interests and skills in 'systematic' subjects such as engineering, science, and computing, and are less interested or skilled in dealing with people and social relationships.

--- **Key research in the field** ---

Greenberg, D. M., Warrier, V., Allison, C. and Baron-Cohen, S. (2018). Testing the Empathizing-Systemizing theory of sex differences and the Extreme Male Brain theory of autism in half a million people. *Proc Natl Acad Sci USA*, 115 (48), pp. 12152–7.

Objective

The two theories and predictions had mostly been tested in relatively small data-sets, limiting their generalisability. To address this, the researchers tested the predictions of these two theories in two large independent datasets, with very different recruitment strategies.

Method

More than 670,000 individuals (including 36,648 autistic individuals) primarily from the United Kingdom completed short versions of the EQ, AQ, SQ-R (henceforth SQ), and a measure of sensory perception (the Sensory Perception Quotient or SPQ) as a part of a Channel 4 TV documentary titled 'Are you autistic?' The SPQ was used considering the new symptom B criteria in the Diagnostic and Statistical Manual of Mental Disorders ('Hyper- or hypo-reactivity to sensory input or unusual interest in sensory aspects of the environment') to examine the role of sensory sensitivity in relation to the E-S and EMB theories.

Findings

Ten predictions of the E-S and the EMB theories were investigated and typical females on average showed higher scores on short forms of the Empathy Quotient (EQ) and Sensory Perception Quotient (SPQ), and typical males on average showed higher scores on short forms of the Autism Spectrum Quotient (AQ) and Systemising Quotient (SQ). Typical sex differences in these measures were attenuated in autistic individuals. Analysis of 'brain types' revealed that typical females on average were more likely to be Type E (EQ > SQ) or Extreme Type E and that typical males on average were more likely to be Type S (SQ > EQ) or Extreme Type S.

Conclusion

In the largest study to date of autistic traits, the researchers tested 10 predictions from the Empathising–Systemising (E-S) theory of sex differences and the Extreme Male Brain (EMB) theory of autism. They confirmed that typical females on average are more empathic, typical males on average are more systems-oriented, and autistic people on average show a 'masculinised' profile.

Critical Autism Studies

Critical Autism Studies (CAS) is a broad umbrella term that encompasses the work of activists and academics interested in disrupting the dominant view of autism as a fixed, neurological deficit, instead focusing on autism as an identity that is discursively produced within specific sociocultural contexts. It is a relatively new field of scholarly thought that originated in 2010 (O'Dell et al., 2016). The three main components of this interdisciplinary approach are scrutiny of the power relationships within autism research and practice; the promotion of positive accounts of autism that confront the prevailing negative views that influence how autism is considered; and the development of research methods and theoretical approaches to autism study that are inclusive and valuing (Davidson and Orsini, 2013).

Central to this conceptualisation of autism as a neurobiological disorder is the shared understanding of the 'deficient' and 'lacking' nature of autism. In recent years, neurobiology and 'neuroculture' have become hugely powerful ways of understanding identity and citizenship (Ortega and Vidal, 2011). Adherents of CAS suggest that the neurobiological assumptions do not fully account for the skills, ability and identity of people with autism. Within neurobiological discourse, autism is primarily described by psychiatrists, psychologists, and neuroscientists as a neurobiological disorder, as abnormalities in social interaction, emotional expression and recognition, and communication (Noterdaeme and Hutzelmeyer-Nickels, 2010). In relation to this chapter, there have been several cognitive theories discussed including Weak Central Coherence (Happé and Frith, 2006), Executive Dysfunction (Diamond, 2013) and Theory of Mind (Premack and Woodruff, 1978). Such findings have focused upon the functioning of the social brain typically using functional neuroimaging (fMRI) (Frith and Frith, 2010).

Looping

Hacking's (1995) concept of 'looping' suggests that the classifications and categories we use to define populations transform not only the categories but also the populations so defined. Hacking identifies the importance of looping in relation to the classification and

(Continued)

categorisation that happens to people who are different (O'Dell et al., 2016). An example of looping is the use of formal classifications of autism which have changed significantly since autism was first described. With each change of diagnostic criteria, what is and is not the 'official' version of autism changes. These changes can be experienced as very threatening to previously diagnosed people (and their families), not the least because diagnosis impacts on self-identity, place in the autistic community, and eligibility for support. Looping stages includes developing or changing diagnostic criteria, medicalising, searching for biological causes and genetic explanations and the implementation of treatments and interventions. However, it also emphasises the value and importance of listening to the opinions of autistic people and through autobiography, autistic people challenge what non-autistic people think they know about autism (Hacking, 2009).

Woods (2017) states that looping effects have caused the evolution and commodification of the autism humankind by the autism industry and gives the example of Pathological Demand Avoidance (PDA). He describes the notion of humankinds as including behaviour, acts or temperament, which can be used to classify sorts of people who are studied within social sciences. Humankinds are kinds that we would like to categorise and generate general and accurate knowledge about which can be used to predict how an individual will react, and autism is an example of humankind. He goes on to suggest that PDA status as humankind is contested. Although not recognised in either ICD-11 or DSM-5, the autism industry does recognise it as a humankind. By reinforcing the deficit model of autism, PDA allows predominant neurotype society to ignore the voice of people of the autism humankind (Mallett and Runswick-Cole, 2012).

Autistic people as researchers

Autistic people describe unique insights about autism derived from the lived experience of being autistic (Huws and Jones, 2015). They report that non-autistic people often do not understand autistic traits such as repetitive body movements and self-regulation strategies. Rather than developing a community of practice between researchers and the autistic population, Milton (2014) argues that autistic people have often become distrustful of researchers and their aims and are frequently frozen out of the processes of knowledge production. He argues that the involvement of autistic scholars in research and improvements in participatory methods is a necessity.

Within Critical Autism Studies, Davidson and Orsini (2013) state the importance of exploring power relationships that construct autism; enabling narratives that challenge the dominant negative medical autism discourses; and the creation of theoretical and methodological approaches that are emancipatory and value the highly individual nature of autism. For example, an autistic researcher pointed out that reduced Theory of Mind, which has been postulated to be a core deficit within autistic people, is not an impairment that resides within autistic people but rather a mutual difficulty relating, as neurotypical people also face often unacknowledged challenges understanding the minds of autistic people (Milton, 2012).

Gillespie-Lynch et al. (2017) conducted an online survey of 636 autistic and non-autistic adults' scientific knowledge about autism, how they define autism, and their endorsement of stigmatising conceptions of autism. They found that autistic partici-pants exhibited more scientifically based knowledge, were more likely to describe autism experientially or as a neutral difference, and were more often opposed to the medical model, with the suggestion that autistic adults should be considered autism experts and involved as partners in autism research. Jones et al. (2013) interviewed nine autistic college students at a specialised college for autistic people who revealed that they felt that only autistic people could truly understand autism. However, they felt that each autistic person could only speak about their own form of autism rather than about autism more generally. Fletcher-Watson et al. (2019) advocate the use of participatory research incorporating the views of autistic people and their allies about what research gets done, how it is done and how it is implemented. A key principle of participatory research is the recognition, and undermining, of the traditional power imbalance between researcher and participant. Arnstein (1996) refers to a ladder of participation to illustrate different types of participation in terms of increasing power, ranging from having no power or partnership in research, through tokenism, to a partnership model. Fletcher-Watson et al. (2019) argue that much of autism research involves no power, or only tokenistic forms of power for the autistic community and that there should be more of a focus upon inclusive participatory research.

Participatory research is also covered in Chapter 2.

Case study

John is a 24-year-old autistic adult, and he is applying for a job which he is capable of being successful in. He knows that he has skills and attributes that he thinks would add value to the workplace including:

- reliability, punctuality, and loyalty;
- honesty;
- different and creative approaches to working;
- high levels of concentration and commitment;
- resourcefulness and a logical way of thinking;
- good working memory and knowledge around specialist areas;
- respect for rules and boundaries.

However, he is worried about the interview as he concerned about eye contact and nonverbal communication. In the past, when someone has asked him a question it may not have elicited any response and gave the impression that he is rude or does not understand that there is more information wanted by the interviewer. Also, if he were to be successful, he is worried about settling in and overcoming some of the barriers he has faced in the past, such as the ones outlined in this chapter.

(Continued)

> • What advice could you give to both John and his future employer to enable these barriers to be overcome, helping him to secure and persevere in the job?

Key points

- There are several researched psychological theories which aim to shed light upon some of the characteristics associated with autism
- No one theory can explain all the characteristics associated with autism
- It is important to review the theories in the light of enhanced capabilities in autistic individuals
- Critical Autism Studies aims to disrupt the dominant view of autism as a fixed, neurological deficit
- Autistic people should be seen as important researchers in the field, as they offer unique insights derived from their lived experience

Questions to consider

- What impact will Critical Autism Studies have on the future direction of research into autism?
- There are more psychological theories associated with neurobiology and the social brain including the Diametric Mind Theory, Social Motivation Hypothesis, Intensive World Hypothesis, and the Mirror Neuron Hypothesis. Should research be focused upon these approaches, rather than the traditional theories?
- How could you get the message out that autistic people may display a range of strengths and abilities that can be directly related to their diagnosis?

Further reading

Fletcher-Watson, S. and Happé, F. (2019). *Autism: A new introduction to psychological theory and current debate.* London: Routledge.

Based on Francesca Happé's best-selling textbook, this completely new edition provides a concise overview of contemporary psychological theories about autism. Fletcher-Watson and Happé explore the relationship between theories of autism at psychological (cognitive), biological and behavioural levels and consider their clinical and educational impact. The authors summarise what is known about the biology and behavioural features of autism and provide concise but comprehensive accounts of all influential psychological models.

MacLeod, A. (2019) Interpretative Phenomenological Analysis (IPA) as a tool for participatory research within Critical Autism Studies: A systematic review. *Research in Autism Spectrum Disorders*, 64 (3), pp. 49–62.

Interpretative Phenomenological Analysis is potentially useful for gaining an insight into the lived experience of autistic individuals and aligns well with participatory approaches. This paper provides the first systematic review of IPA studies that have employed a participatory approach and considers their contribution to Critical Autism Studies. Databases were examined to identify details of the methodology, findings, and recommendations to consider each in relation to the underpinning philosophies of IPA and participatory research respectively, and their relationship to the stated aims of Critical Autism Studies.

IPA is also covered in Chapter 2.

Runswick-Cole, K., Mallett, R. and Timimi, S. (Eds) (2016). *Re-Thinking Autism: Diagnosis identity and equality.* London: Jessica Kingsley Publishers.

This book discusses several issues which are debated, including whether there is any such thing as autism; whether autism can have a neurobiological basis when there is no conclusive evidence of differences in the brain and no conclusive evidence that autism is genetic in origin; what is the point of a diagnosis of autism; and that there are no treatments that have been proven to work with all autistic children. A direct attack on the neurodiversity movement, a political identity movement which claims that autism is a neurobiological difference, the book argues that autistic people are not disabled by their autism but by society.

References

Aljunied, M. and Frederickson, N. (2013). Does central coherence relate to the cognitive performance of children with autism in dynamic assessments? *Autism*, 17 (2), pp. 172–83.

Alsaedi, R. H., Carrington, S. and Watters, J. J. (2020). Behavioral and neuropsychological evaluation of executive functions in children with autism spectrum disorder in the Gulf region. *Brain Sci*, 10 (2), 120.

Ardila, A. (2019). Executive dysfunction in subcortical diseases. In A. Ardila, S. Fatima and M. Rosselli (Eds), *Dysexecutive Syndromes: Clinical and experimental perspectives.* Cham: Springer, pp. 143–53.

Arnstein, S. (1969). A ladder of citizen participation. *AIP Journal*, 35 (4), pp. 214–16.

Baddeley, A. (1996). Exploring the central executive. *The Quarterly Journal of Experimental Psychology A: Human Experimental Psychology*, 49A (1), pp. 5–28.

Baron-Cohen, S. (2002). The extreme male brain theory of autism. *Trends in Cognitive Sciences*, 6 (6), pp. 248–54.

Baron-Cohen, S. (2003). *The Essential Difference: The truth about the male and female brain.* New York: Basic Books.

Baron-Cohen, S., Cassidy, S., Auyeung, B., Allison, C., Achoukhi, M., Robertson, S., Pohl, A. and Lai, M. C. (2014). Attenuation of typical sex differences in 800 adults with autism vs. 3,900 controls. *PLoS One*, 9 (7), e102251.

Baron-Cohen, S., Leslie, A. M. and Frith, U. (1985). Does the autistic child have a 'theory of mind'? *Cognition*, 21 (1), pp. 37–46.

Baron-Cohen, S., Scott, F. J., Allison, C., Williams, J., Bolton, P., Matthews, F. E. and Brayne, C. (2009). Prevalence of autism-spectrum conditions: UK school-based population study. *Br J Psychiatry*, 194 (6), pp. 500–9.

Booth, R. and Happé, F. (2010). 'Hunting with a knife and … fork': Examining central coherence in autism, attention deficit/hyperactivity disorder, and typical development with a linguistic task. *J Exp Child Psychol*, 207 (4), pp. 377–93.

Bowler, D. M. (1992). 'Theory of mind' in Asperger's Syndrome. *J Child Psychol Psychiatry*, 33, pp. 877–93.

Chamberlain, R., McManus, I. C., Riley, H., Rankin, Q. and Brunswick, N. (2013). Local processing enhancements associated with superior observational drawing are due to enhanced perceptual functioning, not weak central coherence. *Q J Exp Psychol (Hove)*, 66 (7), pp. 1448–66

Craig, F., De Giacomo, A., Savino, R., Ruggiero, M., Russo, L., Fanizza, I., Margari, L. and Trabacca, A. (2019). The empathizing-systemizing theory and 'extreme male brain' (EMB) theory in parents of children with autism spectrum disorders (ASD): An explorative, cross-sectional study. *J Autism Dev Disord*, 49 (10), pp. 4067–78.

Craig, F., Margari, F., Legrottaglie, A. R., Palumbi, R., de Giambattista, C. and Margari, L. (2016). A review of executive function deficits in autism spectrum disorder and attention-deficit/hyperactivity disorder. *Neuropsychiatr Dis Treat*, 12, pp. 1191–202.

Crespi, B., Read, S., Ly, A. and Hurd, P. (2019). AMBRA1, autophagy, and the extreme male brain theory of autism. *Autism Res Treat*, 1968580, pp. 1–6.

Davidson, J. and Orsini, M. (Eds) (2013). *Worlds of Autism: Across the spectrum of neurological difference*. Minneapolis: University of Minnesota Press.

Davis, R. and Crompton, C. J. (2021). What do new findings about social interaction in autistic adults mean for neurodevelopmental research? *Perspect Psychol Sci*, 16 (3), pp. 649–53.

Diamond, A. (2013). Executive functions. *Annu Rev Psychol*, 64, pp. 135–68.

Fletcher-Watson, S., Adams, J., Brook, K., Charman, T., Crane, L., Cusack, J., Leekam, S., Milton, D., Parr, J. R. and Pellicano, E. (2019). Making the future together: Shaping autism research through meaningful participation. *Autism*, 23 (4), pp. 943–53.

Frith, U. and Frith, C. (2010). The social brain: Allowing humans to boldly go where no other species has been. *Philos Trans R Soc Lond B Biol Sci*, 365 (1537), pp. 165–76.

Frith, U. and Happé, F. (1994). Autism: Beyond 'theory of mind'. *Cognition*, 50 (1–3), pp. 115–32.

Gernsbacher, M. A. and Yergeau, M. (2019). Empirical failures of the claim that autistic people lack a theory of mind. *Archives of Scientific Psychology*, 7 (1), pp. 102–18.

Gilbert, S. J., Bird, G., Brindley, R., Frith, C. D. and Burgess, P. W. (2008). Atypical recruitment of medial prefrontal cortex in autism spectrum disorders: An fMRI study of two executive function tasks. *Neuropsychologia*, 46 (9), pp. 2281–91.

Gillespie-Lynch, K., Kapp, S. K., Brooks, P. J., Pickens, J. and Schwartzman, B. (2017). Whose expertise is it? Evidence for autistic adults as critical autism experts. *Front Psychol*, 8, 438.

Goldman-Rakic, P. S. (1995). Cellular basis of working memory. *Neuron*, 14 (3), pp. 477–85.

Goodkind, M., Eickhoff, S. B., Oathes, D. J., Jiang, Y., Chang, A., Jones-Hagata, L. B., Ortega, B. N., Zaiko, Y. V., Roach, E. L., Korgaonkar, M. S., Grieve, S. M., Galatzer-Levy, I., Fox, P. T. and Etkin, A. (2015). Identification of a common neurobiological substrate for mental illness. *JAMA Psychiatry*, 72 (4), pp. 305–15.

Greenberg, D. M., Warrier, V., Allison, C. and Baron-Cohen, S. (2018). Testing the Empathizing-Systemizing theory of sex differences and the Extreme Male Brain theory of autism in half a million people. *Proc Natl Acad Sci USA*, 115 (48), pp. 12152–7.

Hacking, I. (1995). The looping effects of human kinds. In D. Sperber, D. Premack and A. J. Premack (Eds), *Causal Cognition: A multidisciplinary debate*. Oxford: Clarendon Press/Oxford University Press, pp. 351–94.

Hacking, I. (2009). Autistic autobiography. *Philosophical Transactions of the Royal Society: Biological Sciences*, 364 (1522), pp. 1467–73.

Happé, F. G. E. (1997). Central coherence and theory of mind in autism: Reading homographs in context. *British Journal of Developmental Psychology*, 15 (Pt 1), pp. 1–12.

Happé, F. and Frith, U. (1996). The neuropsychology of autism. *Brain: A Journal of Neurology*, 119 (4), pp. 1377–400.

Happé, F. and Frith, U. (2006). The weak coherence account: Detail-focused cognitive style in autism spectrum disorders. *J Autism Dev Disord*, 36 (1), pp. 5–25.

Hill, E. L. (2004). Evaluating the theory of executive dysfunction in autism. *Developmental Review*, 24 (2), pp. 189–233.

Huws, J. C. and Jones, R. S. (2015). 'I'm really glad this is developmental': Autism and social comparisons – an interpretative phenomenological analysis. *Autism*, 9 (1), pp. 84–90.

Jones, R., Huws, J. and Beck, G. (2013). 'I'm not the only person out there': Insider and outsider understandings of autism. *International Journal of Developmental Disabilities*, 59 (2), pp. 134–44.

Krahn, T. M. and Fenton, A. (2012). The extreme male brain theory of autism and the potential adverse effects for boys and girls with autism. *J Bioeth Inq*, 9 (1), pp. 93–103.

Livingston, L. A., Carr, B. and Shah, P. (2019). Recent advances and new directions in measuring theory of mind in autistic adults. *Journal of Autism and Developmental Disorders*, 49, pp. 1738–44.

Lopez, B. R., Lincoln, A. J., Oznoff, S. and Lai, Z. (2005). Examining the relationship between executive functions and restricted, repetitive symptoms of Autistic Disorder. *J Autism Dev Disord*, 35 (4), pp. 445–60.

Loth, E., Gomez, J. C. and Happé, F. (2011). Do high-functioning people with autism spectrum disorder spontaneously use event knowledge to selectively attend to and remember context-relevant aspects in scenes? *Journal of Autism and Developmental Disorders*, 41 (7), pp. 945–61.

Lovaas, O. I., Koegel, R. L. and Schreibman, L. (1979). Stimulus overselectivity in autism: A review of research. *Psychological Bulletin*, 86, pp. 1236–54.

Mallett, R. and Runswick-Cole, K. (2012). Commodifying autism: The cultural contexts of 'disability' in the academy. In D. Goodley, B. Hughes and L. Davis (Eds), *Disability and Social Theory*. London: Palgrave Macmillan.

May, K. and Kana, R. (2020). Frontoparietal network in executive functioning in autism spectrum disorder. *Autism Res*, 13, pp. 1762–77.

Milton, D. E. M. (2014). Autistic expertise: A critical reflection on the production of knowledge in autism studies. *Autism*, 18 (7), pp. 794–802.

Morton, J. and Frith, U. (1995). Causal modeling: A structural approach to developmental psychopathology. In D. Cicchetti and D. J. Cohen (Eds), *Developmental Psychopathology, Vol. 1. Theory and methods*. London: John Wiley and Sons, pp. 357–90.

Mottron, L. and Burack, J. A. (2001). Enhanced perceptual functioning in the development of autism. In J. A. Burack, T. Charman, N. Yirmiya and P. R. Zelazo (Eds), *The Development of Autism: Perspectives from theory and research*. Mahwah, NJ: Lawrence Erlbaum Associates Publishers, pp. 131–48.

Mottron, L., Dawson, M., Soulières, I., Hubert, B. and Burack, J. (2006). Enhanced perceptual functioning in autism: An update, and eight principles of autistic perception.
J Autism Dev Disord, 36 (1), pp. 27–43.

Noterdaeme, M. and Hutzelmeyer-Nickels, A. (2010). Early symptoms and recognition of
pervasive developmental disorders in Germany. *Autism*, 14 (6), pp. 575–88.

O'Dell, L., Bertilsdotter Rosqvist, H., Ortega, F., Brownlow, C. and Orsini, M. (2016).
Critical autism studies: Exploring epistemic dialogues and intersections, challenging
dominant understandings of autism. *Disability and Society*, 31 (2), pp. 166–79.

Ortega, F. and Vidal, F. (2011). *Neurocultures: Glimpses into an expanding universe*. New
York: Peter Lang.

Premack, D. and Woodruff, G. (1978). Does the chimpanzee have a theory of mind?
Behav Brain Sci, 1 (4), pp. 515–26.

Radenovic, L. (2010). Impaired concept acquisition in children with ASD: Beyond the
enhanced perceptual processing hypothesis. *Procedia – Social and Behavioral
Sciences*, 5, pp. 69–73.

Rajendran, G. and Mitchell, P. (2007). Cognitive theories of autism. *Developmental
Review*, 27 (2), pp. 224–60.

Rao, V. S., Mysore, A. V. and Raman, V. (2016). The neuropsychology of autism – A
focus on three major theories. *J Indian Assoc Child Adolesc Ment Health*, 12 (2),
pp. 162–99.

Shah, A. and Frith, U. (1983). An islet of ability in autistic children: A research note. *Child
Psychology & Psychiatry & Allied Disciplines*, 24 (4), pp. 613–20.

Warrier, V. and Baron-Cohen, S. (2018). Genetic contribution to 'theory of mind' in adolescence. *Sci Rep*, 8 (1), 3465.

Wen, W. and Wen, S. W. (2014). Expanding upon the 'extreme male brain' theory of
autism as a common link between other major risk factors: A hypothesis. *Med
Hypotheses*, 82 (5), pp. 615–18.

Wimmer, H. and Perner, J. (1983). Beliefs about beliefs: Representation and constraining
function of wrong beliefs in young children's understanding of deception. *Cognition*,
13 (1), pp. 103–28.

Witkin, H. A., Oltman, P. K., Raskin, E. and Karp, S. A. (1971). *A Manual for the Embedded
Figures Test*. Palo Alto, CA: Consulting Psychologists Press.

Woods, R. (2017). Pathological demand avoidance: My thoughts on looping effects and
commodification of autism. *Disability & Society*, 32 (5), pp. 753–8.

EIGHT

Educational choice and support

Introduction

Where children and young people are educated is an important aspect in the lives of the individual concerned, their families, allies, and educational practitioners. This chapter explores one of the key issues in this area, such as that of the most appropriate context for educating autistic individuals, the standing of mainstream and special education, and the importance of Education, Health and Care plans. The impact that the COVID-19 pandemic had on education is considered and the Government response to research findings. High-quality teaching which is responsive to children's individual needs is examined with respect to Initial Teacher Education. It is also important to consider the role of multi-agencies in supporting autistic adults.

———————————————— Learning objectives ————————————————

This chapter will:

- Invite you to evaluate the role of mainstream and specialist provision in the education of autistic children and young people
- Help you to consider the role and impact of Education, Health and Care plans and educational support
- Invite you to review the impact COVID-19 had on autistic children, young people and adults
- Help you consider the impact autism may have on adults
- Introduce you to the role that Initial Teacher Education has on supporting autistic learners

———————————————————— Key terms ————————————————————

Mainstream school, special school, Education, Health and Care plan, COVID-19, support in adulthood, Initial Teacher Education

---
Pause for reflection

- Why do you think there are so many choices parents, children and young people face when deciding the most appropriate setting in supporting their needs?
- Where would they look for information to enable their decision?
- Does it really matter where education and support take place?

The All-Party Parliamentary Group on Autism (APPGA) (2017) reported on how the education system in England works for children and young people on the autism spectrum. They concluded that for many children on the autism spectrum and their families, it is a struggle to get the right school place, an assessment of their needs, additional support from health services, access to out-of-school support, and other support. It points to staff often lacking the skills needed to put in place the right plans and support for autistic young people, which can result in them missing out on opportunities.

Their recommendations to the Government included building upon the inclusion of autism in Initial Teacher Training courses and on the work of the Autism Education Trust, making provision for a specialist curriculum for all pupils on the autism spectrum who need one, setting out strategies for improving autism awareness and understanding across a whole school to help reduce bullying and improve inclusion.

In the 'Supporting SEND' report (Ofsted, 2021), the principal ways in which schools work to meet the needs of pupils and meaningfully include them in the classroom and wider school life were discussed. This involved developing deep understandings of the strengths and needs of each pupil, making clear and well-thought-through adjustments to the curriculum and having high expectations for the outcomes they can achieve, academically and across their wider school life. Schools should also aim to ensure that pupils felt included with their peers while receiving interventions or other forms of support. Where staff did not understand pupils well, those pupils' needs were identified less readily. The curriculum was therefore not planned appropriately, and help could therefore not support pupils' learning as effectively. Sometimes, staff faced challenges developing their own understanding of pupils with SEND. Factors such as staff knowledge and pupils' coping mechanisms affected accurate and timely identification of needs.

Mainstream or specialist provision?

Parents are faced with several options when choosing a school for their child. In addition to mainstream and special schools, some schools have bases or units specifically for autistic children and young people. Depending on their needs, it may also be appropriate to consider residential schools or home education for your child. There is a legal duty to ensure that all children are educated in a mainstream setting, except for the following circumstances: a mainstream school would not meet the child's needs; the education of the other children at the school would be affected; or the placement would be too expensive. Also, an Educational, Health and Care plan is usually needed to access a placement at a special school (National Autistic Society [NAS], 2020).

An increasing number of children are dual registered, spending part of the week in a special school and part in a mainstream school. Some with minor needs may spend most of their time in a mainstream school but with specialist input from a special school. Good Schools Guide (2022) suggests that there are advantages in special schools, including class sizes are smaller, even exceeding one-to-one help in some cases; work is geared to the child's individual needs and linked carefully to their own targets; children have a peer group with similar needs, so they don't feel different and find it easier to make friends; staff generally have an excellent understanding of the needs of the children and how best to teach them; and that progress is very carefully tracked and monitored.

The inclusion of autistic children into mainstream schools has been argued to improve their quality of life, educational performance, and social development. Kurth and Mastergeorge (2010) examined the academic profiles of autistic adolescents who had been educated in inclusive and self-contained settings using three measures: cognitive assessments, adaptive behaviour, and academic achievement. Findings indicate significant between group differences (inclusion versus self-contained) in academic achievement measures. Students who were included in general education obtained significantly higher scores on tests of achievement, including subtests measuring abstract and inferential skills; however, all students demonstrated emerging academic skills on standardised measures. However, Waddington and Reed (2017) found that mainstream children have no greater academic success than children in specialist provision. They suggest that mainstreaming practice varied across local authorities. However, there were significant differences in the severity of autism across the school placements.

Those children in special schools generally had more severe autism, and had poorer social relating, and social skills, than those children placed in mainstream schools. The SEND Code of Practice (2015) (DfE and DoH, 2015) sets out a 'graduated approach' to removing barriers and supporting pupils' learning with special provision. This is designed to be a responsive, spiral system of regular and personalised assessment, targeted action, and review. The Code of Practice also requires each local authority to publish its own 'Local Offer', describing the support and provision available for children and young people with an identified SEN.

─────────────────── Case study ───────────────────

Jane is autistic and just about to start school for the first time. She has an EHC plan, and her parents are searching for information before they and her decide as to where she might be educated. They know that there is a range of schools, including mainstream, specialist, and residential settings. They know that their local authority has a Local Offer.

- Visit the Local Offer website of a local authority and identify what support is available to Jane and her family in making that decision.
- What other aspects of the Local Offer might be relevant to them as a family?

Mainstreaming is also thought to increase the social awareness of inclusion. Although the definitions of inclusion vary (e.g. children included for play times and meals versus children included all day), the fundamental concept is that children identified with special educational needs ought to be educated in the same setting as their mainstream peers. Symes and Humphrey (2011) researched the increased number of Teaching Assistants (TAs) being deployed into mainstream classrooms to support autistic pupils. Evidence suggested, however, that pupils who have a TA may underperform academically, receive less attention from their teachers and be isolated from their peer group. Issues relating to the deployment and training of these staff, and their relationships with class teachers, have been raised as contributing to the negative impact of TAs. The factors perceived as facilitating or hindering the ability of TAs to effectively include autistic pupils included access to expertise, communication within school and teaching staff awareness. Most TAs worked with just one pupil at a time and worked in a variety of lessons. Their role primarily involved helping pupils to stay focused and follow instructions and many had no experience of autism prior to starting their job. The amount of training received varied, but all felt that generic training about autism was not helpful and a lack of time for joint planning with teachers was raised as a key concern.

Hours of access to Learning Support Assistants (LSAs) were negatively correlated with academic outcomes for those children placed in mainstream schools. For example, Osborne and Reed (2011) suggested that having an LSA can create a barrier between students and their classmates and can stall pupils' progress by consistently decreasing the challenges of the work in the classroom. Such findings have been found previously and have formed the basis of several criticisms regarding the use of LSA support. Their research examined the factors promoting inclusion of autistic young people in mainstream secondary schools and noted high levels of behavioural difficulties in these pupils. The size of the secondary school, and the class size, impacted on the pupils with autism, and the number of other pupils with Special Educational Needs (SEN) statements and the number of support staff per pupil were both positive factors in school progress for autistic children. Support teachers and assistants helped to reduce emotional and behavioural difficulties, but also reduced improvements in pro-social behaviour. Good staff-training promoted the pupils' social behaviours and their sense of school belonging. In summary, social-emotional behaviours are better facilitated in mainstream secondary schools with larger numbers of other children with SEN statements, individual support, which helps emotional and behavioural difficulties, but does not facilitate social behaviours, good teacher-training, which facilitates social behaviours, and a sense of school belonging. Ainscow (2000) also raises a concern that having an LSA means that the teacher is less involved with the student, which may mean that the child with SEN is benefiting less from their teacher's expertise than other pupils in the class.

Humphrey (2008) suggests that there is growing concern about these children's educational experiences in mainstream provision. Research suggests that such pupils make easy targets for bullies and are considered difficult to teach by teachers. Furthermore, autistic pupils are more than 20 times more likely to be excluded from school than those without special educational needs. The National Autistic Society (NAS) and the All-Party Parliamentary Group on Autism (APPGA, 2017) published their latest survey of children with autism and their parents, including the following findings:

- Seven in ten children and young people said that their peers do not understand them and five in ten said that their teachers do not know how to support them.
- 70 per cent of parents said they waited more than six months for support for their child, with 50 per cent waiting more than a year.
- 42 per cent of parents said their request for a SEN assessment was refused on the first time of asking.
- 40 per cent of parents said that their child's school place does not fully meet their needs with fewer than five in ten teachers confident about supporting a child on the autism spectrum.

Croydon et al. (2019) suggest that including autistic children and young people in mainstream schools is notoriously difficult, especially so for those with additional intellectual, communication and behavioural needs. Their study sought to understand the perceived impact on selected students from special schools who are transferred to dedicated 'satellite' classes in local, mainstream partner schools, while continuing to receive the tailored curriculum and specialist teaching of the originating school. They conducted interviews with 19 London-based young autistic people, their parents/carers, and teachers to understand their experiences of transitioning from specialist to satellite mainstream provision, who overwhelmingly welcomed the prospect of transition and its perceived benefits in the short and longer term. Young people and families celebrated achieving access to 'more normal places and things', 'seeing what others are doing', and greater autonomy, without losing the trusted expert support of their special school. Young people also felt a deep sense of belonging to their new mainstream school, despite only being minimally included in regular mainstream classes and activities. Teachers were equally positive and felt that their students had responded to higher expectations in their new mainstream schools, reportedly resulting in better behavioural regulation and more sustained attention in the classroom.

In a review of research literature into stakeholder attitudes to inclusion of autistic students in mainstream schools, Roberts and Simpson (2016) found that while there is a general philosophical commitment to the inclusion of students with autism in mainstream schools in line with a rights-based approach to education of children with disabilities, there are significant barriers in practice. These included peers experiencing frustration and difficulty understanding why the student with autism was treated differently.

Pause for reflection

- Considering your own educational journey, what do you think is the role of Teaching or Learning Support Assistants in classroom support?

Education, Health and Care plans

An Education, Health and Care plan (EHCP) is a legal document detailing education, health and social support needs for children and young people (CYP) with SEND. The SEND Code of Practice (DfE and DoH, 2015) saw the introduction of EHCPs, which replaced statements of special educational needs. The plan is a document for children and young people up to the age of 25 who need extra support above the special needs provision that the school should offer as standard. The plan outlines the young person's needs and the additional support that should be put in place to meet those needs (DfE, 2014).

In 2001, the earlier SEND Code of Practice outlined the need for schools to make 'reasonable adjustments' for students with additional needs and outlined a graduated response which included School Action and School Action Plus levels. The child progressed through the tiers of interventions and approaches that had been put in place, but progress was still minimal. If the child did not make the required progress, they may have had a statutory assessment and been Statemented (Tutt and Williams, 2015). This was like an EHCP, but there was less emphasis placed on obtaining the child's and family's views. The Lamb Inquiry (2009) identified the unhappiness felt by parents of children with SEND due to their minimal involvement in their child's education, and suggested this as a vital area in need of change. As well as this, the government identified the previous system as over-complicated and ineffective (Tutt and Williams, 2015). They wanted the young people's plans to be more accessible and user-friendly for both their families and the school. They also recognised the difficulty in transitioning from children to adult services, so extended the age range of people with EHCPs up to 25. This meant that pre-16 and post-16 services were able to work collaboratively to support the young person's transition.

- If a school identifies a student with a long-term special need who may require support over and above the notional special needs budget that they have, they can submit a Request for Statutory Assessment notice, which will be forwarded to a nominated team at their local authority.
- The request will be considered by a panel of professionals, who will have received information from the school about the student, including assessment data and reports from external agencies. The panel will consider whether the school has completed their graduated response with the student, a tiered system of support that demonstrates how their notional SEN budget has been used with the student, and how the increased budget will be used. Within 6 weeks, the panel will have made the decision as to whether the student will be formally assessed.
- The formal assessment will involve collating further reports from the family, the young person, the school and external agencies that have been involved with the student. A draft plan will be issued, clearly outlining targets and provision, to the young person, their family and the school and they have 15 days to respond if they feel any changes need to be made.
- Once this is confirmed, the EHCP is finalised and issued.

EHCPs, and the needs assessment process through which these are made, were introduced as part of the Children and Families Act (2014). The Act, and an accompanying SEND Code of Practice (2015) (DfE and DoH, 2015), sets out how local authorities must deliver these, including developing the plan, maintaining and supporting participation, and these collaboratively with children, young people and parents, and securing the best possible outcomes for the child/young person. It is drawn up by the local authority after an Education, Health and Care needs assessment of the child or young person has determined that an EHCP is necessary, and after consultation with relevant partner agencies and with the children/young people, and parents. The annual review is the statutory process of looking at the needs, provision and outcomes specified, and deciding whether these need to change. The first review must be held within 12 months of the plan being finalised with subsequent reviews held within 12 months of the previous review. The following steps must take place in an annual review:

- The LA must consult with the parent of the child or young person (and with the school or institution being attended if there is one) about the EHC plan, and take account of their views, wishes and feelings.

- An annual review meeting must take place to discuss the EHC plan.
- Information must be gathered from parents and young people and from professionals about the EHC plan and then circulated two weeks before the meeting.
- After the meeting a report of what happened must be prepared and circulated to everyone who attended or submitted information to be discussed.
- After the meeting the LA reviews the EHC plan.
- The LA must notify the parent of the child or young person of their decision within four weeks of the meeting. (NAS, 2022)

The yearly annual review meeting means that the information is kept current and relevant. Targets are reviewed and adjusted, ensuring that progress is monitored. At these meetings, the family can meet with the professionals involved with their child and ask questions or have discussions. This has been reported by parents to be extremely valuable and helps them feel involved and informed (Roulstone et al., 2016). Suni and Cochrane (2020) suggest that while parental involvement has improved, and there is some evidence of multi-agency work, the views of children and young people continue to be marginalised, and EHCPs are highly variable in quality, indicating that person-centred approaches are not yet fully implemented. For an autistic CYP, an EHCP will give them a voice and view of their education and what works best. They will be able to express what they like and dislike about education and what they want others to know about them (Tutt and Williams, 2015). Additionally, the involvement of their family will mean that strategies and approaches could be used at home, providing continuation of support (Pearlman and Michaels, 2019). As well as this, with the confirmation of an EHCP, the school may be able to seek and fund additional provisions that could benefit them, such as cognitive behavioural therapy, specialist teaching, short breaks, or other alternative therapies (Crane and Boesley, 2018).

However, some groups of educators have expressed frustration with the process, calling it bureaucratic, costly and time inefficient, and Keer (2019) states that it can add more work to an already over-capacity teacher's role and can mean that they become 'bogged down' in paperwork. This could lead to children and families not receiving the support needed, or their wishes and opinions not being included in the process. Crane and Boesley (2018) reported that SENCos felt a lack of engagement from health and social care professionals, with Hobbs (2019) suggesting that healthcare professionals were not attending reviews due to shortage of staff, time constraints and insufficient funding to be effective. Palikara et al. (2009) also state that professionals reported difficulties working together with other agencies.

The most recent statistics (DfE, 2021a) show that there are 163,041 autistic pupils in schools in England, an increase of 7 per cent from 2020, with 70 per cent educated in mainstream schools. The number of autistic pupils with EHCPs totalled 92,572 and autism is the most common type of need for pupils who have a statement of special educational needs or an EHCP. Autism is the primary need for

27 per cent of these pupils – 31 per cent of boys with a statement or EHCP, and 16 per cent of girls. Most of the identified pupils are classed as requiring 'SEN support', typically provided by schools. The NAS (2021) School Report surveyed 3,470 parents and carers of autistic children and young people and found that 1 in 4 were satisfied with the SEN support their child was receiving, 50 per cent were dissatisfied with the process, and only 1 in 8 felt that their child's needs were being met fully at school, with a lower number indicating that they had been met across all services.

The impact of the COVID-19 pandemic

────────────── Key research in the field ──────────────

Taylor, J. L., Adams, R. E., Pezzimenti, F., Zheng, S. and Bishop, S. L. (2022). Job loss predicts worsening depressive symptoms for young adults with autism: A COVID-19 natural experiment. *Autism Res*, 15 (1), pp. 93–102.

Objective

Autistic adults experience high rates of both unemployment and depression. Though job loss predicts increased risk of depression in the general population, studies have yet to directly examine this relationship among individuals with ASD. With the backdrop of rising unemployment due to COVID-19, the researchers used a longitudinal design to examine whether employment changes predicted increasing depressive symptoms among young autistic adults with ASD.

Method

Online surveys were collected from young adults with ASD at two times: just before widespread social distancing measures were adopted in the United States, and again 10 weeks later. Both time points included measurement of depressive symptoms (Beck Depression Inventory-2). At Time 2, COVID-related employment changes and the perceived impact of those changes on wellbeing were collected.

Findings

Of the young adults who were employed at Time 1 (n = 144), over one-third (37.5%) reported employment changes during the first 2 months of COVID-19. Most of this change was job loss or reductions in hours or pay ('job loss/reduction'). Controlling for Time 1 depressive symptoms, young adults who experienced job loss/reduction had significantly higher depressive symptoms at Time 2 than those without an employment change. Individuals' perceived impact of employment change also predicted depressive symptoms.

(Continued)

Conclusion

Autistic adults who lost their jobs or experienced reductions in pay or hours during the first 2 months of COVID-19 had worsening depression compared to adults who did not have job changes. Findings suggest that increasing access to employment may help alleviate poor mental health among autistic adults.

The impact of the recent COVID-19 pandemic on families with an autistic child has been researched extensively in the UK and other countries. Meral (2021) investigated the impact of the lockdown and curfew associated with the COVID-19 coronavirus pandemic on the family functioning of children with autism in Turkey. There were some negative effects on education, such as lack of online resources and support and the lack of meeting up with peers. However, the study also found that there was increased family interaction, verbal interaction and that children were more skilful to meet their own self-care skills. The Social Care Institute for Excellence (SCIE) (2021) published a COVID-19 guide for carers and family supporting adults and children with learning disabilities or autistic adults and children, in which they emphasise strategies such as the establishing of different routines, including exercise, social contact and good sleep routines, and explaining in simple terms why things need to be different for a time, e.g. there is a virus that might make us ill, so we are trying to keep safe and that the restrictions are not forever.

Simpson and Adams (2022) carried out an online survey in which parents (n = 180) of school-aged children (9.3–16.5 years) on the autism spectrum in Australia were asked an open-ended question on how the COVID-19 pandemic had impacted on their child's education experience. Nearly half (48 per cent) of the parents reported only negative impacts, 26 per cent only positive impacts, 12 per cent a mix of positive and negative impacts, and 9 per cent little or no impact. Kalb et al. (2021) found that the COVID-19 pandemic may disproportionately impact parents of autistic children. Loss of services and supports, heightened fears about increased infection rates, and disruption of daily routines likely adversely affect the wellbeing of autistic children and their families. Results demonstrated substantially higher levels of psychological distress, particularly those related to feelings of panic, among parents raising an autistic child during the pandemic. The report 'Understanding Progress in the 2020/21 Academic Year' (DfE, 2021b) identified that pupils with an identified SEND do not appear to have been affected during that year by the pandemic to a greater extent in reading and mathematics than the average pupil. However, 'Left stranded: The impact of coronavirus on autistic people and their families in the UK' (NAS, 2020) found that:

- 9 in 10 autistic people worried about their mental health during lockdown; 85 per cent said their anxiety levels got worse;

- autistic people were 7 times more likely to be chronically lonely than the general population; and 6 times more likely to have low life satisfaction (comparisons using ONS data);
- 1 in 5 family members responding to the survey had to reduce work due to caring responsibilities;
- 7 in 10 parents say their child has had difficulty understanding or completing schoolwork and around half said their child's academic progress was suffering;
- some schools have refused to allow young people with autism to come back even when schools have re-opened;
- others haven't put in place the individual plans that children with autism need to cope with another massive change to their routines.

The 'National Strategy for autistic children, young people, and adults: 2021 to 2026' (Department of Health and Social Care [DHSC] and DfE, 2021) reported that the COVID-19 pandemic has exacerbated challenges many autistic people already faced, such as loneliness and social isolation, and anxiety. While reasons for this vary, the research found that many autistic people have struggled with understanding restrictions and practising infection control measures. In addition, the pandemic has created new issues for autistic people, for example in being able to shop at super-markets due to new social distancing measures. At the same time, the research also showed the benefits of lockdowns for some autistic people, who have been better able to engage in virtual spaces, have felt less societal pressure and have been able to avoid anxiety-inducing activities like using public transport.

Exercise

The strategy sets out six key areas in which to make improvements for autistic people. These are:

1 Improving understanding and acceptance of autism within society.
2 Improving autistic children and young people's access to education and supporting positive transitions into adulthood.
3 Supporting more autistic people into employment.
4 Tackling health and care inequalities for autistic people.
5 Building the right support in the community and supporting people in inpatient care.
6 Improving support within the criminal and youth justice systems.

Examine two of the themes and summarise how these will impact upon the life of someone with autism and their allies and families.

The strategy can be found at: www.gov.uk/government/publications/national-strategy-for-autistic-children-young-people-and-adults-2021-to-2026/the-national-strategy-for-autistic-children-young-people-and-adults-2021-to-2026

- What are the main issues we need to consider when examining the impact autism may have on adults?
- Other than education, which other agencies need to be involved in support?
- Are there any issues with respect to accessing a range of services?

Support in adulthood

The National Institute for Health and Care Excellence (NICE) (2021) identifies several steps which adults may follow if they think they may have autism. If the adult, or a healthcare professional, family member, partner, or carer, think that they have autism, and were not diagnosed as a child, they should be offered an assessment. Even if they were diagnosed with autism as a child, an assessment in adulthood may be offered if they are being transferred from a service for children to an adult service. Some diagnostic teams accept self-referrals, but in most areas, adults will need a referral from their GP. Professionals will ask about and assess behaviour in social situations, early life, life at home, college, or work, and if there are any mental and physical health problems, learning disabilities, problems with speech and language, or sensory sensitivities.

If there is a diagnosis of autism, adults will be offered another appointment to discuss the diagnosis, what it means for them, any concerns they have and care and support for the future. Individuals should be offered this appointment even if they have decided not to have further care and support.

Professionals will then put together a plan for care that considers needs (such as any communication needs, or other needs related to any sensory sensitivities) and those of the family, partner, or carer.

What kind of care to have and support options available will depend on several other factors, including previous support, any learning disability or physical or mental health problem, sensory sensitivities and any problems that could lead to a crisis. Information about the care and support options available is provided along with a 'health passport', which is a card that lists the care and support the person is having and other details in their care plan. Details are given with respect to recognised national or local organisations and websites that provide information for autistic people, and about self-help groups, support groups and one-to-one support.

Autistic adults may need a wide range of support to live as independently and happily as possible, either from social care services, from benefits or from housing. The APPGA's 'The Autism Act, 10 Years On' (2019) report found that ten years after the introduction of the Autism Act (2009), thousands of autistic adults are living without the range of support they may need from social care, benefits, or housing, because care staff do not understand their needs and the right specialist and lower-level services are not available. Many do not get any help until they reach crisis point. Support for autistic adults has got worse, particularly for those who need social care, over the last 10 years. The APPGA have found alarming levels of unmet need, with 71 per cent of autistic adults telling us they are living without the support they need. Those who need 'preventative' support are not getting it because the services all too often are not available.

Autistic people may need a wide range of support, from a little help to organise and keep on top of things, to intensive packages of personal care. Specialist Autism Teams (SATs) were recommended by the National Institute for Health and Care Excellence (NICE) and in the Autism Act statutory guidance. NICE defined SATs as specialist community-based, multi-disciplinary services providing or coordinating diagnosis and assessments, holistic care, and support (addressing health, social care, housing, welfare, or employment needs), support to family members and carers, and supporting mainstream services caring for autistic adults. Few local areas in England currently have these teams but where they do exist, they are specifically for autistic adults without learning disabilities (LD), and this is because commissioners and practitioners feel there is no provision for this group.

Beresford et al. (2020) evaluated these teams, with staff in these services reporting a growing demand. They found evidence of measurable benefit for some people. Service characteristics, such as a wide range of skills and a holistic approach, appear to support positive impacts and are highly valued by service users. However, achieving some of these benefits may lead to higher costs, and so these approaches may not always be considered sufficiently worthwhile. They also compared people diagnosed by a SAT with those receiving a diagnostic assessment but no post-diagnosis support. The two groups differed in how they felt about their diagnosis. This seems to be because SATs provide extended support to help people understand, accept, and see the positive sides of their diagnosis. This makes people feel more able to manage everyday life and, for some, address mental health or other concerns.

The APPGA's 'The Autism Act, 10 Years On' (2019) report showed that autistic children and young people often find it difficult to get the help they need at school due to poor understanding of autism among education staff. It also highlighted that fewer than 5 in 10 education staff were confident about supporting autistic children and young people, and this can result in missed opportunities to help children reach their potential or prevent children's needs or distressed behaviour from escalating. The inquiry's survey of around 11,000 autistic adults and families in England found:

- 71 per cent (2 in 3) of autistic adults in England aren't getting the support they need;
- 26 per cent (1 in 4) of autistic adults need support to live more independently; just 5 per cent (1 in 20) get this;
- while 20 per cent (1 in 5) of all autistic adults need support with day-to-day tasks, like washing, cooking, and going out of the house, only 6 per cent (just over 1 in 20) get this;

- 38 per cent (nearly 2 in 5) of autistic adults need support from social groups; only 16 per cent have this support;
- 29 per cent (nearly 3 in 10) of autistic adults need buddying or befriending; just 4 per cent (1 in 25) get this.

───────────────── Case study ─────────────────

Mohammed is a 27-year-old man who lives independently and is autistic. He has a best friend, Steve, who will shop for him and take him to the local coffee shop, which he enjoys. However, he can feel anxious and overwhelmed when shopping or going out into the community, especially if his friend leaves him alone at any time during the outing. He would love to be able to share the responsibility of shopping for food and planning a day out with his friend, as he is concerned that Steve does all the planning but lacks the confidence and understanding of how to do these 'things that most people do for themselves'.

- What steps could both Mohammed and Steve take to support the activities they enjoy?
- Are there any agencies, including the local authority, who could offer advice?

Initial Teacher Training

The APPGA has long been calling for teachers and other school staff to have better training and support to teach and support children on the autism spectrum. The APPGA were pleased, following a campaign by the National Autistic Society and Ambitious about Autism, the Government agreed that autism should be included in a new framework of content for Initial Teacher Training from September 2018. It has been compulsory since September 2018 for all English Initial Teacher Training (ITT) courses to include content around autism to all their students. The aim is to improve Newly Qualified Teachers' (NQTs) understanding of autism and how being autistic may affect pupils' experiences of school. The training also aims to equip NQTs with practical teaching strategies to use in the classroom.

High-quality teaching which is responsive to children's individual needs is particularly important for autistic children and others with SEND. Headteachers and local authorities are usually best placed to decide the training needs of their staff, in line with local needs and circumstances and the Government stated that it does not propose to make training in autism mandatory for staff in mainstream schools. All schools are expected to ensure that their staff have a good understanding of pupils' SEND and can adapt their teaching accordingly. Schools are required to support this through their performance management and continuous professional development processes. The DfE has been funding the Autism Education Trust (AET) since 2011 to deliver autism awareness training to staff in early years settings, schools, and colleges. The AET actively promote improved autism practice within settings and improved educational access and provide a range of practical resources to inform practice at both setting and practitioner levels. They promote communities of practice to facilitate mutual support and shared learning. The AET have also developed national standards for autism support and a progression framework for those who work with children who have autism.

Ofsted (2021) has highlighted that curriculum knowledge is not the only area that training could fruitfully focus on. They found that many school staff used labels, such as autism, attention deficit and hyperactivity disorder (ADHD) and dyspraxia, to describe children with SEND. This suggests that practitioners should be familiar with the wide-ranging debate around the use of labels for SEND and the potential problems this can create for effective inclusive practice and possibly for pupils themselves. They should understand that assigned labels are not the focus. Instead, it is more important to understand pupils as individuals with unique strengths, removing barriers to learning and providing support that meets needs and makes a positive difference. Roberts and Simpson (2016) suggest that level of knowledge and understanding of autism of school staff emerged as the primary issue, with all stakeholders identifying the need for more training.

In the report 'Support for pupils with special educational needs and disabilities in England', the National Audit Office (2019) identified that how well pupils with SEND are supported affects their wellbeing, educational attainment, and long-term life prospects. Some pupils with SEND are receiving high-quality support that meets their needs, whether they attend mainstream schools or special schools. However, the significant concerns that have been identified indicate that many other pupils are not being supported effectively, and that pupils with SEND who do not have EHC plans are particularly exposed. The system for supporting pupils with SEND is not, on current trends, financially sustainable. Many local authorities are failing to live within their high-needs budgets and meet the demand for support. Pressures such as incentives for mainstream schools to be less inclusive, increased demand for special school places, growing use of independent schools and reductions in per-pupil funding are making the system less, rather than more, sustainable.

The statutory Teachers' Standards (DfE, 2011 updated 2021) state that teachers must have a clear understanding of the needs of all pupils, including those with SEND, and must be able to use and evaluate distinct teaching approaches to engage and support them. As part of their initial training, trainee teachers must satisfy the Teachers' Standards, which include a requirement that they have a clear understanding of the needs of all pupils, including those with autism, and that they are able to use and evaluate distinct teaching approaches to engage and support them. In 2016, the Department for Education accepted the recommendations of an expert group tasked with developing a framework of core content for ITT (DfE, 2016).

The recommendations included that training providers should ensure that trainees understand the principles of the SEND Code of Practice, are confident working with the four broad areas of need it identifies, and are able to adapt teaching strategies to ensure that pupils with SEND can access and progress within the curriculum. In an annual survey (DfE, 2018), 53 per cent of newly qualified teachers said that their training equipped them well to teach pupils with SEND and while classroom teachers in mainstream schools generally said that they can identify pupils with SEND, they were less confident in their ability to meet those pupils' needs.

Key points

- There are a range of settings in which autistic children and young people are educated
- Research suggests that there are advantages and issues with Education, Health and Care plans which replaced statements and learning difficulty assessments
- COVID-19 had a major impact on the lives of autistic children, young people, and adults
- Research states that a large percentage of autistic adults are not receiving the support they need
- There is an increased recognition that both qualified and initial teacher trainees need to have a clear understanding of the needs of all pupils, including those with SEND

Questions to consider

- Why must we consider the fact that autism is neurodevelopmental and can impact on an individual throughout their life?
- How can the support for autistic children, young people and adults become more 'joined up'?
- What lessons can be learned from the COVID-19 pandemic with respect to autism?

Further reading

Denning, C. B. and Moody, A. K. (2018). *Inclusion and Autism Spectrum Disorder: Proactive strategies to support students.* New York; London: Routledge, Taylor and Francis.

This title demonstrates specific user-friendly and evidence-based strategies that classroom teachers can implement to proactively set up and deliver classroom instruction that will maximise the chances of success for students with autism spectrum disorder (ASD). Teachers in inclusive environments are facing increasing pressure to meet the needs of diverse classrooms that include more students with ASD. This easy-to-use, research-based professional guide provides teachers with the activities and specific strategies they need, along with detailed descriptions that support immediate implementation.

Cameron, L. A., Borland, R. L., Tonge, B. J. and Gray, K. M. (2022). Community participation in adults with autism: A systematic review. *Journal of Applied Research in Intellectual Disabilities*, 35 (2), pp. 421–47.

This systematic review aimed to explore how adults with autism participate in the community, the impact of community participation on quality of life and mental health, and factors that support and hinder participation. Sixty-three reports were included, reporting on 58 studies. Solitary activities, organised group activities, community activities, religious groups and online social participation were identified. The relationship between community participation and quality of life was examined. Barriers and facilitators to increased community participation were identified and it was concluded that adults with autism participate in a range of independent and community activities.

Robinson, D., Moore, N. and Hooley, T. (2017). Ensuring an independent future for young people with special educational needs and disabilities (SEND): A critical examination of the impact of education, health and care plans in England. *British Journal of Guidance and Counselling*, 46 (4), pp. 479–91.

This article examines the implications of the new Education, Health and Care (EHC) planning process for career professionals in England. There is much to recommend the new process as it represents a shift to a more holistic and person-centred approach. However, there are four main criticisms which can be made of the new process: (1) the policy has an excessive focus on paid work as an outcome, which is unrealistic (for some young people); (2) the resourcing in local authorities is too limited to successfully operationalise the policy; (3) there is a lack of clarity about the professional base delivering EHC planning (especially in relation to the career elements); and (4) the policy is too narrowly targeted.

References

Ainscow, M. (2000). The next step for special education. *British Journal of Special Education*, 27 (2), pp. 76–80.

All-Party Parliamentary Group on Autism (APPGA) (2017). *Autism and Education in England 2017.* [online] Available at: www.autism-alliance.org.uk/wp-content/uploads/2018/04/APPGA-autism-and-education-report.pdf [Accessed 05.11.2021].

All-Party Parliamentary Group on Autism (APPGA) (2019). *Autism Act 10 Years On.* [online] Available at: https://pearsfoundation.org.uk/wp-content/uploads/2019/09/APPGA-Autism-Act-Inquiry-Report.pdf [Accessed 07.11.2021].

Beresford, B., Mukherjee, S., Mayhew, E., Heavey, E., Park, A-L., Stuttard, L., Allgar, V. and Knapp, M. (2020). Evaluating specialist autism teams' provision of care and support for autistic adults without learning disabilities: The SHAPE mixed-methods study. *Health Services and Delivery Research*, 8 (48).

Children and Families Act (2014). [online] Available at: www.legislation.gov.uk/ukpga/2014/6/contents [Accessed 08.11.2021].

Crane, L. and Boesley, L. (2018). 'Forget the Health and Care and just call them Education plans': SENCOs' perspectives on Education, Health and Care plans. *Journal of Research in Special Educational Needs*, 18 (51), pp. 36–47.

Croydon, A. Remington, A., Kenny, L. and Pellicano, E. (2019). 'This is what we've always wanted': Perspectives on young autistic people's transition from special school to mainstream satellite classes. *Autism & Developmental Language Impairments*, 4, pp. 1–16.

Department for Education (2011 updated 2021). *Teachers' Standards.* [online] Available at: www.gov.uk/government/publications/teachers-standards [Accessed 03.01.2022].

Department for Education (2014). *Children with Special Educational Needs and Disabilities (SEND)*. [online] Available at: www.gov.uk/children-with-special-educational-needs/extra-SEN-help [Accessed 12.11.2021].

Department for Education (2016). *Initial Teacher Training: Government response to Carter review*. [online] Available at: https://www.gov.uk/government/publications/initial-teacher-training-government-response-to-carter-review [Accessed 03.02.2022].

Department for Education (2018). *Newly Qualified Teachers (NQTs): Annual survey 2017*. [online] Available at: www.gov.uk/government/publications/newly-qualified-teachers-nqts-annual-survey-2017 [Accessed 14.12.2021].

Department for Education (2021a). *Special Educational Needs in England: January 2021*. [online] Available at: www.gov.uk/government/statistics/special-educational-needs-in-england-january-2021 [Accessed 12.05.2021].

Department for Education (2021b). *Understanding Progress in the 2020/21 Academic Year'*. [online] Available at: https://assets.publishing.service.gov.uk/government/uploads/system/uploads/attachment_data/file/1062293/Understanding_Progress_in_the_2020_21_Academic_Year_Initial_findings_from_the_spring_term.pdf [Accessed 29.11.2021].

Department for Education and Department of Health (2015). *Special Educational Needs and Disability Code of Practice: 0 to 25 years*. [online] Available at: www.gov.uk/government/publications/send-code-of-practice-0-to-25 [Accessed 25.06.2021].

Department of Health and Social Care and Department for Education (2021). *National Strategy for Autistic Children, Young People, and Adults: 2021 to 2026*. [online] Available at: www.gov.uk/government/publications/national-strategy-for-autistic-children-young-people-and-adults-2021-to-2026 [Accessed 21.01.2022].

Good Schools Guide (2022). *Find the Best School for Your Child*. [online] Available at: www.goodschoolsguide.co.uk/ [Accessed 04.01.2022].

Hobbs, S. (2019). *What are the pros and cons of keeping EHCPs?* [online] Available at: https://headteachersroundtable.wordpress.com/2019/12/11/what-are-the-pros-and-cons-of-keeping-ehcps/ [Accessed 23.02.2022].

Humphrey, N. (2008). Including pupils with autistic spectrum disorders in mainstream schools. *Support for Learning*, 23 (1), pp. 41–7.

Kalb, L. G., Badillo-Goicoechea, E., Holingue, C., Riehm, K. E., Thrul, J., Stuart, E. A., Smail, E. J., Law, K., White-Lehman, C. and Fallin, D. (2021). Psychological distress among caregivers raising a child with autism spectrum disorder during the COVID-19 pandemic. *Autism Research: Official Journal of the International Society for Autism Research*, 14 (10), pp. 2183–8.

Keer, M. (2019). *EHCPs in 2019: Bedded in, or bogged down?* [online] Available at: www.specialneedsjungle.com/ehcps-in-2019-bedded-in-or-bogged-down/ [Accessed 12.12.2021].

Kurth, J. and Mastergeorge, A. M. (2010). Individual education plan goals and services for adolescents with autism: Impact of age and educational setting. *Journal of Special Education*, 44 (3), pp. 146–60.

Lamb, B. (2009). *Lamb Inquiry Special Educational Needs and Parental Confidence*. Annesley: DCSF Publications.

Meral, B. F. (2021). Parental views of families of children with autism spectrum disorder and developmental disorders during the COVID-19 pandemic. *J Autism Dev Disord*, 52 (4), pp. 1712–24.

National Audit Office (2019). *Support for Pupils with Special Educational Needs and Disabilities in England*. [online] Available at: www.nao.org.uk/wp-content/uploads/2019/09/Support-for-pupils-with-special-education-needs.pdf [Accessed 24.10.2021].

National Autistic Society (NAS) (2020). *Left Stranded: The impact of coronavirus on autistic people and their families in the UK*. [online] Available at: www.autism.org.uk/what-we-do/news/coronavirus-report [Accessed 02.02.2022].

National Autistic Society (NAS) (2021). *School Report 2021*. [online] Available at: www.autism.org.uk/what-we-do/news/school-report-2021 [Accessed 04.12.2021].

National Autistic Society (NAS) (2022). *Annual Review*. [online] Available at: www.autism.org.uk/advice-and-guidance/topics/education/extra-help-at-school/northern-ireland/annual-review [Accessed 12.02.2022].

National Institute for Health and Care Excellence (NICE) (2021). *Autism Spectrum Disorder in Adults: Diagnosis and management*. [online] Available at: www.nice.org.uk/guidance/cg142 [Accessed 12.11.2021].

Ofsted (2021). *Supporting SEND*. [online] Available at: www.gov.uk/government/publications/supporting-send/supporting-send [Accessed 27.11.2021].

Osborne, L. A. and Reed, P. (2011). School factors associated with mainstream progress in secondary education for included pupils with autism spectrum disorders. *Research in Autism Spectrum Disorders*, 5 (3), pp. 1253–63.

Palikara, O., Lindsay, G. and Dockrell, J. E. (2009). Voices of young people with a history of specific language impairment (SLI) in the first year of post-16 education. *Int J Lang Commun Dis*, 44, pp. 56–78.

Pearlman, S. and Michaels, D. (2019). Hearing the voice of children and young people with a learning disability during the Educational Health Care Plan (EHCP): Hearing the voice of children. *Support for Learning*, 32 (2), pp. 148–61.

Roberts, J. and Simpson, K. (2016). A review of research into stakeholder perspectives on inclusion of students with autism in mainstream schools. *International Journal of Inclusive Education*, 1 (18), pp. 1084–96.

Roulstone, S., Harding, S. and Morgan, L. (2016). *Exploring the Involvement of Children and Young People with Speech, Language and Communication Needs and Their Families in Decision Making: A research project*. London: The Communication Trust.

Simpson, K. and Adams, D. (2022). Brief report: Covid restrictions had positive and negative impacts on schooling for students on the autism spectrum. *Journal of Autism and Developmental Disorders*, 3, pp. 1–7.

Social Care Institute for Excellence (SCIE) (2021). *Coronavirus (COVID 19): Insights and experiences*. [online] Available at: www.scie.org.uk/care-providers/coronavirus-covid-19/blogs [Accessed 01.02.2022].

Suni, A. and Cochrane, H. (2020). Education, health and care plans: What do we know so far? *Support for Learning*, 35 (3), pp. 372–88.

Symes, W. and Humphrey, N. (2011). The deployment, training and teacher relationships of teaching assistants supporting pupils with autistic spectrum disorders (ASD) in mainstream secondary schools. *British Journal of Special Education*, 38 (2), pp. 57–64.

Taylor, J. L., Adams, R. E., Pezzimenti, F., Zheng, S. and Bishop, S. L. (2022). Job loss predicts worsening depressive symptoms for young adults with autism: A COVID-19 natural experiment. *Autism Res*, 15 (1), pp. 93–102.

Tutt, R. and Williams, P. (2015). *The SEND Code of Practice 0–25 Years: Policy, provision and practice.* London: SAGE.

Waddington, E. M. and Reed, P. (2017). Comparison of the effects of mainstream and special school on National Curriculum outcomes in children with autism spectrum disorder: An archive-based analysis. *Journal of Research in Special Educational Needs,* 17 (21) pp. 132–14.

NINE
Transitions

Introduction

For people on the autism spectrum, transitions can present both challenges and opportunities. Fayette and Bond (2018) discuss how autistic individuals accessing the correct support and provision is vital to their transition into adulthood and many children and young people are not accessing support discussed in statutory guidance, ultimately resulting in poor adult outcomes. Deweerdt (2014) suggests that many professionals do not have the understanding and training of different disabilities, with Marsh et al. (2017) stating that autistic children and young people face more challenges which require more intensive support as transitioning into a new setting is difficult due to their unique social, communication and behavioural difficulties. A late diagnosis could mean that an individual may experience bullying, peer rejections and self-confidence issues which can then lead to mental health difficulties, affecting a person's ability to access employment settings, further education, and necessary support.

—————————————— Learning objectives ——————————————

This chapter will:

- Introduce you to the importance of transitions for autistic children, young people and adults
- Invite you to consider how individuals can be supported in making transitions at various life stages
- Introduce you to reflect on the role of multi-agencies in transitions and the response to COVID-19
- Invite you to review the importance and barriers affecting transition into employment for autistic individuals

—————————————— Key terms ——————————————

Transitions, multi-agencies, COVID-19, education, employment, barriers, adulthood, university

- What do you think are the key issues autistic children and young people face in educational transitions?
- What are the benefits and barriers which autistic young people and adults face in gaining and sustaining employment?

Supporting transitions

Families of autistic individuals must navigate several forms of transition at one time including status transitions (e.g. getting a job, entering post-secondary education); family life transition (e.g. new daily family routines); and bureaucratic transitions (e.g. moving from children to adult service systems) (Blacher, 2001). With respect to schools, school fit has been described as the match between a student's school and their psychosocial needs (e.g. for emotional support, self-esteem, competence, and autonomy) (Bahena et al., 2016). Stage environment fit (SEF) theory (Eccles and Midgley, 1989) suggests that change in students' attitudes to school following transition is not necessarily a feature of the move itself, but is the result of a mismatch between the emotional, cognitive and social needs of the individual student and the environment of the school to which they transition. These interactions included the fit or misfit between the child's needs for safety, relatedness, autonomy, competency, enjoyment and identity development, and their experiences of teachers and peers, school environment, curriculum, and pedagogy (Stack et al., 2021). For a successful transition, there needs to be full involvement from a range of services, involving both the individual and their family.

Codd and Hewitt (2020) interviewed ten parents to get detailed personal experiences regarding the transition process. Most of the support came from the school setting, but adult services support often seemed confusing. The parents had an overall negative response to transitioning support and policy; many of them felt isolated and deemed the local authorities to be untrustworthy. One parent highlighted how children's services was very clearly laid out but when it came to the transition into adulthood it is very 'foggy' and 'disjointed' (p. 4).

Gaona et al. (2020) interviewed individuals currently going through a transition into either further education or employment. Similarly to Codd and Hewitt (2020), individuals felt great uncertainty and sadness when discussing their transition, due to the lack of consistent support and poor self-confidence. However, they did find that some were feeling positive about new opportunities.

Cheak-Zamora et al. (2015) discuss how people with a SEND must have the correct support; if not, this could lead to difficulties in behaviour and communication which then affects their overall psychological and mental stability. They conducted focus groups of both autistic children and young people aged 15–22 and their caregivers to discuss their thoughts and feelings regarding transitioning. The language used tended to include terms such as 'impossible', 'absolutely stuck', 'running across brick walls' (p. 551). Indeed, many parents stated how the only aspect of transitioning that they were confident in was what they themselves had taught their children, for example basic life skills such as cooking and finance management.

Beresford et al. (2013) reported on autistic individuals and their transitioning to adult services. Through surveys, parents believed that their role within the transition process varied depending on the amount of support they received from care services. Parents with overall more positive experiences with transitioning had a stronger support network and were able to make informed decisions alongside their child. It is important to involve parents throughout all of the stages of transition.

Pause for reflection

- Who do you think should be involved in supporting transition throughout the lifespan of an autistic individual?
- Why is it important that planning for transition is a key priority for the range of services involved?

The importance of multi-agency working to support transition

The Children Act 1989 established the statutory requirement for inter-agency collaboration and joint working in relation to children and young people, requiring professionals to 'work together better'. Sloper (2004) identifies three types of working together:

1   Multidisciplinary, where the focus tends to be on priorities of that agency and coordination with other agencies is rare.
2   Interdisciplinary, in which individual professionals from different agencies separately assess the needs of child and family, and then meet to discuss findings and set goals.
3   Transdisciplinary, where different agencies work together jointly, sharing aims, information, tasks and responsibilities and families are seen as equal partners.

Within the new EHC plans, multi-agency working was to be enhanced to improve accessible support for children and young people and they aim to put children and families at the centre of transition planning. Atkinson (2002) highlights important models of multi-agency working and how professionals come together for different reasons, the three main being: improve services, direct outcomes, and prevention.

Regarding the transition process, professionals share the roles and responsibilities of support to come to a collective agreement on best practice for the child at the centre of care, with multi-agency working being useful for decision making regarding the future, as well as the safeguarding of these vulnerable individuals (Home Office, 2014). It is important to examine the impact of multi-agency working on the life of autistic individuals. Multi-agency working is used to gather an overview of a child's current care provisions and where there may need to be improvements in support (NSPCC, 2019).

Solomon (2019) highlights how understanding the family is important to reaching the best outcomes, suggesting how the family itself may deal with issues such as finance and employment be taken into account, and that multiple assessments and interventions taking place will lead to a collaborative advantage. These assessments and interventions can help to support the family with factors such as housing and funding needs. He refers to those with complex needs requiring more multi-agency interventions when compared to those without. For example, an individual with autism will need additional support with communication and understanding. Therefore, professionals such as speech and language therapists and educational psychologists working together would be an advantage to overall support and development. Everitt (2010) suggests different agencies working together are more effective than each agency working separately, and the best outcomes are achieved when professionals work together to fully support child and family (Greco et al., 2005). Working collaboratively is difficult and there are many barriers to a coordinated multi-agency approach (Everitt, 2010; Horwath and Morrison, 2007; Solomon, 2019), including:

- lack of funding and training;
- lack of information sharing across agencies and services;
- lack of ownership among senior managers and competitive relationships;
- duplicated assessments to identify needs and subsequent provision;
- poorly coordinated integrated activities across agencies;
- too much 'buck passing' and referring on of clients between agencies;
- lack of continuity and inconsistent levels of service provision;
- unclear accountability;
- issues of accountability;
- lack of common language.

NICE Guidance (2014) highlights the use of 'multi-agency local autism teams' suggesting that due to the rising prevalence rates of autism, specific multi-agency teams are useful. Beresford et al. (2013) also report how transitioning teams were useful in creating positive transition outcomes; further suggesting that autistic individuals struggle with social interaction and relationships and there is a need for a consistent transition team. However, Beresford et al. (2013) support Solomon (2019) in highlighting the difficulties within multi-agency working, stating that there was a high turnover of staff which is out of the children and families' control. Consistency of staff supports the strength of multi-agency working, transition staff working along-side other professionals strengthens the knowledge and understanding, but Beresford et al. (2013) report that the organisation and links within transition teams is 'very poor' and inconsistent.

A vital part of multi-agency working with autistic children, young people and adults is their protection and 'The National Strategy for Autistic Children, Young People and Adults: 2021 to 2026' (DfE and DHSC, 2021) discusses that as well as protection, professionals should also be trained in autism to fully understand the needs of the individual, how to appropriately communicate and ultimately fully support them throughout their lives. Thom et al. (2020) highlight how during transitioning, adults lose a lot of their established support as much of this is acquired through educational settings. Therefore, individuals will lose the support of agencies such as CAMHS (Child and Adolescent Mental Health), directly impacting their mental health and wellbeing. Mental health can have a major impact on employment, those with a mental illness are more likely to become unemployed and fewer than 40 per cent of employers would be willing to consider employing someone with a mental health condition (Mental Health Foundation, 2012).

NICE (2016) states that if professionals such as a school SENCo (Special Educational Needs Coordinator) and a CAMHS professional have good communication and frequent meetings, this can reduce waiting times for processes such as diagnosis and adulthood transition. However, Sinai-Gavrilov et al. (2019) discuss how multi-agency working is helpful in theory, but due to the lack of training in autism there is often a gap in knowledge. Brookman-Frazee et al. (2012) also suggest that there is a lack of time for EHC processes, which results in less time for positive communication across agencies. There are often difficulties within multi-agency working as sectors work differently; for example, the health sector is very 'structured' while education is more complex. Greco et al. (2005) discovered through a survey of families that two-thirds reported services working collaboratively made a positive difference to their lives. However, the most success was found regarding their health needs and access to education, whereas families still faced issues regarding social and emotional difficulties.

─────────── Multi-agency response: COVID-19 pandemic ───────────

The Care Quality Commission and Ofsted (2020) produced a COVID-19 series: briefing on special educational needs and disabilities provision. In it, they identified some key factors in multi-agency responses to the pandemic:

1   Flexibility: A cross-cutting theme of responding to the pandemic was the importance of services' ability to be flexible in their responses, and to adapt quickly.
2   Response time: Many agencies credited working quickly with other organisations to come up with innovative ways to deliver services as being a critical feature of their response.

(Continued)

3   Digital delivery: The overarching characteristic of service delivery within lockdown was the use of digital technology to offer virtual interventions to children and families. These ranged from taking multi-agency meetings online, telehealth systems to deliver therapy or 1-to-1 work, social work 'home' visits carried out via video messaging services, online parenting classes and many others.

4   Co-production of knowledge: Co-production of knowledge and guidance with children and families was considered important to meaningfully offer intervention and to better understand their experiences during the pandemic.

Baginsky and Manthorpe (2021) sought to understand how those working in Children's Social Care (CSC) made the transition from being an office-based agency to one where most social workers were based at home and to understand how CSC perceived the impact on children and their families. They found that multi-agency working had improved, with greater involvement of general practitioners and paediatricians.

Transition to school

Starting school is a major event in any child's life and while for children with disabilities this transition can be challenging (Quintero and McIntyre, 2011), this is particularly significant for autistic children. The unique social, communication and behavioural issues that they experience may present additional barriers to a positive start to school. There may be behavioural problems, bullying or peer rejection, for example. The transition process begins at pre-school age whereby the child is prepared for school while also evaluating if the child is ready, described as 'school readiness'. This is defined by two characteristic features on three dimensions. The characteristic features are 'transition' and 'gaining competencies', and the dimensions are 'children's readiness for school', 'schools' readiness for children', and 'families and communities' (UNICEF, 2012). While autistic children show basic academic school readiness, they may not be ready in the areas of social skills and daily living skills. McAlister and Peterson (2012) examined the link between early childcare experiences, friendship quality, Theory of Mind (ToM) and school readiness, and found poorer positive friendship quality, ToM and school readiness in autistic children.

Transition from primary to secondary school

Considering the key characteristics of autism, such as difficulties with change, rigid thinking styles, social interaction difficulties and sensory challenges, it is not unusual that autistic students can be particularly vulnerable transferring to a new school (Richter et al., 2019). The transition from primary to secondary school is a landmark moment in a child's life (Zeedyk et al., 2003) and has been the focus of several research studies. The move to a new school, with new teachers, new routines and new friends, can be an exciting time, affording many opportunities. Equally, it can also present considerable challenges. The loss of familiar places, structures and people, together with a 'fear of the unknown', particularly of greater academic and social demands and the prospect of bullying, can be daunting for children on the cusp of adolescence (Evangelou et al., 2008). Although many children adapt well to these changes, others struggle to adjust resulting in issues such lowered self-esteem, anxiety and a reduction in academic achievement. Dillon and Underwood (2012) confirmed that transition was problematic in the first year of secondary school, although there were signs of integration by the second year with the establishment of friendship groups, and peer acceptance appeared to be the key criterion for successful transition. Thus, there is considerable heterogeneity within the transition requirements of autistic students (Dillon and Underwood, 2012).

Transitioning between activities in lessons, or moving between different schools, has been shown to have an impact on individuals. The school environment itself can also present challenges for autistic children. Secondary schools are often physically larger than the previous primary school, are noisy and chaotic and can be overwhelming. Transitions between classes occur frequently throughout the school day, which may be difficult for autistic children to adjust to without appropriate support. Belonging to a friendship group for most children and young people may be an important step in developing interpersonal relationships with an increased population of learners. Autistic children often report on having few friends, but Calder et al. (2013) found that in a group of autistic children aged between 9 and 11 years, they generally reported satisfaction with their friendships and no child was socially isolated, and although adults played an active role in supporting children's friendships, this sometimes conflicted with what the children wanted. Makin and Pellicano (2017) examined the factors that influence a successful school transition for autistic children in one local education authority in England by talking to 15 children, their parents and teachers. They reported negative experiences of their transition to secondary school – regardless of the type of secondary provision (mainstream or specialist) to which they transferred. Transition success appeared to be predominantly related to several school- and system-level factors, including tensions over school choice, delays in placement decisions, lack of primary preparation and communication between schools.

Exercise

The Autism Educational Trust publish a pack which contains practical strategies, resources and case-studies to support transition from early years to primary school and from primary to secondary school – with examples and templates. It can be found at:

www.autismeducationtrust.org.uk/sites/default/files/2021-09/supporting-learners-with-autism-during-transition.pdf

You are tasked with supporting the transition of an autistic child or young person from early years to primary school, or from primary to secondary school. Using the pack, plan an induction activity to the new school which involves both the school and the family.

Autistic children are particularly vulnerable to negative transition experiences as changes in routine can be especially difficult. Fortuna (2014) suggests that the issue of school transition from primary to secondary for autistic students is a complex one and there are challenges for all parties involved. For example, parents are anxious about their children's school move and need reassurance and want to feel involved and informed in their children's progress throughout and want their views to be valued and taken seriously. School staff can often underestimate the difficulties of the students, and for the students themselves, the process of transition is daunting and provides a wide range of mixed feelings.

The transition may not always be a negative experience for autistic pupils though, and Mandy et al. (2015) highlight the need to examine school-based practices that may support successful transitions from primary to secondary school. Their findings were not consistent with the expectation that the ecological shift from primary to secondary mainstream education would precipitate a marked increase in problems. Parents did not observe a decline in the adaptive function of their children as they moved from primary to secondary school. Although autistic students are at considerably higher risk of complications during the primary–secondary transition, these risks can be mitigated by environmental or familial protective factors (Hannah and Topping, 2013). Some of these students have reported experiences of transition that were positive and better than anticipated and in line with their typically developing counterparts. Differences have been observed between the positive experiences of those transferring to a specialist provision, or to a supportive mainstream setting, compared to the negative experiences of those moving to mainstream with no support.

Stack et al. (2021) explored the perceptions of autistic children on the topic of which features of school environment fitted more or less well with their needs, as they transferred from primary to secondary school. Carrying out semi-structured interviews to gather the experiences of six students and their parents, before and after the transition to secondary school, they found that participants voiced more positive perspectives of secondary school than primary school. They suggested that inclusion and integration of autistic students in mainstream secondary schools at transition can be a positive experience when the school environments are a good fit with the individual needs of each child. This 'school fit' has been described as the match between a student's school and their psychosocial needs (e.g. for emotional support, self-esteem, competence and autonomy). Peer relations were important and identified as a critical factor influencing positive or negative transition expectations and outcomes, and the importance of peer relationships and peer support was identified by parents of autistic children as central to a child's school experience.

Eccles and Roeser (2009) suggest that the issues might not be down to the transition itself, rather the result of a mismatch between the emotional, cognitive and social needs of the individual student and the environment of the new school. There are many facilitators which can aid successful transitions, including:

- visiting their new secondary schools in advance to become familiar with the new environment, meet their new teachers and gain an insight into the new subjects they would be studying;
- parents and children could be involved in suggesting strategies to help prepare for the transition and adapt to daily life in secondary school;
- a range of visual supports including maps, pictures, diaries and planners also help with organisation;
- mentoring from an older student could be beneficial;
- the identification of a base where they could access additional supports or a quieter space where they could eat their lunch away from the noise of the mainstream school.

Deacy et al. (2015) recommend structuring the transition programme over a three-year timescale, starting two years before the transition. The framework consists of the 'Planning for Transition' stage, focusing on the skills that will be necessary over the transition period and the need to devise oral and written communication systems. The importance of 'Building Relationships' needs to be recognised through the creation of a transition team in both schools and a key member of staff who is part of the transition team should be identified. The 'Transition Programme' may contain aspects of a generic programme and an 'Individualised Approach', which is based on assessment and identification of individual strengths and challenges and the use of evidence-based practices.

───────── **Key research in the field** ─────────

Nuske, H. J., McGhee Hassrick, E., Bronstein, B., Hauptman, L., Aponte, C., Levato, L., Stahmer, A., Mandell, D. S., Mundy, P., Kasari, C. and Smith, T. (2019). Broken bridges – new school transitions for students with autism spectrum disorder: A systematic review on difficulties and strategies for success. *Autism*, 23 (2), pp. 306–25.

Aim

Transitioning to a new school is often challenging for students with autism spectrum disorder. Few studies have examined the transition needs of students with autism spectrum disorder or the benefits of specific supports. This review synthesises research findings on the difficulties that school transitions pose for students with

(Continued)

autism spectrum disorder and their parents and teachers, and the strategies used to support students and parents during school transition.

Method

The review included 27 studies (10 examining the transition to primary school, 17 the transition to secondary school), with data from 443 students with autism spectrum disorder, 453 parents, and 546 teachers, across four continents (North America, Europe, Africa, and Australia).

Results

Studies reported that children with autism spectrum disorder struggled with anxiety and increased social pressure, their parents felt overwhelmed with complex placement decisions and worried about the well-being of their children, and teachers strove to provide appropriate supports to their students with autism spectrum disorder, often with inadequate resources.

Conclusions

Findings indicated that the most useful strategies involved helping the student adjust to the new school setting, individualising transition supports, clarifying the transition process for parents, and fostering communication both between the sending and receiving schools, and school and home.

Case study

Hirvikoski and Blomqvist (2015) demonstrated that autistic people were more stressed and found it harder to cope than their neurotypical counterparts. Everyday places such as supermarkets, streets and hospitals can be forbiddingly noisy or unpredictable. It is not a world designed by or for autistic people.

Jadwiga has moved into Year 12 at her local secondary school. She has managed the transition from the more structured curriculum of her GCSE to her A-level studies, which involve more independent working. She has just been offered a part-time job at a local supermarket but is concerned about making the move to this environment.

- What advice could you give to both her and her potential employer?

Transition to adult services

Transition from children to adult services was an underpinning principle of SEND reform as initiated with the Children and Families Act 2014 and the accompanying guidance documents including the SEND Code of Practice (2015) (DfE and DoH, 2015). There were several issues identified, namely:

- difficulties maintaining consistent staffing over the transition period;
- lack of communication between professionals in different services;
- different services switching to adult services at different ages;
- fewer, less well-resourced services in adulthood;
- paying for services that were free as a child;
- carers feeling excluded from consultations about their now-adult family member.

NICE (2016) state that children's and adults' services should both take responsibility for transition, should work together to ensure a smooth and gradual move from children's to adults' services and work closely with GPs and any other support services, including education, health and social care.

However, transition for autistic children and young people is further exacerbated by a range of autism-specific features that create extra barriers, including the removal of a structure which schools provide, the need to cope with change that can be an issue, and the possibility of falling through the gaps in adult services (Allard, 2009). Taylor and Marrable (2011) argue that for many autistic people, and their families and friends, it is a wearying battle to get the care they need. Barriers to receiving services include a lack of awareness about autism, the 'invisibility' of autism as a condition, and that receiving support can rely on good social communication and social interaction skills when completing forms or taking part in assessments.

A significant transition faced by many people with autism as they get older comes when their parent carers are no longer able to support them at home. Many autistic people continue to live at home with carers well into adulthood, and parent carers are therefore likely to be nearing and entering old age while still providing care to people with often very high needs. Hines et al. (2014) carried out in-depth interviews with 16 older parents of autistic adults and their narratives reflected the notion that much of their experience was a delicate balancing act as they attempted to manage their offspring's symptoms of autism while achieving a degree of fulfilment in their own lives. Parents did not believe that formal services had adequately supported their ability to provide care while meeting other needs within the family context.

A crisis, such as the death of a parent/carer, may result in many autistic people finding themselves quickly placed in settings that may be expensive, distant or inappropriate. Other people may be left living at home without adequate support. Dillenburger and McKerr (2011) found that parents worry a lot about the future and what will happen when they can no longer look after their sons and daughters with disabilities, which is a key cause for stress and concern for parents and carers as they approach older age. Preventative services will be particularly important for older adults with autism who are not eligible for social care support. Furthermore, special consideration is needed when planning for the transition into older age and the increased likelihood of other health issues, particularly when family may not be around to support adults with autism.

Transition to university

──────────────────────── Pause for reflection ────────────────────────

Going to university can be a stressful and exciting period in the life of any student.

• What should universities do to ensure that the transition into Higher Education is successful for all students and inclusive?

The transition period from secondary to post-secondary education is a critical time for autistic students as it prepares them for Higher Education (HE) and should provide the structure needed to reduce stress and anxiety. Cai and Richdale (2016) found that many students had no formal transition planning, and they did not feel adequately prepared. Where preparations were made, parents were often significantly involved, as well as teachers and careers advisors. As autistic students typically experience stress levels exceeding those of their neurotypical students (Glennon, 2001), transition is even more likely to affect adjustment, indicating the importance of appropriate transition planning. Effective transition planning should identify the services to be provided and those responsible for implementing them, timelines, intended outcomes, and monitoring and follow-up procedures (Roberts, 2010).

Autistic people may have skills particularly suited to HE, such as proficient memory skills, a focus on detail, and creative thoughts, as well as passionate interests and a strong desire to acquire accurate knowledge (Drake, 2014). Jansen et al. (2018) report that social challenges and increased mental health concerns have been reported and suggest that knowledge about the full spectrum of problems can be the first step towards a better match between the individual problems and the reasonable accommodations offered to increase the participation chances and success rate. Gurbuz et al. (2019) found that autistic students self-reported poorer social skills compared to non-autistic students and the biggest challenges were difficulties with social interactions, loneliness, and lack of interpersonal skills. However, the autistic students reported enjoyment in their academic work, said they received good academic grades, or had good study habits. The authors suggest that we need to consider the opportunity to capitalise on the academic strengths of autistic students and these were self-reported in their research skills, written abilities, analytical thinking, understanding complex ideas, and an ambition to learn their subject of interest.

Beardon and Edmonds (2007) examined overarching themes relating to difficulties encountered at university, these being social interaction, course/curriculum structure, the social environment of the university and understanding of autism. Difficulties identified with social interaction were concerned with the necessity of communicating with others (in, for example, group work). It was suggested that support to understand non-autistic people's behaviour may benefit people on the autism spectrum, while support to understand autism may help non-autistic individuals. In terms of the environment, participants identified difficulties with expectations, activities and sensory experiences. Again, education of the autistic individual about non-autistic behaviours, and vice versa, was identified as a way of minimising the impact of this. Some participants reported that they faced challenges arising from their own and others' understanding of autism. Factors related to the course and curriculum structure, such as rigidity in assessment modes/criteria and bureaucratic requirements, were found to present challenges to some of the participants. Suggested approaches to minimising the stress caused by these challenges were clear communication and mentoring.

Madriaga and Goodley (2010) interviewed eight students with Asperger syndrome, recognising the students themselves as central to the experience. The study found that students initially regarded starting university as a positive experience, viewing attending university as an opportunity to move on from past negative experiences (supporting the view that transition can present both challenges and opportunities). Some of the participants reported experiencing social isolation, whereas others did not report difficulties in social interaction. Participation in social situations, such as attending freshers' fairs and living in shared accommodation, were not found to remedy social isolation due to the high levels of stress they could produce. Facilitators identified by participants included having effective mentoring and teaching staff being adaptable to different learning styles.

Hastwell et al. (2013) identified four main factors that influenced student experience at university: social interaction, the university environment, understanding of autism and academic engagement. One difficulty identified was living in shared accommodation, which could be very noisy, making studying difficult and very stressful. Many of the autistic participants in this study identified that a lack of understanding and empathy caused difficulties at university, with others making assumptions and underestimating their abilities The researchers developed an acronym to encompass principles of good practice for positive university transitions for people on the autism spectrum – REAL (reliable, empathic, anticipatory, logical).

Difficulties encountered at university concern the social environment, the institutional environment, academic expectations, and people's understanding of autism. The move to university can, therefore, be a challenging transition, or it may be viewed as an opportunity to start a new phase in their lives. Madriaga and Goodley (2010) found that barriers were encountered in lectures, such as not providing handouts prior to the lecture and not encouraging participation of students, group work and assessment. They concluded that the barriers identified result from unsuitable social, physical and institutional environments and not 'deficits' or 'impairments'. Cage et al. (2020) examined the factors that affect university completion for autistic people and found that they may be less likely to complete their university studies and those who did not complete had a poorer academic experience, found the transition more diffi-cult, and felt less organisational and social identification at university.

Transition into employment

With regard to transitioning into employment, the lack of appropriate employment opportunities, and insufficient support to gain and maintain employment, are key barriers to paid work. Voluntary work is frequently identified both as a route into paid employment, as well as being a positive and meaningful day-time activity. According to the British Association for Supported Employment (BASE, 2021), employment rates for people with disabilities have been on a downward trend year on year. The latest figures for 2020–21 show another drop after a brief upturn in 2017–18.

In 2020–21, 5.1 per cent of adults with learning disabilities aged 18–64 and known to Councils with Adult Social Services Responsibilities (CASSRs) were in paid employ-ment. The gender breakdown was male 5.7 per cent, female 4.4 per cent. The Office for National Statistics (ONS) (2021) identify that 22 per cent of autistic people are reported as being in paid work. Autistic adults face significant challenges entering the workforce and maintaining meaningful employment (Taylor et al., 2015). A survey by the National Autistic Society (Bancroft et al., 2012) found that although 53 per cent of autistic adults would like access to employment support, only 10 per cent get it, and that generic employment support programmes can be difficult to access.

Employment is not only important from an economic standpoint, but it is also a vital part of an individual's wellbeing. Independence, self-esteem, community engagement and social status are all related to an individual's capacity to work, and employment has a positive effect on physical and mental health, and the desire to be employed is common in autistic people (Chen et al., 2015). Furthermore, those who are employed are more likely to experience a better quality of life and improved cognitive and mental health outcomes than those who are not employed. However, successfully navigating traditional job interviews, complex work environments, including often challenging social dynamics, varied communication requirements and need for flexibility, could be difficult in both gaining and keeping a job.

Barriers to employment

There are several barriers to employment for autistic young people and adults – employment may not be considered as a post-school option and some schools and colleges find it hard to source work experience placements for young autistic people. Research shows that work experience is an important factor both in gaining future employment and in helping to consider different work options, and this also applies to young disabled people. However, some schools and colleges offer well-structured modules from established work preparation programmes, while others rely on their own work awareness curricula or provide no input at all. Families may also have concerns about employment as an option for their son or daughter as they fear that the young person, or family, will be financially worse off in paid work, or that the young person will not cope well in a work environment (Graetz, 2010). Employer attitudes may also be a barrier for young people moving into work and they may be fearful of the behaviour traits of autistic people and of the effect of these on their business, resources and other employees and may thus be unwilling to consider employing them (Forsythe et al., 2008). Applying for a job and getting to an interview may find autistic people having difficulties in 'selling themselves' in a positive and confident way (understanding body language, maintaining appropriate eye contact, varying the tone of their voice, and finding the appropriate level of formality) (Townsley et al., 2014).

Once in a job there are many social barriers, such as not understanding the subtle, unwritten, or hidden messages in workplace communication; difficulties in establishing relationships and interacting with colleagues may lead to their exclusion by colleagues or managers, misunderstandings, or crises, and can cause people with autism to leave jobs they enjoy, or to be dismissed. Richards (2012) found that many were excluded by everyday management practices such as task-based meetings, annual performance reviews and team-building events. Some people also face cognitive barriers to maintaining employment, such as difficulty in the planning, sequencing of activities and literal thinking (Patterson and Rafferty, 2010). The workplace environment may also cause issues, with sensory overload and confusions associated with fluorescent lighting and the hum of electrical appliances such as computers. Reactions to stressful social situations can lead to inappropriate behaviour, such as verbal outbursts, or challenging behaviour as a response to the feeling of being anxious or overwhelmed.

Case study

Brian works at a law firm as a paralegal. He has a previous diagnosis of Asperger syndrome. Since starting work at the firm, Brian had a lot of difficulty managing his time. He was consistently behind on his work targets and had lots of late deadlines flagged up. He began to make mistakes and when he asked for help, he had coaching in the office, which proved an inefficient way of learning for him as there were too many distractions. When he asked more experienced colleagues for help, he found that each one gave a slightly different answer.

(Continued)

You have been asked to be a mentor for Brain to support his role in the firm. Under each of the following headings: environment, work tasks and working with others, identify:

1   An issue.
2   Factors to be considered.
3   Potential adjustments.

———————————————————— Key points ————————————————————

- For autistic people, transitions at every stage in their lives can present both challenges and opportunities
- Multi-agencies, including health and social services along with local authorities, need to collaborate to support transitions
- Support for older autistic adults, including the role and importance of carers, needs to be planned with their views and wishes at the forefront
- Transition is a process and period of change
- The time between childhood and adulthood and the planning and transferring from children's education, health and care services and support involves managing new relationships to ensure a smooth transition to adult education, employment independent living, health and social care services and support including end of life provision

———————————————————— Questions to consider ————————————————————

- What do you think are the main barriers and facilitators involved in the process of transition?
- How do we ensure that there is a joined-up approach to supporting autistic individuals, their allies and families?
- Where would you as a teacher or potential employer signpost an autistic individual to in order to gain an understanding of the process of transitions?

———————————————————— Further reading ————————————————————

Murin, M., Mandy, W. and Hellriegel, J. (2016). *Autism Spectrum Disorder and the Transition into Secondary School: A handbook for implementing strategies in the mainstream school setting*. London: Jessica Kingsley Publishers.

An effective evidence-based programme, this practical handbook provides everything schools need to make the transition from primary to secondary school as smooth and successful as possible for children with autism spectrum disorder (ASD). After explaining how to create individualised transition plans for each child and describing how staff can collaborate successfully with parents and carers, the second part of the book contains a wealth of practical, photocopiable resources for use directly with pupils on the autism spectrum.

Pesonen, H. V., Waltz, M., Fabri, M., Lahdelma, M. and Syurina, E. V. (2021). Students and graduates with autism: Perceptions of support when preparing for transition from university to work. *European Journal of Special Needs Education*, 36 (4), pp. 531–46.

Despite the steps taken to improve support in universities, many students and graduates with autism face a substantial employment gap when completing university as compared to any other student group with disabilities. Utilising a participatory approach, perceptions of autistic students and graduates about the employment support they received when preparing for university-to-work transition were sought. The study involved semi-structured interviews with 30 university students and graduates from Finland, France, the Netherlands, and the UK. Findings indicate that organisational enablers consisting of career-focused support and internships and practicums facilitated preparation for employment. Supportive and caring relationships emerged as forms of support that included mentors, committed and caring academics, and family members. Further, the findings indicated the aspiration for individualisation that consists of improving work and academic support, and awareness and understanding.

Richter, M., Popa-Roch, M. and Clément, C. (2019). Successful transition from primary to secondary school for students with autism spectrum disorder: A systematic literature review. *Journal of Research in Childhood Education*, 33 (3), pp. 382–98.

The transition from primary to secondary school is a sensitive phase in the life of a child, especially within vulnerable groups such as autistic children. Characteristics, such as the refusal to change or social interaction difficulties, present challenges to the transition not only for the students themselves, but also for their parents and the teachers involved in the transition process. For the literature review, 16 studies focusing on the primary–secondary transition for autistic children were selected. Based on criteria existing in the literature for students without special needs, the selected articles were analysed for identifying factors that enable a successful transition for children. The literature review confirms these criteria to a major extent, but also modifies and adds new criteria, which involve all main stakeholders and the transition preparation.

References

Allard, A. (2009). *Transition to Adulthood: Inquiry into transition to adulthood for young people with autism*. London: The National Autistic Society.

Atkinson, M. (2002). *Multi-agency Working: A detailed study*. Slough: National Foundation for Educational Research.

Baginsky, M. and Manthorpe, J. (2021). The impact of COVID-19 on children's social care in England. *Child Abuse Negl*, 116 (2), 104739.

Bahena, S., Schueler, B. E., McIntyre, J. and Gehlbach, H. (2016). Assessing parent perceptions of school fit: The development and measurement qualities of a survey scale. *Appl Dev Sci*, 20 (2), pp. 121–134.

Bancroft, K., Batten, A., Lambert, S. and Madders, T. (2012). *The Way We Are: Autism in 2012*. [online] Available at: https://cnnespanol.cnn.com/wp-content/uploads/2017/04/50th-survey-report-2012.pdf [Accessed 15.02.2022].

Beardon L. and Edmonds G. (2007). *ASPECT Consultancy Report. A national report on the needs of adults with Asperger syndrome.* [online] Available at: www.shu.ac.uk/theautismcentre [Accessed 28.03.2022].

Beresford, B., Moran, N., Sloper, P., Cusworth, L., Mitchell, W., Spiers, G., Weston, K. and Beecham, J. (2013). *Transition to Adult Services and Adulthood for Young People with Autistic Spectrum Conditions* (Working paper no: DH 2525, Department of Health Policy Research Programme Project reference no. 016 0108).

Blacher, J. (2001). Transition to adulthood: Mental retardation, families, and culture. *American Journal on Mental Retardation,* 106 (2), pp. 173–88.

British Association for Supported Employment (BASE) (2021). *Employment Rates for People with Disabilities 2020-21.* [online] Available at: www.base-uk.org/employment-rates [Accessed 27.02.2022].

Brookman-Frazee, L., Stahmer, A. and Lewis, K. (2012). Building a research-community collaborative to improve community care for infants and toddlers at-risk for autism spectrum disorders. *Journal of Community Psychology,* 40 (6), pp. 715–34.

Cage, E., De Andres, M. and Mahoney, P. (2020). Understanding the factors that affect university completion for autistic people. *Research in Autism Spectrum Disorders,* 72, 101519.

Cai, R. Y. and Richdale, A. L. (2016). Educational experiences and needs of higher education students with autism spectrum disorder. *J Autism Dev Disord,* 46 (1), pp. 31–41.

Calder, L., Hill, V. and Pellicano, E. (2013). 'Sometimes I want to play by myself': Understanding what friendship means to children with autism in mainstream primary schools. *Autism,* 17 (3), pp. 296–316.

Care Quality Commission and Ofsted (2020). *COVID-19 series: Briefing on local areas' special educational needs and disabilities provision, October 2020.* [online] Available at: https://assets.publishing.service.gov.uk/government/uploads/system/uploads/attachment_data/file/933499/SEND_COVID-19_briefing_October_2020.pdf [Accessed 02.02.2022].

Cheak-Zamora, N. C., Teti, M. and First, J. (2015). 'Transitions are scary for our kids, and they're scary for us': Family member and youth perspectives on the challenges of transitioning to adulthood with autism. *J Appl Res Intellect Disabil,* 28 (6), pp. 548–60.

Chen, J. L., Leader, G., Sung, C. and Leahy, M. (2015). Trends in employment for individuals with autism spectrum disorder: A review of the research literature. *Rev J Autism Dev Disord,* 2, pp. 115–27.

Children Act (1989). [online] Available at: www.legislation.gov.uk/ukpga/1989/41/contents [Accessed 12.02.2022].

Codd, J. and Hewitt, O. (2020). Having a son or daughter with an intellectual disability transition to adulthood: A parental perspective. *British Journal of Learning Disabilities,* 49 (1), pp. 39–51.

Deacy, E., Jennings, F. and O'Halloran, A. (2015). Transition of students with autistic spectrum disorders from primary to post-primary school: A framework for success. *Support for Learning,* 30 (4), pp. 292–304.

Department for Education (DfE) and Department for Health and Social Care (DHSC) (2021). *The National Strategy for Autistic Children, Young People and Adults: 2021 to 2026.* [online] Available at: www.gov.uk/government/publications/national-strategy-for-autistic-children-young-people-and-adults-2021-to-2026/the-national-strategy-for-autistic-children-young-people-and-adults-2021-to-2026 [Accessed 27.03.2022].

Deweerdt, S. (2014). *Autism characteristics differ by gender, studies find.* [online] Available at: www.spectrumnews.org/news/autism-characteristics-differ-by-gender-studies-find/ [Accessed 13.11.2021].

Dillenburger, K. and McKerr, L. (2011). 'How long are we able to go on?' Issues faced by older family caregivers of adults with disabilities. *British Journal of Learning Disabilities*, 39 (1), pp. 29–38.

Dillon, G. V. and Underwood, J. D. M. (2012). Parental perspectives of students with autism spectrum disorders transitioning from primary to secondary school in the United Kingdom. *Focus on Autism and Other Developmental Disabilities*, 27 (2), pp. 111–21.

Drake, S. (2014). College experience of academically successful students with autism. *Journal of Autism*, 1 (5), pp. 1–4.

Eccles, J. S. and Midgley, C. (1989). Stage/environment fit: Developmentally appropriate classrooms for early adolescence. In R. E. Ames and C. Ames (Eds), *Research on Motivation in Education, Vol. 3*. New York: Academic Press, pp. 139–86.

Eccles, J. S. and Roeser, R. W. (2009). Schools, academic motivation, and stage-environment fit. In R. M. Lerner and L. Steinberg (Eds), *Handbook of Adolescent Psychology: Individual bases of adolescent development*. Hoboken, NJ: John Wiley & Sons Inc, pp. 404–34.

Evangelou, M., Taggart, B., Sylva, K., Melhuish, E., Sammons, P. and Siraj-Blatchford, I. (2008). *What Makes a Successful Transition From Primary to Secondary School?* Nottingham: Department for Children, Schools and Families.

Everitt, J. (2010). *A Critical Evaluation of the Effectiveness and Efficiency of Multiagency Working: A literature review.* MA thesis, Staffordshire University, Stoke-on-Trent.

Fayette, R. and Bond, C. (2018). A systematic literature review of qualitative research methods for eliciting the views of young people with ASD about their educational experiences. *Eur J Special Needs Educ*, 33, pp. 349–65.

Forsythe, L., Rahim, N. and Bell, L. (2008). *Benefits and Employment Support Schemes to Meet the Needs of People with an Autistic Spectrum Disorder.* London: Inclusion Research and Consultancy.

Fortuna, R. (2014). The social and emotional functioning of pupils with an autistic spectrum disorder during the transition between primary and secondary schools. *Support for Learning*, 29 (2), pp. 177–91.

Gaona, C., Castro, S. and Palikara, O. (2020). The views and aspirations of young people with autism spectrum disorders and their provision in the new Education, Health and Care plans in England. *Disabil Rehabil*, 42 (23), pp. 3383–94.

Glennon, T. J. (2021). The stress of the university experience for students with Asperger syndrome. *Work*, 17 (3), pp. 183–90.

Graetz, J. E. (2010). Autism grows up: Opportunities for adults with autism. *Disability & Society*, 25 (1), pp. 33–47.

Greco, V., Sloper, P., Webb, R. and Beecham, J. (2005). *An Exploration of Different Models of Multi-Agency Partnerships in Key Worker Services for Disabled Children: Effectiveness and costs.* [online] Available at: www.york.ac.uk/inst/spru/pubs/pdf/keyworker.pdf [Accessed 11.01.2022].

Gurbuz, E., Hanley, M. and Riby, D. M. (2019). University students with autism: The social and academic experiences of university in the UK. *J Autism Dev Disord*, 49, pp. 617–31.

Hannah, E. F. and Topping, K. F. (2013). The transition from primary to secondary school: Perspectives of students with autism spectrum disorder and their parents. *International Journal of Special Education*, 28 (1), pp. 145–57.

Hastwell, J., Harding, J., Martin, N. and Baron-Cohen, S. (2013). *Asperger Syndrome Student Project, 2009-12: Final project report, June 2013*. [online] Available at: www.disability.admin.cam.ac.uk/files/asprojectreport2013.pdf [Accessed 21.01.2022].

Hines, M., Balandin, S. and Togher, L. (2014). The stories of older parents of adult sons and daughters with autism: A balancing act. *J Appl Res Intellect Disabil*, 27 (2), pp. 163–73.

Hirvikoski, T. and Blomqvist, M. (2015). High self-perceived stress and poor coping in intellectually able adults with autism spectrum disorder. *Autism*, 19 (6), pp. 752–7.

Home Office (2014). *Multi Agency Working and Information Sharing Project: Final report*. [online] Available at: https://assets.publishing.service.gov.uk/government/uploads/system/uploads/attachment_data/file/338875/MASH.pdf [Accessed 15.12.2001].

Horwath, J. and Morrison, T. (2007). Collaboration, integration and change in children's services: Critical issues and key ingredients. *Child Abuse and Neglect*, 31 (1), pp. 55–69.

Jansen, D., Emmers, E., Petry, K., Mattys, L., Noens, I. and Baeyens, D. (2018). Functioning and participation of young adults with ASD in higher education according to the ICF framework. *Journal of Further and Higher Education*, 42 (2), pp. 259–75.

Madriaga, M. and Goodley, D. (2010). Moving beyond the minimum: Socially just pedagogies and Asperger's syndrome in UK higher education. *International Journal of Inclusive Education*, 14 (2), pp. 115–31.

Makin, C., Hill, V. and Pellicano, E. (2017). The primary-to-secondary school transition for children on the autism spectrum: A multi-informant mixed-methods study. *Autism and Developmental Language Impairments*, 2, pp. 1–18.

Mandy, W., Murin, M., Baykaner, O., Staunton, S., Hellriegel, J., Anderson, S. and Skuse, D. (2015). The transition from primary to secondary school in mainstream education for children with autism spectrum disorder. *Autism*, 20 (1), pp. 5–13.

Marsh, A., Spagnol, V., Grove, R. and Eapen, V. (2017). Transition to school for children with autism spectrum disorder: A systematic review. *World J Psychiatry*, 7 (3), pp. 184–96.

McAlister, A. R. and Peterson, C. C. (2012). Siblings, theory of mind, and executive functioning in children aged 3–6 years: New longitudinal evidence. *Child Development*, 84 (4), pp. 1442–58.

Mental Health Foundation (2012). *Employment is vital for maintaining good mental health*. [online] Available at: www.mentalhealth.org.uk/blog/employment-vital-maintaining-good-mental-health [Accessed 21.02.2022].

National Institute for Health and Care Excellence (NICE) (2014). *Implementation Pack: Developing a multi-agency local autism team*. [online] Available at: www.nice.org.uk/guidance/qs51/resources/local-team-information-sheet-pdf-122808925 [Accessed 09.01.2022].

National Institute for Health and Care Excellence (NICE) (2016). *Transition from Children's to Adults' Services for Young People Using Health or Social Care Services*. [online] Available at: www.nice.org.uk/guidance/ng43/evidence/full-guideline-pdf-2360240173 [Accessed 11.01.2022].

National Society for the Prevention of Cruelty to Children (NSPCC) (2019). *Multi-agency Working*. [online] Available at: https://learning.nspcc.org.uk/child-protection-system/multi-agency-working-child-protection [Accessed 23.01.2022].

Nuske, H. J., McGhee Hassrick, E., Bronstein, B., Hauptman, L., Aponte, C., Levato, L., Stahmer, A., Mandell, D. S., Mundy, P., Kasari, C. and Smith, T. (2019). Broken bridges – new school transitions for students with autism spectrum disorder: A systematic review on difficulties and strategies for success. *Autism*, 23 (2), pp. 306–25.

Office for National Statistics (ONS) (2021). *Outcomes for Disabled People in the UK: 2021*. [online] Available at: www.ons.gov.uk/peoplepopulationandcommunity/healthandsocialcare/disability/articles/outcomesfordisabledpeopleintheuk/2021 [Accessed 01.03.2022].

Patterson, A. and Rafferty, A. (2010). Making it to work: Towards employment for the young adult with autism. *International Journal of Language and Communication Disorders*, 36 (1), pp. 475–80.

Quintero, N. and McIntyre, L. L. (2011). Kindergarten transition preparation: A comparison of teacher and parent practices for children with autism and other developmental disabilities. *Early Childhood Education Journal*, 38 (6), pp. 411–20.

Richards, J. (2012) Examining the exclusion of employees with Asperger syndrome from the workplace. *Personnel Review*, 41 (5), pp. 630–46.

Richter, M., Popa-Roch, M. and Clément, C. (2019). Successful transition from primary to secondary school for students with autism spectrum disorder: A systematic literature review. *Journal of Research in Childhood Education*, 33 (3), pp. 382–98.

Roberts, K. D. (2010). Topic areas to consider when planning transition from high school to postsecondary education for students with autism spectrum disorders. *Focus on Autism and Other Developmental Disabilities*, 25 (3), pp. 158–62.

Sinai-Gavrilov, Y., Gev, T., Mor-Snir, I. and Golan, O. (2019). Seeking team collaboration, dialogue and support: The perceptions of multidisciplinary staff-members working in ASD preschools. *J Autism Dev Disord*, 49 (11), pp. 4634–45.

Sloper, P. (2004). Facilitators and barriers for co-ordinated multi-agency services. *Child: Care, Health and Development*, 30 (6), pp. 571–80.

Solomon, M. (2019). Becoming comfortable with chaos: Making collaborative multi-agency working work. *Emotional & Behavioural Difficulties*, 24 (4), pp. 391–404.

Stack, K., Symonds, J. E. and Kinsella, W. (2021). The perspectives of students with autism spectrum disorder on the transition from primary to secondary school: A systematic literature review. *Research in Autism Spectrum Disorders*, 84 (4), 101782.

Taylor, I. and Marrable, T. (2011) *Access to Social Care for Adults with Autistic Spectrum Conditions*. London: SCIE.

Taylor, J. L., Henninger, N. A. and Mailick, M. R. (2015). Longitudinal patterns of employment and postsecondary education for adults with autism and average-range IQ. *Autism: The International Journal of Research and Practice*, 19 (7), pp. 785–93.

Thom, R. P., Hazen, M. M., McDougle, C. J. and Hazen, E. P. (2020). Providing inpatient medical care to children with autism spectrum disorder. *Hosp Pediatr*, 10 (10), pp. 918–24.

Townsley, R., Robinson, C., Williams, V., Beyer, S. and Christian-Jones, C. (2014). *Employment and Young People with Autistic Spectrum Disorders: An Evidence Review*.

[online] Available at: https://dera.ioe.ac.uk/20174/3/140602-employment-young-people-autism-evidence-review-en.pdf [Accessed 23.02.2022].

United Nations Children's Fund (UNICEF) (2012). *The State of the World's Children 2012.* [online] Available at: www.unicef.org/media/89226/file/The%20State%20of%20the%20World's%20Children%202012.pdf [Accessed 27.02.2022].

Zeedyk, M. S., Gallacher, M., Henderson, G., Hope, G., Husband, B. and Lindsay, K. (2003). Negotiating the transition from primary to secondary school: Perceptions of pupils, parents and teachers. *School Psychology International*, 24 (1), pp. 67–79.

TEN

Pedagogical approaches in autism

Introduction

This chapter follows on from Chapter 5, which focused upon evidence-based strategies surrounding working with autistic learners in the classroom. The focus of this chapter is to examine some of the teaching approaches involved in working with autistic learners. There are a range of approaches which teachers have in their 'toolbox', including general approaches such as Intensive Interaction and specific strategies such as the use of Token Economies. The concept of the inclusive classroom and the view that what constitutes effective pedagogy for autistic learners is also effective for others in the classroom will be discussed. While there may be strategies to support issues involved in Executive Functioning or Theory of Mind for example, teachers must be aware of the importance to focus upon the individual learner, including their strengths, what motivates them and how assessment of the learning is carried out. One size does not fit all.

--------------------- Learning objectives ---------------------

This chapter will:

- Introduce you to a range of general and specific approaches that could be used with autistic learners
- Invite you to evaluate the debate surrounding specialist or inclusive pedagogy
- Introduce you to consider differing approaches to assessment of what has been learned
- Help you to consider how different strategies can be matched to communication, cognitive and behavioural issues associated with autism being a continuum of need

--------------------- Key terms ---------------------

Inclusive and specialist pedagogy, labelling, Quality First Teaching, Universal Design for Learning (UDL), differentiation, Inclusive Pedagogical Approach in Action (IPAA) framework,

(Continued)

Intensive Interaction, SPELL (Structure, Positive, Empathy, Low arousal, Links), Power Cards, Token Economies, Executive Functioning, Theory of Mind, Central Coherence, Assessment of Learning, Assessment for Learning, Objects of Reference, Makaton, Hybrid Learning Model

----------------------------------- Pause for reflection -----------------------------------

- You have just been told that you will be teaching an autistic child in your class. What would be your priorities to ensure that you understand about any issues or strengths that this child may have and how might this affect how you start to plan your lesson?
- How would you include them in the session activities?

Difficulties for students with autism may present as follows:

- speech and language difficulties and a lack of desire to communicate;
- over- or under-stimulation in the classroom, as well as an inability to integrate sensory information from different sources;
- inability to read social cues, feel empathy or develop social skills resulting in difficulty making friends, or to engage with others in learning tasks;
- lack of flexibility of thought and imagination leading to problems understanding and interpreting the world around them;
- preference for highly structured environments and routines, combined with a resistance to change challenging behaviours.

Specialist or inclusive pedagogy?

Norwich and Lewis (2007) contend that there is insufficient evidence to support specialist pedagogy for categories of SEN and that in supporting learners with SEN, teachers draw on continua of strategies which reflect the adaptations of common teaching methodologies. Teaching at various points on the continua may look different but not qualitatively different to warrant specialist pedagogies (Brennan et al., 2021). Individualised interventions, based on a response to a particular impairment or specific difficulty, can compound the problem of difference by marking the learner as different. Lewis and Norwich (2005) found little evidence to support the notion of one, or several, SEN-specific pedagogies, and although they suggest that there is increasing support for the recognition of common pedagogic needs, how this is translated at the level of the individual learner will reflect the capabilities of that individual. Others regard the separation of knowledge and pedagogy as potentially detrimental and assert that scientific knowledge about types of SEN is important in meeting the needs of all learners (Mintz and Wyse, 2015). They argue for a concept of special pedagogy which refers to specialist knowledge of diagnostic categories and knowledge of the learner's individual needs. Teachers often adapt strategies when working with different groups of children but once a learner is identified or diagnosed as having an SEN, they can feel inadequately prepared to meet the needs of such learners (Florian, 2014).

Labelling

Lewis and Norwich (2005) conceptualise two possible positions that are taken in the field of SEN, specifically in terms of pedagogy, the 'dilemma of difference'. If we identify individuals as being autistic, we run the risk of stigmatising and marginalising learners in ways that may limit their opportunities and may lead to 'othering'. Yet, if we do not, then it is less likely that additional educational resources will be identified and ensured for them. However, inaccurate labels may lead to inappropriate interventions or assumptions about what a learner can and cannot do and what they do and do not need. There may be a focus on the 'label' rather than on the capabilities and complexities of an individual learner.

Riddick (2012) suggests that a label emphasises the existing negative attitudes and by assigning categories to certain learners predisposes educators to believe that they cannot effectively teach all learners together, or that they lack the knowledge to work with pupils who belong to that category. There may be advantages of labelling in that a label can give us an accurate understanding of a child's learning differences and hence be a starting point for addressing their needs appropriately. It may enable access to 'gatekeepers' of resources such as medical practitioners and advocacy groups. Labels can lead to a greater self-understanding and empowerment and used as mediators in explaining behaviour that might seem unacceptable to the wider public, perhaps leading to greater understanding.

Quality First Teaching

Under the SEND Code of Practice (2015), schools and their staff are legally required to provide 'reasonable adjustments' to avoid educational disadvantages (DfE and DoH, 2015). As the professional responsible and accountable for the progress of all the children they teach, the class teacher is expected to deploy the best strategy for their whole class. If the quality of universal provision is high, the need for targeted provision is likely to be less, as more of the pupils will have most of their learning needs met. Consistent and sustained use of classroom strategies to meet the needs of all pupils is likely to reduce the need for multiple targeted intervention groups and allow pupils to learn in a more inclusive way.

According to the SEND Code of Practice 0–25 (2015) (DfE and DoH, 2015), this is high-quality, inclusive teaching which ensures that planning and implementation meets the needs of all pupils, and builds in high expectations for all pupils, including those with SEN. It is about the day-to-day interactions that take place in the classroom and the different pedagogical approaches teachers use to engage and motivate learners, which ensure good pupil progress. Teachers are responsible and accountable for the progress and development of the pupils in their class, including where pupils access support from teaching assistants or specialist staff. Quality First Teaching (QFT) derives from the notion of personalised learning which sees the importance of highly focused lesson design with sharp objectives, pupil involvement, interaction and engagement with their learning. Also, there is an emphasis on learning through dialogue, with regular opportunities for pupils to talk both individually and in groups, along with an expectation that pupils will accept responsibility for their own learning and work independently. Quality First Teaching emphasises the importance of student–teacher relationships through higher expectations and support for all (North Yorkshire County Council, 2020) and encourages inclusivity through adapted pedagogy appropriate for all children regardless of diagnosis. The essential features of this strategy are:

1   Design clear lesson plans.
2   Create opportunities to engage with students.
3   Use models, explanations and questions appropriately to grow critical-thinking skills.
4   Ensure opportunities for individual and group interactions.
5   Expect students to take responsibility for their own learning.
6   Offer regular authentic praise and encouragement to motivate.

Inclusive pedagogy

Whether teachers are using the Quality First Approach, tailored intervention support or an individualised programme, it is important that autistic learners feel included in the classroom. Children with autism have a right to be within inclusive classrooms. There are many benefits to having inclusive classrooms, including reducing stigma surrounding autism, creating respectful relationships between all students within a classroom, teaching all students how to act positively with others, and increasing knowledge of autism. To best create an inclusive classroom, teachers should continue differentiating instruction and should teach to a student's interests and needs (Beghin, 2021). Examples of inclusive pedagogy include Universal Design for Learning (UDL), Differentiated Instruction (DI) and the Inclusive Pedagogical Approach in Action (IPAA) framework.

Universal Design for Learning (UDL)

Universal Design for Learning (UDL) is a comprehensive framework that is used to support teachers to address diversity of learning in the classroom. It was developed by researchers (Rose and Meyer, 2002) at the Center for Applied Special Technology (CAST) and is based on decades of neuroscience research, which led to the assumption of variability in life and learning (Carrington et al., 2020). The UDL framework has three guiding principles that help educators to support all learners by providing multiple ways of engaging students, representing knowledge, and demonstrating understanding. These guiding principles are underpinned by nine guidelines, which are broken into 31 checkpoints that support students to access, build, and internalise skills. These highlight ways in which educators can design learning environments and programmes that are accessible for all students and may guide them to set learning goals and plan curricula, assessment, teaching strategies, and resources to meet individual learning needs.

Providing autism-specific examples of UDL goes a little bit against the grain, since it is about design, which is inclusive of everyone. Understanding characteristics typical of people on the spectrum, while respecting that every single individual is unique, provides a starting point for thinking about including autistic people when developing UDL (Milton et al., 2016). Milton et al. (2016) suggest that there are three principles involved relating to multiple means of engagement, representation of material and expression of knowledge. Guidelines for these principles include the provision of a range of options, including the provision of options for recruiting interest, sustaining effort and self-regulation, and options for the use of language, symbols, and executive functions.

Differentiated Instruction

The specific skills or difficulties of autistic learners can be addressed by employing a variety of methods to differentiate (or vary) the depth or breadth of the information or skills to be taught; the instructional approaches used with the student, as well as the materials used to deliver or illustrate the content and the products of the learning situation. Teachers need to utilise flexible strategies that will both engage and support the needs of students on the autism spectrum as well as the class (Graham et al., 2020). Researchers have identified strategies that have a strong evidence base for supporting the learning needs of autistic children (see Chapter 5). These include strategies that provide structure, visual information, and build on special interests to promote learning. For example, learners could be grouped for ability or peers; there could be differentiated instructions; assessments could involve personalised choice and a variety of methods; tasks could be matched to the learner's needs and interests; and feedback could be targeted at individual needs.

———————————————— Case study ————————————————

Mitch is 15 years old, autistic and attends a mainstream school, where he is particularly interested in sports and plays football for the school team. He is friends with Frankie (discussed in Chapter 7) and they regularly play football together at home. He lacks motivation when things start to go wrong in his studies, has difficulty in organising himself, following verbal instructions, time management and

(Continued)

working as part of a team. Amir, who is Mitch's PE teacher, wants him to become more of a team player, as this is vital if he is to remain in the football squad.

Amir understands the concept of inclusion and wants Mitch to be part of the PE lessons where he will develop his skills in working with others. He has been asked to produce a lesson plan which is differentiated for the group, including Mitch, along the lines of aims and outcomes, teaching and learning strategies and assessment.

- How should Amir go about planning a PE lesson which evidences differentiation and allows Mitch to take part in the session alongside his peers?
- How would this evidence inclusivity?

The Inclusive Pedagogical Approach in Action (IPAA) framework

The Inclusive Pedagogical Approach in Action (IPAA) framework emerged as a support mechanism for teachers to develop responses to individual differences in ways that do not marginalise any learner (Spratt and Florian, 2015). The IPAA framework identifies three key assumptions that teachers must hold to enact inclusive pedagogy while also acknowledging the challenges of meeting the needs of all learners. First, teachers must believe in the concept of transformability, which refers to the belief that a child's capacity to learn is not static nor pre-determined but can be transformed by the actions undertaken by the teacher in developing teaching and learning (Hart and Drummond, 2014). The second assumption of the IPAA refers to fostering teachers' beliefs in their ability to teach students with SEN. Associated with the second assumption is the view that difficulties in learning are not within the learner but are problems for the teacher to solve. In this context, teachers must be prepared to commit to supporting the learning of all (Florian, 2014).

Wilkinson and Twist (2010) state that teaching strategies often recommended for use with autistic pupils are those that are sensitive to the specific strengths and issues related to the disorder and include a clearly defined teaching structure and daily routine with the use of visual cues where appropriate; the use of unambiguous classroom language with clear explanation of rules and regulations in class; and sharing the purpose of activities and assessments as well as their intended outcomes. There are some established approaches for teaching students with autism. Some teachers prefer to concentrate on one strategy, while others will use ideas taken from several approaches.

──────────── Key research in the field ────────────

Goodall, C. (2018). 'I felt closed in and like I couldn't breathe': A qualitative study exploring the mainstream educational experiences of autistic young people. *Autism & Developmental Language Impairments*, 3, pp. 1–16.

Objective

This study discusses the educational experiences of 12 autistic young people (aged 11–17 years) from their perspectives and how education could be improved to better support others with autism.

Method

A qualitative participatory approach was used with 12 autistic young people (aged 11–17 years), seven attended an Alternative Education Provision (having come from mainstream schools) and five were home schooled. The approach incorporated a range of methods, including individual semi-structured interviews, diamond ranking activities and draw-and-tell activities.

Findings

The young people offered insights into how education has been for them in mainstream school, mostly negative, but with islets of positive experience. Several described themselves as being socially, emotionally and physically isolated from peers, with loneliness and bullying experienced by some. Participants felt unsupported and misunderstood by teachers within a social and sensory environment. Some spoke of the dread they felt before and during school and the negative impact their experiences in mainstream has had on their wellbeing.

Conclusion

The participants demonstrate that mainstream is not working for all and that changes such as smaller class sizes, flexible pedagogy and understanding could improve education for autistic learners.

General approaches

The TEACCH structured teaching approach, PECS and Social Stories™ are discussed in Chapter 5. Two other approaches are discussed below.

Intensive Interaction

Intensive Interaction is one of the most important advances of the past 20 years. It has made a significant contribution to the development of effective communication curricula for those with complex learning and communication difficulties (Nind and Hewett, 1988; Nind and Hewett, 2005). The prime focus is on mirroring body language and vocalisations to achieve long-term communication skills (Berridge and Hutchinson, 2021) and is especially beneficial for children who are less included in a class environment (Tee and Reed, 2017). While some studies define Intensive Interaction as a strategy for developing communication (Nind and Hewett, 2005), others perceive it as a means for social inclusion.

(Continued)

It is particularly useful for children with pre-verbal, pre-linguistic, pre-intentional behaviour and/or those who are difficult to reach (often those with complex needs or autism). It is based on conventional parent/infant models of interaction and focuses on the communication process from birth. It emphasises that communication is a two-way process and should be nurtured and enjoyed from the start of a child's life. By doing this, we become flexible and responsive partners. This encourages children to engage fully and empowers them to understand that they can affect the actions of those around them.

SPELL (Structure, Positive, Empathy, Low arousal, Links)

The NAS (2022) suggest that this is a framework rather than an approach. SPELL was developed through evidence-based practice to understand and respond to the needs of autistic children and adults. It focuses on five principles that have been identified as vital elements of best practice in autism and emphasises ways of how to change the environment and our approaches, to meet the specific needs of autistic children and adults.

Structure. Structure can aid personal autonomy and independence by reducing dependence on others. Examples include using timetables to help the student to predict what's happening next, using visual cues (symbols and pictures) to support understanding and structuring communication using language that is clear, precise and concrete.

Positive (approaches and expectations). Establish and reinforce self-confidence and self-esteem by building on natural strengths, interests, and abilities. Expectations should be high but realistic and based on careful assessment, using reward strategies and motivators and providing positive alternatives to behaviour and using strengths or special interests when planning activities.

Empathy. To reduce the gap in the double-empathy problem, including developing and sharing of a pupil profile.

Low arousal. Approaches and the environment need to be calm and ordered paying attention to noise levels, colour schemes, odours, lighting and clutter.

Links. Creating and maintaining links between the individual, their wider support networks, and the community. Autistic people, their parents or advocates should be seen as partners. There are benefits of sharing information and working alongside the individual, their families, and other professionals.

Strategies

There are a number of well-documented strategies to support autistic learners, these include helping build up relationships and develop their communication skills, using an alternative communication method such as the Picture Exchange Communication System (PECS); using visual schedules, objects, pictures, symbols, words, etc.; breaking down tasks into small steps; designated workstations in the classroom for different activities; creating an autism-friendly environment by taking care over lighting and cutting down on glare; keeping to pale colours with matt finishes and adding soft furnishings, such as cushions and carpeting, to dampen noise; and providing opportunities for 'learning through doing'.

Pause for reflection

It is important to recognise both the strengths and challenges an autistic learner may present to gain an understanding of what pedagogical approaches or strategies may be useful.

- How would you go about setting up a one-page profile, or pen portrait of such an individual?

Sharing

Autistic learners experience challenges joining or inviting class friends to participate in fantasy play activities and cooperative games which have an element of sharing. They struggle to act on communicative cues given by their peers that may include the sharing of apparatus, sharing of attention and sharing of emotions and ideas during these play activities (Gillis and Butler, 2007). The ability to share is not only an important element in cooperative games and fantasy play activities, but it contributes to social and communicative skills, which form the basis of healthy and positive peer relations (Lang et al., 2014). Wolfberg et al. (2012) warn that autistic children do not necessarily prefer solitary play but that they articulate their play interests and socialising needs in ways that are their own and this sets them apart from their friends. The exclusion of these learners in play and social activities affects their formation of friendships negatively and autistic learners may experience feelings of rejection.

Prompting independence

Badiah (2018) states that it is important that teachers guide autistic learners to become more autonomous, especially in their socialising interactions with their peers and other people in their community alongside the need to be taught functional communication skills to become more independent. For learners to become more autonomous, social instructions need to be given in different situations and environments, preparing the learner to adapt to a variety of instructions, activities and locations. Techniques to assist learners to become more self-reliant include use of visual cues, a list or schedules depicting the various activities to be engaged with as well as facilitating the changeover from one activity to another. Iovannone et al. (2003) emphasise that the learning environment should be structured and enable learners to envisage what is currently being taught, as well as to predict what the following activity will entail and how the knowledge and/or skills that have been taught can be generalised to another environment or situation.

Managing behaviour

Autistic learners can display complicated behavioural manners due to the possible manifestation of anxiety disorders and they may experience an overload of senses, a deviation from everyday schedules and practices, and social bewilderment. Other non-social deficits include inability to show facial expressions and empathy, verbal intonation and making eye contact, looking through or beyond a person (Daou et al., 2014). Challenging behaviours occur at high rates among autistic individuals and include aggression, self-injurious behaviour (SIB), stereotypical behaviour, pica, and vomiting/rumination. There are several strategies commonly used in setting behavioural targets in both mainstream and specialist classrooms; for example, the use of Token Economies.

Token Economy Strategies

Token Economy Strategies (TES) are a form of behaviour modification that uses positive reinforcement to engage children to achieve tasks, improve academic performance or increase desirable behaviours. This is achieved by collecting tokens after desired behaviour occurs – tokens are later exchanged for back-up reinforcers or rewards, an activity, item, or privilege at a chosen time. TES are very effective approaches to modify behaviour (Jones et al., 1977). This can be a positive intervention that can be successfully used in all educational settings to aid practitioners to support autistic children, for maintaining appropriate behaviours in individuals. The purpose of them is to reinforce and strengthen behaviour, since tokens are a way of 'paying' children for completing tasks or showing positive behaviour. The children can purchase a desired activity or item (back-up reinforcer) through collection of tokens. The basic principle is that by engaging in desired behaviours, also known as target behaviours, a child earns a certain number of tokens and can then exchange these tokens to gain access to back-up reinforcers effectively.

Targets for desired behaviours are set and once the child displays the behaviour they are reinforced with tokens (secondary reinforcers) which are then exchanged for rewards (primary reinforcers). This strategy increases the frequency of desired behaviours and reduces undesired behaviours. Tokens could be objects such as marbles, counters, stickers, or printed cards with pictures (Educate Autism, 2022) and charts/boards could be used for visual reinforcement.

Token Economies are one of the most used measures for encouraging improvement in behaviour, but teachers have been concerned that students may become dependent on these systems and will only work constantly for tangible tokens or back-up rewards, making it difficult to 'fade' the incentive and expect the behaviour to continue.

Developing social skills

Autistic learners can experience challenges with respect to their social development, including limited interactive communication skills, restricted eye contact during social interaction, limited sharing and being aggressive. Iovannone et al. (2003) state that the pivotal role by teachers is to ensure that their interactions with autistic learners who experience interactive communication and social skills challenges, should meet the needs of each learner's specific and distinctive needs for growth to occur. They recommend that multiple approaches and methodologies such as personalised assistance, regular and organised coaching and tutoring, as well as creating clear and logical learning situations with a practical and purposeful approach to challenges be utilised by teachers.

Lack of social relationships in childhood can lead to a decline in employment, a decrease in independent life and life expectancy, and severe mental health problems (such as depression, suicidal desires, and anxiety). In addition, autistic children are also vulnerable to be bullied by their peers. Problems in communication, including the failure to read and interpret the body language, feelings and meanings of their peers may also complicate social interactions and friendships. Badiah (2018) suggests that social skills being modelled and taught in social groups is an effective strategy to be employed in classrooms and there are several narrative techniques to address issues with social interactions, including Comic Strip Conversations and Power Cards.

Comic Strip Conversations

Developed by Carol Gray (Gray, 1998), Comic Strip Conversations (CSC) use visual aids in the form of cartoons which help portray the thoughts and feelings of others in different social situations. The technique uses simple line drawings of people, speech bubbles and thought bubbles to show how individuals in the same situation may have different thoughts and feelings and therefore act differently. It is based on the belief that visual supports are useful in structuring the learning of children and comprehending and recognising the motivations and beliefs of others.

Comic Strip Conversations generally consist of simply drawn stick figure characters used to identify individuals within the situation, annotated with speech and thought bubbles. A symbols dictionary is provided, containing simple symbols, including those to identify location, talking, listening, interrupting, and thinking (Ahmed-Husain and Dunsmuir, 2014). The child is encouraged to complete as much as possible for themselves, with a supporting adult using question prompts to help the child to identify key elements of the incident, such as the setting, those present, what happened, what was said and what was thought (Vivian et al., 2012). The process of CSC provides detailed visual frameworks from which to revisit and analyse specific elements of overall challenging situations to identify potential solutions (Ahmed-Husain and Dunsmuir, 2014). The aim is to teach autistic learners how to manage the consequences and avoid them in future, or used repeatedly, where recurring issues or potential problems can be analysed and referred to, similarly to social stories.

Power Cards

Power Cards are a visual aid strategy which embodies a child's specialist interest – a unique characteristic of children with autism – to assist them in making sense of challenging situations they face daily. For example, social situations, routines, understanding the meaning of language and a hidden curriculum they face wherever they go (Gagnon, 2002). The Power Card strategies are special interest visual aids used to teach and reinforce academic, behavioural, and social skills to those with autism. The strategy uses a social narrative technique which capitalises on a child's special interest to teach applicable engagement in procedures, social interaction, and communication (Daubert et al., 2015).

Each Power Card contains a character related to the child's interest and a brief social narrative, written at the child's level of understanding, to model how a character would use behaviour or a skill in a situation that is familiar to the child. Power Cards can be used to target a wide range of behaviours and social interactions such as self-regulation of emotional outbursts, enhance reciprocal discourse, improve responsiveness to interactions (Keeling et al., 2003), improve playground behaviour (Spencer et al., 2008) and model instruction compliance (Daubert et al., 2015).

Creating a Power Card requires the formulation of a brief personalised narrative, detailing the situation or behaviour identified as a target for intervention based on difficulties experienced by the child, before summarising the strategy on a small card containing the image of the character. The narrative is written from the perspective of the special interest character or hero, identified as significant to the child, experiencing the same difficulty and a three- to five-point action plan of the steps they take in their attempt to solve it is identified (Daubert et al., 2015).

Assessment

Assessment of autistic pupils is often not achieved through a tick list or prescriptive set of tasks. It relies on careful observation, identification of concepts or skills which require further exploration, dialogue with parents and other professionals, and reflective interpretation of this information. Teachers should identify what is intrinsically motivating for the pupil as they are unlikely to respond to extrinsic or social motivators, and support them to notice and comment on their own performance and behaviour in relation to specific or agreed targets. The Scottish Government (2022) suggests that the assessment of autism in children and young people in schools is a process rather than an end-product and should support the learner's next steps for learning. It needs to be a holistic and collaborative process which takes place over a period, drawing on a range of observational and assessment methods. Whichever approach teachers adopt, assessment is used to ascertain if learning has taken place.

Assessment of Learning (AoL) ties into behaviourist approaches to planning, using skills such as chaining and task analysis and measures performance and whether targets were met at the end of a certain time (Cartwright and Wind-Cowie, 2005).

Imray and Hinchcliffe (2014) state that pupils' progress must be clear, achievable, and quantifiably measurable, so setting targets is often used. SMART targets (Specific, Measurable, Achievable, Realistic, Time Bound) can be set, but these can tend to be limiting to pupils' progress and don't promote learning if they are not able to be met. Lacey (2010) suggests that there should be SCRUFFY targets (Student led, Creative, Relevant, Unspecified, Fun, For Youngsters) as they are a more relevant method of assessment for autistic individuals and those with complex needs, because they allow for autonomy and flexibility.

AoL is used to confirm what students know, to demonstrate whether they have met curricular targets and to make decisions about a student's further programmes or placements. It is used to summarise achievements to record and report on learning (Harlen, 2007). For autistic individuals, AoL is likely to be used to assess against targets on their Individual Education Plans, for example. Summative assessment is often used in this type of assessment; this is done at the end of a topic, term or other period that shows what a pupil has achieved in this period.

Assessment for Learning (AfL) is the process of seeking and interpreting evidence for use by learners and their teachers to decide where the learners are in their learning, where they need to go and how best to get there (Assessment Reform Group, 2002) and is seen in the interactionist approach to learning where the learner decides on the pace and direction of teaching. Meijer (2003) suggests that there seems to be agreement that what is good for SEN students is good for all students and that general AfL methods can be used with SEN if they are modified and adjusted to meet their needs. For example, teachers should give a longer wait time to autistic and other SEN learners in general after asking verbal questions which can be supported with different stimuli and different ways of responding. With autistic children, it has been suggested that teachers should use only brief and clear questions, avoiding idioms and metaphorical questions, and feedback should be kept short and unambiguous (Florian and Black-Hawkins, 2011).

Pause for reflection

- How does the setting of targets relate to the strengths of an autistic student?
- Are there any issues that might arise, such as the non-achievement of the targets?
- How might AoL address some of these?

Pedagogy to support Executive Functioning

Executive Functioning is discussed in Chapter 7 and there are several strategies which can be used to support this process when working with autistic learners. Executive functions are a set of cognitive skills that are used for both planning and carrying out tasks, organising and regulating behaviour over time. Most researchers agree that issues with working memory, mental flexibility and inhibition (Happé et al., 2006), along with attention and planning are all important aspects. There are several strategies to support Executive Functioning. For example, graphic organisers and visual timetables and giving prompts may support the initiation of a task; supporting flexibility with planning for change alongside the teaching of coping skills; giving step-by-step instructions to aid working memory and using checklists to support organisation and planning.

Case study

James is 12 years old. He has a diagnosis of autism and attends a mainstream secondary school. He enjoys Art and ICT and has been provided with a classroom assistant for 20 hours per week. He finds it difficult to organise himself and his belongings, as well as meeting deadlines. He is reluctant to acknowledge help from others as he thinks it makes him stand out from the class. He spends most of his time alone despite wanting to make friends but not knowing how to. His parents have said that he is becoming increasingly withdrawn and spends large amounts of time alone, usually online. James has indicated that he is aware that he has autism but will not talk to anyone about it. Staff feel that it is possible that his difficulty in establishing and maintaining friendships has had a negative impact on his self-esteem. His difficulties with planning and organisation mean that he gets into trouble for forgetting homework, which also damages his perception of school.

- If you were James' teacher, who would you approach to support him with the issues outlined above?
- What would be your priority(ies) with respect to both academic and social skills?
- How would you incorporate his love of Art and ICT into an inclusive curriculum?

Pedagogy to support Theory of Mind

Theory of Mind (ToM) facilitates children's understanding of knowledge state and change as well as teaching and learning intention in various aspects, including knowing you do not know; knowing what other people know; knowing that other people do not know what you know; and knowing how knowledge comes about (Wang et al., 2016). This mind-oriented teaching and learning concept challenges both the traditional behaviourist and interactionist perspectives. In everyday interaction with young children, for example, adults could use more mental state discourse such as believe, guess, think, and reason with children and talk about what they know and how they know what they know. Using picture books is a good source of mental state talk since the image in picture books can supplement the text to materialise mental states, therefore making it easier for young children to follow the inference process. Other strategies include talking about events in personal life history which helps children to understand how knowledge and memory of those events come about. Playful interactions such as pretend play, guessing games, hide-and-seek, and drama all have the potential to develop into an enriched mental state discourse involving desire, intention, knowledge, ignorance, and false belief.

Swettenham (1996) used a 'picture in the head' strategy to develop the analogy that people have photos in their heads. This strategy draws on a domain of intact cognition in autism (understanding photographic representations) to bypass a cognitive impairment in a certain domain (understanding mental state representations). All the children were able to understand photographic misrepresentation during teaching and, following specific teaching, they could use the strategy of visualising photos in characters' heads to predict the character's behaviour. Wellman et al. (2002) explored the usefulness of 'thought bubbles', such as those that appear in comics and cartoons, to train ToM and it was found that autistic children could understand and make use of the strategy.

Pedagogy to support Central Coherence

Our Central Coherence (CC) ability enables us to see 'the big picture', to understand context and to use context to draw meaning. It is the ability to understand the 'gist' of a conversation or event. Autistic learners tend to focus on the detail rather than the whole picture which can mean they can fail to understand the actual meaning or appreciate the nature of a situation or context. Close attention to detail can, of course, also be a major strength. Capabilities/deficits in weak CC are distinct from co-existing deficits in ToM and EF. Autistic children do well on tasks where a local processing bias is advantageous, but perform poorly on tasks requiring integrative processing, compared with their typically developing peers of similar age, gender, and ability (Pellicano, 2010), and may have difficulty accessing and building background knowledge.

A strategy that can be used to access and build upon background knowledge for autistic students is priming with visual supports. Nguyen et al. (2015) identify a strategy for reading information about birds by priming the students by first placing two pictures from the text on separate index cards. Then each picture card would be presented to the student and say, 'Look at this picture. This is a nest. Look at this picture. This is an egg' (Williamson and Carnahan, 2010). Next, the key vocabulary from the text using picture-to-text matching would take place by matching picture and word card. Accessing and building upon students' background knowledge enables them to identify details from the text through pictures and words.

Other strategies include:

- supporting choices by using visual prompts;
- identifying the main idea in new information;

- making learning intentions explicit and rehearsing the main idea of the lesson;
- making links to be covered in the lesson explicit;
- use of mind maps to help illustrate connections between ideas;
- forewarning of changes and events;
- use of Social Stories™.

Visual support

There are several visual support strategies when working with autistic learners, including visual schedules, choice boards, tools to give information, tools to manage behaviour, Social Stories™ and other visual communication supports. Visual strategies can be used to support communication, help students organise their thinking, give choices or communicate rules and identify what is happening, what is not happening and what is changing, as well as supporting transitions among others. A wide range of items can be used as visual supports. For example:

- tactile symbols;
- objects of reference;
- photographs;
- videos;
- real objects;
- coloured pictures;
- plain squares of coloured card;
- line drawings;
- symbols or words.

There are several visual strategies to support communication which are used in a range of contexts including Makaton and Objects of Reference.

Makaton

Makaton is a form of communication that uses signs and spoken word to aid conversation and allows the participants to learn and develop crucial conversational skills such as listening, paying attention, remembering, and recalling. The complete Makaton Language Programme comprises two vocabularies:

- A Core Vocabulary of essential words or concepts presented in stages of increasing complexity. The Core Vocabulary is taught first and is the foundation of the programme.
- A much larger, open-ended, topic-based resource vocabulary providing an enormous bank of further signs and symbols covering broader life experiences and used in association with the Core Vocabulary as required.

Makaton symbols and signs are matched to all the concepts in the two vocabularies to be used with speech, the written word or on their own. They provide a visual representation of language which increases understanding and makes expressive communication easier. Lal (2010) demonstrated the benefits of Makaton in the classroom and that language acquisition was equally as important as mathematics, literacy, and science skills, and vital for social and emotional development. Mitha et al. (2009) discuss one school who adopted a whole-school approach to Makaton which improved communication between staff and pupils, which, in turn, increased the pupils' confidence, concentration and empowerment. Makaton was seen as improving communication because it was simple to use, adaptable, used multiple senses and it was very pupil centred.

A dominant feature of Makaton appears to be its ease of use, with some phrases or sentences needing only one or two signs to relay a message. It appears that using Makaton from a young age encourages important social elements of communication like eye contact and paying attention. It was also suggested that babies used pointing to communicate and express (Ford, 2006).

Makaton can be used in the classroom in many ways to help learners have a greater understanding and facilitate learning:

- Teachers can use elements of Makaton when delivering all sessions or in assemblies for a whole-school approach.
- Makaton signs can be printed and stuck around the school and classroom, so learners are constantly exposed to them, making them easier to remember and understand.
- A Makaton board can be used in classrooms to spread awareness of Makaton, a sign of the week can be included so learners are constantly exposed to new signs.

See the Makton website for further information: https://makaton.org/

Objects of Reference

Objects of Reference are objects that can be used to represent an activity, person or place. These objects stand for something in the same way that words do. By using objects of reference at every opportunity, the learner begins to link the word, the object, and the activity together. When objects of reference are understood, they support the ability to anticipate, sequence events and make choices. Examples of activities and objects of reference:

- Brushing teeth: Toothbrush.
- Brushing hair: Hairbrush/comb/bobbles.
- Bath/wash: Sponge, towel, bubble bath.
- Drink: Cup/bottle.
- Mealtime: Plate/spoon.
- Going outside: Coat/shoes.
- Going shopping: Shopping bags.

(Continued)

It is suggested that 3–5 objects of reference are used to start with, so they are not too confusing and that objects are used for everyday activities such as going outside, mealtimes, seeing a favourite person, or a favourite game. Steps involved include:

1   Show the object of reference.
2   Let the child hold it.
3   Use a key word or phrase which may be linked to the object and activity.
4   Use a sign or touch cue.
5   Show them the person, object, place, or activity which is related to the object.
6   Remove the object during the activity.

(NHS South Yorkshire Foundation Trust, 2022).

Adapted from CallScotland: Objects of reference, Ideas for Schools (2014).

Rowland and Schweigert (2000) state that tangible symbols make relatively low demands on cognitive processing as they are permanent, there is no necessity to recall from memory, they can readily be handled, manipulated, and require only a simple motor response to be utilised effectively. With respect to care staff working with adults, Jones et al. (2002) suggest that this technique instructs and motivates care staff and provides a means by which the use of objects of reference by individual clients may be assessed and planning for the development of their communication may be informed.

Exercise

Often, teachers will use a linear or structured approach when planning a lesson which includes:

*   details of the learning outcomes;
*   how learning outcomes are going to be shared with learners;
*   assessment criteria and opportunities;
*   methods of feedback;
*   how differentiation is to be incorporated for the range of learners;
*   learning opportunities;
*   an evaluation or plenary activity.

Alongside knowledge and understanding, the acquisition of skills may also be important and for SEN and autistic learners, these could be at three levels: emerging, consolidating and established.

An alternative model to the structured approach to lesson planning is the Hybrid Learning Model (HLM). The HLM (University of Ulster, 2022) can be used to describe learning activities as a series of understandable and universal set of learning events where the teachers and students experience, and roles are clearly defined at each stage. It proposes a 'palette' of 8 specific ways, referred to as Learning Events, of learning/teaching that the teacher or learning designer can use to describe any point in the development and analysis of learning activities. The learning events include imitates, practices, creates, explores, etc. Alongside each learning event are verbs which can be allocated to a particular event, including present, report, analyse, explain, justify, etc. It can be accessed from:

http://cetl.ulster.ac.uk/elearning/documents/About-HLM.pdf

www.ulster.ac.uk/__data/assets/pdf_file/0004/595732/LE-Full-List.pdf

- Use the HLM to plan an inclusive activity or lesson for a group of learners.

Key points

- There are a range of pedagogical approaches used in supporting autistic learners, but it is important that these are matched to individual needs
- Strategies utilised include those to support aspects of cognition, communication, visual support and behaviour
- Inclusive practices can occur in a range of contexts and involve aspects of differentiating including grouping, resources, assessment methods and support, among others
- Often the use of targets and other behaviourist approaches may not be appropriate for autistic learners and other approaches can be used
- As autism is recognised as a spectrum, it is important to match the strategy to where the learner's needs are located

Questions to consider

- It is often thought that teachers need to use strategies to 'normalise' autistic learners into a neurotypical mould. What are the implications for such a statement?
- How could you reconcile the need to use some strategies specific for the needs of autistic learners with the danger of 'othering'?
- Assessment is important in evidencing learning, and often involves observation, but what types of observational assessment could you use?

Further reading

Conn, C. (2019). *Autism, Pedagogy and Education: Critical issues for value-based teaching.* Cham, Switzerland: Palgrave Macmillan.

This book discusses critical issues concerning autism and education, and what constitutes effective pedagogy for this group of learners. Autism is a high-profile area within the discipline of special education, and the issue of how to teach autistic learners remains a contested one: recent theorising has questioned a techno-rationalist approach that places the burden of change on the autistic pupil. The author explores the values that underpin educational approaches within existing pedagogical practice: while these approaches have their individual merits and shortcomings, this book introduces and expands upon a strengths-based approach.

Connor, D. (2018). *Supporting Children with Autism in the Primary Classroom: A practical approach.* Abingdon: Routledge.

This book offers a wealth of strategies to support autistic children in the mainstream classroom. Each chapter addresses some of the most common social, practical and behavioural difficulties that a child may face at school, and details tried and tested approaches for improving their

(Continued)

experiences and outcomes. Topics discussed include: classroom layout, timetables and rules, effective communication, supporting learning and setting targets, breaks, unstructured times and school trips and challenging behaviours.

Radley, K. C., Dart, E. H., Brennan, K. J., Helbig, K. A., Lehman, E. L., Silberman, M. and Mendanhall, K. (2020). Social skills teaching for individuals with autism spectrum disorder: A systematic review. *Advances in Neurodevelopmental Disorders*, 4 (3), pp. 215–26.

Social skills teaching (SST) is a commonly implemented intervention strategy with individuals with autism spectrum disorder (ASD). Given the myriad of strategies that may be utilised within SST, a systematic review was conducted to identify intervention studies published between 1998 and 2018. A total of 12 intervention categories were identified. Video modelling represented the most frequently researched intervention between 1998 and 2018, with didactic instruction and the provision of rules representing the least frequently studied procedure.

References

Ahmed-Husain, S. and Dunsmuir, S. (2014). An evaluation of the effectiveness of Comic Strip Conversations in promoting the inclusion of young people with autism spectrum disorder in secondary schools. *International Journal of Developmental Disabilities*, 60 (2), pp. 89–108.

Assessment Reform Group (2002). *Assessment for Learning*. [online] Available at: www. hkeaa.edu.hk/doclibrary/sba/hkdse/eng_dvd/doc/Afl_principles.pdf [Accessed 03.04.2022].

Badiah, L. I. (2018). *The Importance of Social Skills for Autism*. Proceedings of the 2nd INDOEDUC4ALL – Indonesian Education for All, Banjarmasin, 18 October, pp. 20–4.

Beghin, H. (2021). The benefits of inclusion for students on the autism spectrum. *BU Journal of Graduate Studies in Education*, 13 (2), pp. 12–16

Berridge, S. and Hutchinson N. (2021). Staff experience of the implementation of intensive interaction within their places of work with people with learning disabilities and/ or autism. *J Appl Res Intellect Disabil*, 34 (1), pp. 1–15.

Brennan, A., King, F. and Travers, J. (2021). Supporting the enactment of inclusive pedagogy in a primary school. *International Journal of Inclusive Education*, 25 (13), pp. 1540–57.

CallScotland (2014). *Using Objects of Reference Possible Problem Areas*. Available at: www.callscotland.org.uk/common-assets/quick-guides/QG-1408114357.pdf Accessed 01.11.2021].

Carrington, S., Saggers, B., Webster, A., Harper-Hill, K. and Nickerson, J. (2020). What Universal Design for Learning principles, guidelines, and checkpoints are evident in educators' descriptions of their practice when supporting students on the autism spectrum? *International Journal of Educational Research*, 102, 101583.

Cartwright, C. and Wind-Cowie, S. (2005). *Profound and Multiple Learning Difficulties, (SEN)*. New York: Continuum International Publishing Group.

Daou, N., Vener, S. M. and Poulson, C. L. (2014). Analysis of three components of affective behavior in children with autism. *Research in Autism Spectrum Disorders*, 8 (5), pp. 480–501.

Daubert, A., Hornstein, S. and Tincani, M. (2015). Effects of a modified power card strategy on turn taking and social commenting of children with autism spectrum disorder playing board games. *J Dev Phys Disabil*, 27, pp. 93–110.

Department for Education and Department of Health (2015). *Special Educational Needs and Disability Code of Practice: 0 to 25 years*. [online] Available at: www.gov.uk/government/publications/send-code-of-practice-0-to-25 [Accessed 25.03.2022].

Educate Autism (2022). *Token Economy*. [online] Available at: www.educateautism.com/token-economy.html [Accessed 29.03.2022].

Florian, L. (2014). What counts as evidence of inclusive education? *European Journal of Special Needs Education*, 29 (3), pp. 286–94.

Florian, L. and Black-Hawkins, K. (2011). Exploring inclusive pedagogy. *British Educational Research Journal*, 37 (5), pp. 813–28.

Ford, J. (2006). *Enhancing Parent and Child Communication: Using Makaton signing for babies*. [online] Available at: https://www.katemb.com/wp-content/uploads/ford06babies.pdf [Accessed 29.03.2022].

Gagnon, E. (2002). *Power Cards: Using special interests to motivate children and youth with Asperger syndrome and autism*. Kansas: AAPC Publishing.

Gillis, J. M. and Butler, R. C. (2007). Social skills interventions for preschoolers with autism spectrum disorder: A description of single-subject design studies. *Journal of Early and Intensive Behavior Intervention*, 4 (3), 532–47.

Goodall, C. (2018). 'I felt closed in and like I couldn't breathe': A qualitative study exploring the mainstream educational experiences of autistic young people. *Autism & Developmental Language Impairments*, 3, pp. 1–16.

Graham, L., Medhurst, M., Tancredi, H., Spandagou, I. and Walton, E. (2020). Fundamental concepts of inclusive education. In L. J. Graham (Ed.), *Inclusive Education for the 21st Century: Theory, policy and practice*. Salisbury South Australia: Griffin Press, pp. 27–54.

Gray, C. A. (1998). Social Stories and Comic Strip Conversations with students with Asperger Syndrome and high-functioning autism. In E. Schopler, G. B. Mesibov and L. J. Kunce (Eds), *Asperger Syndrome or High-Functioning Autism? (Current Issues in Autism)*. Boston: Springer.

Happé, F., Booth, R., Charlton, R. and Hughes, C. (2006). Executive function deficits in autism spectrum disorders and attention-deficit/hyperactivity disorder: Examining profiles across domains and ages. *Brain Cogn*, 61 (1), pp. 25–39.

Harlen, W. (2007). *Assessment of Learning*. London: SAGE.

Hart, S. and Drummond, M. J. (2014). Learning without limits: Constructing a pedagogy free from determinist beliefs about ability. In L. Florian (Ed.), *The SAGE Handbook of Special Education* (2nd edition). London: SAGE.

Imray, P. and Hinchcliffe, V. (2014). *Curricula for Teaching Children and Young People with Severe or Profound and Multiple Learning Difficulties: Practical strategies for educational professionals*. London: Routledge/Taylor & Francis Group.

Iovannone, R., Dunlap, G., Huber, H. and Kinkaid, D. (2003). Effective educational practices for students with autism spectrum disorders. *Focus on Autism and Other Developmental Disabilities*, 18, pp. 150–65.

Jones, R. T., Nelson, R. E. and Kazdin, A. E. (1977). The role of external variables in self-reinforcement: A review. *Behavior Modification*, 1 (2), pp. 147–78.

Jones, F., Pring, T. and Grove, N. (2002). Developing communication in adults with pro-found and multiple learning difficulties using objects of reference. *Int J Lang Commun Disord*, 37 (2), pp. 173–84.

Keeling, K., Myles, B. S., Gagnon, E. and Simpson, R. L. (2003). Using the Power Card strategy to teach sportsmanship skills to a child with autism. *Focus on Autism and Other Developmental Disabilities*, 18, pp. 105–11.

Lacey, P. (2010). Smart and scruffy targets. *The SLD Experience*, Issue 57.

Lal, R. (2010). Effect of alternative and augmentative communication on language and social behavior of children with autism. *Educational Research and Reviews*, 5 (3), pp. 119–25.

Lang, R., Machalicek, W., Rispoli, M., O'Reilly, M., Sigafoos, J., Lancioni, G. and Didden, R. (2014). Play skills taught via behavioral intervention generalize, maintain, and per-sist in the absence of socially mediated reinforcement in children with autism. *Research in Autism Spectrum Disorders*, 8, pp. 860–72.

Lewis, A. and Norwich, B. (Eds) (2005). *Special Teaching for Special Children? Pedagogies for inclusion*. Maidenhead: Open University Press.

Meijer, C. J. W. (Ed.) (2003). *Inclusive Education and Classroom Practices*. Middelfart: European Agency for Development in Special Needs Education.

Milton, D., Martin, M. and Melham, P. (2016). Beyond reasonable adjustment: Autistic-friendly spaces and universal design. In D. Milton and N. Martin (Eds), *Autism and Intellectual Disabilities in Adults, Vol. 1*. Hove: Pavilion, pp. 81–6.

Mintz, J. and Wyse, D. (2015). Inclusive pedagogy and knowledge in special educa-tion: Addressing the tension. *International Journal of Inclusive Education*, 9 (11), pp. 1161–71.

Mitha, S., Whiting, M. and Scammell, A. (2009) Using Makaton with children with multi-ple disabilities and visual impairments. *SLD Experience*, 4, pp. 25–8.

National Autism Society (NAS). (2022). *Supporting Autistic People using the SPELL Framework*. [online] Available at: www.autism.org.uk/what-we-do/professional-devel-opment/training-and-conferences/support-spell#:~:text=SPELL%20stands%20for%20 Structure%2C%20Positive,examples%20to%20illustrate%20each%20component. [Accessed 03.01.2022].

NHS South Yorkshire Foundation Trust (2022). *Objects of Reference*. [online] Available at: www.southwestyorkshire.nhs.uk/wp-content/uploads/2020/04/Objects-of-reference. pdf [Accessed 02.12.2021].

Nguyen, N., Leytham, P., Whitby, P. and Gelfer, J. (2015). Reading comprehension and autism in the primary general education classroom. *The Reading Teacher*, 69 (1), pp. 71–6

Nind, M. and Hewett, D. (1988) Interaction as curriculum. *British Journal of Special Education*, 15 (2), pp. 55–7.

Nind, M. and Hewett, D. (2005). *Access to Communication: Developing the basics of com-munication in people with severe learning difficulties through intensive interaction* (2nd edition). London: David Fulton.

North Yorkshire County Council (2020). *Quality First Teaching Guidance*. [online] Available at: https://cyps.northyorks.gov.uk/sites/default/files/SEND/IES%20land-ing%20page/Quality%20First%20Teaching%20Guidance.pdf [Accessed 01.11.2021].

Norwich, B. and Lewis, A. (2007). How specialised is teaching children with disabilities and difficulties? *Journal of Curriculum Studies*, 39 (2), pp. 127–50.

Pellicano, E. (2010). Individual differences in executive function and central coherence predict developmental changes in theory of mind in autism. *Developmental Psychology*, 46 (2), pp. 530–44.

Riddick, B. (2012). Labelling learners with SEND: The good, the bad and the ugly. In A. Squires (Ed.), *Contemporary Issues in Special Educational Needs*. Maidenhead: Open University Press.

Rose, D. H. and Meyer, A. (2002). *Teaching Every Student in the Digital Age: Universal design for learning*. Alexandria, VA: Association for Supervision and Curriculum Development.

Rowland, C. and Schweigert, P. (2000). Tangible symbols, tangible outcomes. *AAC: Augmentative and Alternative Communication*, 16 (2), pp. 61–76.

Scottish Government (2022). *Autism Toolbox*. [online] Available at: www.autismtoolbox. co.uk/ [Accessed 11.04.2022].

Spencer, V. G., Simpson, C. G., Day, M. and Buster, E. (2008). Using the Power Card strategy to teach social skills to a child with autism. *Teaching Exceptional Children Plus*, 5 (1), pp. 1–10.

Spratt, J. and Florian, L. (2015). Inclusive pedagogy: From learning to action. Supporting each individual in the context of 'everybody'. *Teaching and Teacher Education*, 49, pp. 89–96.

Swettenham, J. (1996). Can children with autism be taught to understand false belief using computers? *Journal of Child Psychology and Psychiatry and Allied Disciplines*, 37, pp. 157–65.

Tee, A. and Reed, P. (2017). Controlled study of the impact on child behaviour problems of intensive interaction for children with ASD. *Journal of Research in Special Educational Needs*, 17 (3), pp. 179–86.

University of Ulster (2022). *Hybrid Learning Model (HLM)*. [online] Available at: http:// cetl.ulster.ac.uk/elearning/documents/About-HLM.pdf [Accessed 12.01.2022].

Vivian, L., Hutchins, T. L. and Prelock, P. A. (2012). A family-centered approach for training parents to use comic strip conversations with their child with autism. *Contemporary Issues in Communication Science and Disorders*, 39, pp. 30–42.

Wang, Z., Devine, R. T., Wong, K. K. and Hughes, C. (2016). Theory of mind and executive function during middle childhood across cultures. *J Exp Child Psychol*, 149, pp. 6–22.

Wellman, H. M., Baron-Cohen, S., Caswell, R., Gomez, J. C., Swettenham, J., Toye, E. and Lagattuta, K. (2002). Thought-bubbles help children with autism acquire an alternative to a theory of mind. *Autism*, 6 (4), pp. 343–63.

Wilkinson, K. and Twist, L. (2010). *Autism and Educational Assessment: UK policy and practice*. Slough: NFER.

Williamson, P. and Carnahan, C. (2010). Reading fluency. In C. Carnahan and P. Williamson (Eds), *Quality Literacy Instruction for Students with Autism Spectrum Disorders*. Shawnee Mission, KS: Autism Asperger Publishing, pp. 287–314.

Wolfberg, P., Bottema-Beutel, K. and DeWitt, M. (2012). Including children with autism in social and imaginary play with typical peers (Integrated Play Groups Model). *American Journal of Play*, 5 (1), pp. 55–80.

ELEVEN

International perspectives on autism

Introduction

This chapter takes a comparative approach and examines autism as it is viewed in the 21st century in the UK, Europe, and the wider world. For example, in the UK autism diagnosis now follows internationally agreed criteria and standard procedures; there are several educational strategies and interventions in use in a wide range of educational provision and there have been significant changes in public awareness and perceptions of autism in which autistic people have played a key role. Autism spectrum disorders (ASD) are a group of neurodevelopmental diseases and although the exact cause is unknown, several genetic and non-genetic risk factors have been characterised that, alone or in combination, are implicated in the development of autism, thus the aetiology is likely to be multifactorial. However, there are cultural differences in how autism is recognised, reported, interpreted, and diagnosed. There is a disparity in how low/middle- and high-income countries respond to the needs of autistic individuals, due to a range of issues such as economic factors, culture, and access to services. Rather than focus upon a country-by-country approach, the chapter examines the comparative nature of autism through a thematic analysis, including issues of inclusivity, stigma and teacher attitudes.

--------------------- Learning objectives ---------------------

This chapter will:

- Introduce you to how low/middle- and high-income countries respond to issues surrounding the nature of autism
- Invite you to evaluate how autism is expressed, recognised, interpreted, and reported across a range of countries

(Continued)

- Introduce you to the International Classification of Functioning, Disability and Health (ICF) Core Sets for Autism Spectrum Disorder (ASD)
- Help you to consider how teachers' attitudes towards autism and inclusion impact on the education of autistic children and young people

──────────────── Key terms ────────────────

Low/middle- and high-income countries, symptom expression, recognition, interpretation, stigma, comparative, core sets, diagnosis, attitudes, teachers

──────────────── Pause for reflection ────────────────

- Before you read this chapter, what do you think are the key factors in how countries differ in their understanding of issues surrounding autism?
- What is the importance of comparative research in autism?

Low/middle- and high-income countries

Approximately 90 per cent of autistic individuals live in low/middle-income countries (LMICs) (de Vries, 2016). The clinical characteristics of autism present the same in individuals who live in high-income countries (HICs) and LMICs, and Daley (2002) suggests that autism could be classed as culturally invariant given its biological underpinnings and be seen as a universal disorder which – like schizophrenia – occurs in some form in all cultures, though still susceptible to cultural influences in expression and course. However, the most accurate view of autism is as a biological condition that is culturally shaped in symptoms and course. LMICs represent an heterogeneous group of countries, of vastly different geography and cultures, but classified based on income. The situation for autistic people and their families in many LMICs reflects the problems experienced in developed areas of the world, but with additional cultural, political and economic challenges. For instance, health and financial priorities may focus elsewhere on problems such as infant mortality, malaria and AIDS and may be hampered by inadequate professional training.

The global prevalence of autism is estimated more than 1 per cent and from the evidence reviewed, the median of prevalence estimates of autism spectrum disorders was 62/10,000 (Elsabbagh et al., 2012). However, 95 per cent of autistic individuals and those with other developmental disabilities live in LMICs (Franz et al., 2017), where they are typically either undiagnosed or diagnosed much later than those living in HICs, and where they may receive no or very limited intervention and support. Daley (2004) found that in India, specific symptoms that parents initially recognise may be associated with the speed with which they receive a diagnosis, and that the saliency of symptoms may be culturally shaped. Culturally appropriate screening and diagnostic instruments for autism are lacking in most

LMICs where most of the global autism population lives. Fewer than 20 per cent of the global population live in HICs (World Bank, 2019). Moreover, even within HICs ethnic minorities are underrepresented in autism research (West et al., 2016). As a result of this global imbalance, our knowledge of the symptom expression of autism, the screening and diagnostic instruments used to aid identification and referral, and the interventions developed to support people are likely to be culturally and con-textually biased. Barriers perpetuating this imbalance are the high cost of proprietary tools for diagnosing autism and for delivering evidence-based therapies and the high cost of training of professionals and para-professionals to use the tools (Durkin et al., 2015). de Leeuw et al. (2020) suggest using a conceptual framework to consider the identification, help-seeking, and diagnostic process at four interrelated levels:

1   Expression.
2   Recognition.
3   Interpretation.
4   Reporting of autism symptoms, across differing contexts.

Symptom expression in autism

While the broad symptom domains of autism are universally observed, differences may occur in the behavioural manifestations of autism. Research shows that autis-tic manifestations vary according to age, intellectual ability, and gender within a population. For example, Lai et al. (2015) found that on average, autistic women had higher camouflaging scores than autistic men. Norbury and Sparks (2013) emphasise that as most autism research originates in the West, we have a particular view of what autism is, a particular view about how children behave and interact with adults. It is important to understand that there are cultural differences in how autistic characteristics are demonstrated and how they may differ from those acknowledged in the West. In Ethiopia (Hoekstra et al., 2018), parents indicated that 'greeting others well' is something their autistic child does well, rather than a deficit. They suggest that although the expression of core autism symptoms does not differ markedly from reports in Western countries, due to local belief systems, cultural norms, and low levels of awareness, some symptoms may be missed when using a standard Western autism tool.

In Western cultural contexts, a lack of eye contact is a common characteristic relat-ing to nonverbal behaviour in autism. Madipakkam et al. (2019) note that in their research the autistic group had no preference towards direct gaze and instead showed a tendency to prefer a face with averted gaze, suggesting an unconscious and involuntary avoidance of eye contact. However, cultural differences can also be seen with respect to eye contact and a young child may look at adult faces while having a conversation but may not make direct eye contact because it is considered

(Continued)

disrespectful. There are clear differences in cultural expectations surrounding social communication behaviour; for example, eye contact with adults and pointing with the index finger were deemed to be inappropriate for children from a Chinese cultural background (Zhang et al., 2006). For Chinese children, lack of eye contact with adults or using the index finger to point would be a sign of difference from Western social expectations, not a deficit. In the Chinese culture, making direct eye contact with adults is considered impolite for children. Thus, in a Chinese cultural context, nonverbal communication difficulties characteristic for autism may manifest themselves in atypical eye contact, rather than lack of eye contact. Yet a lack of eye contact is a hallmark of social deficits in people with autism, and as such it is something Western clinicians look for when diagnosing the disorder (Norbury and Sparks, 2013).

Even when the types of symptoms expressed are the same, there may be cultural differences in the frequency and severity of autistic traits or symptoms. Racial differences are documented in the timing and type of autism spectrum disorder diagnosis among White American and African American children. Differences in clinical presentation by race may contribute to these disparities; Sell et al. (2012) compared African American with White American children and reported differences in the frequency of presentation of autistic symptoms: non-functional routines or rituals and the preoccupation with parts of objects were significantly more often reported among White American children.

Recognition

Brett et al. (2016) found that the median age of autism diagnosis in the UK has not reduced in the last decade, being 55 months, in line with figures reported in the US. In countries with a different sociocultural or socioeconomic background, the reported age of first parental concerns tends to be higher. Samms-Vaughan (2014) reviewed seven studies from Colombia, India, Jamaica, Jordan, and Mexico. The mean age of parental concern, at 21–24 months, and mean age of diagnosis, at 45–57 months, were similar in LMICs, but later than in HICs. Both low- and middle-income country groups reported language disorder to be the symptom of initial concern. Similarities in biological aspects of the disorders were noted across the countries, but comparable ages of identification and diagnosis suggest limited resources to be the underlying contributory factor.

Ertem et al. (2018) studied typically developing children from Argentina, India, South Africa, and Turkey and reported that median ages of attainment in the first three years of life were equivalent for all play, expressive language, receptive language, fine motor and gross motor milestones. However, across the four countries the median age of attainment was equivalent for only two of nine milestones in the self-help domain. Recognition of autism symptoms may be affected by cultural differences in what is considered typical behaviour. What is seen as an atypical characteristic in a Western sociocultural context may not be deviating from the local

norms in other sociocultural contexts. One example is how children engage in pretend play and the degree of imagination used during this play which is culturally
influenced. Parents in most societies speak to babies and rightly see them as comprehending interactive partners long before infants produce language, but parents
in some societies think that it is nonsensical to talk to infants before children themselves are capable of speech and so do not speak to them (Bornstein, 2006).

Parents in some societies think of young children as interactive partners and play
with them, whereas parents in other societies think that such behaviour is pointless
and expect children to play with their siblings or peers (Bornstein, 2013). Edwards
(2000) found differences in how children from India, Kenya, and Mexico engaged
in creative-constructive play, fantasy play, role play, and games with rules and that
cultural norms and opportunities determined how the kinds of play were stimulated
by the physical and social environments. Difficulties in sharing imaginative play is
identified as a deficit in autism, thus a lack of imaginary play may be a more salient
symptom of autism in high-income Western countries than in other cultural contexts.

Latino autistic children are under-identified and under-diagnosed and, in a study
comparing reports of autism symptoms by Anglo and Latino mothers, the Latino
mothers reported significantly fewer symptoms (Blacher et al., 2014). Children
suspected of ASD (28 Anglo and 55 Latino) were assessed via the Autism
Diagnostic Observation Schedule (ADOS) and the mother Intake Form. A sub-
sample of 40 children were assessed with the Autism Diagnostic Interview-Revised
(ADI-R). The primary objective was to determine whether Anglo and Latino mothers
differed in their symptom reports, and whether their children differed in the professional classifications.

Anglo mothers reported significantly more developmental concerns and symptoms
than Latino mothers. The authors suggested possible explanations such as Latino mothers were not as aware of the symptoms, and thus do not report them; Latino mothers are
not as concerned as Anglo mothers until social communication deficits become more
apparent; and Latino mothers' parenting practices and cultural beliefs might both mask
the autistic symptomatology. Zuckerman et al. (2014) interviewed 30 parents of typically
developing Latino children in Oregon. They found that parents had poor access to care
as a result of poverty, limited English proficiency, and lack of empowerment to take advantage of services. The diagnostic process itself was slow and confusing. All these factors
led to parents dening that a problem existed and to lose trust in the medical system.

Zakirova-Engstrand et al. (2020) suggest that families' knowledge and cultural perceptions of beliefs about aetiology and prognosis can affect parents' recognition of
the first signs of autism in their children and influence help seeking and treatment
decisions. In multicultural families in Sweden, they found that there were differences
in parents' explanatory models before and after diagnosis. Initial interpretations of
the disorder included medical conditions and reaction to environmental influences,

while genetic, supernatural/religious factors, and vaccinations were mentioned as definite causes after obtaining a clinical diagnosis.

In many developing countries, access to diagnosis is extremely limited, which contributes to strikingly lower prevalence estimates (Elsabbagh et al., 2012). There is also evidence for variations in diagnosis rates between different ethnic communities within a given country (Begeer et al., 2009).

Most diagnostic criteria and tools have been developed in the UK and US and reflect the majority Western understanding of what is typical behaviour and what constitutes significant difference. Beyond the challenge of making diagnosis available wherever it is needed, there is the issue of what diagnostic criteria and instruments are appropriate to use; cultural norms for behaviour must be considered (Norbury and Sparks, 2013).

Interpretation

Pause for reflection

- Why do you think that stigma is a key issue for autistic individuals and their families?
- What are the associated consequences of these?

Stigma towards individuals with autism and their families occurs globally and crosses culture and context and includes felt stigma and enacted stigma or external stigma such as ostracism or discrimination (Brohan et al., 2010). Gillespie-Lynch et al. (2019) suggest that although stigma negatively impacts autistic people globally, the degree of stigma varies across cultures. Prior research suggests that stigma may be higher in cultures with more collectivistic orientations. The study by Gillespie-Lynch et al. aimed to identify cultural values and other individual differences that contribute to stigma among college students in Lebanon and students in the US. Replicating prior work, stigma was lower in women than men and in the US relative to Lebanon. Heightened autism knowledge, quality of contact with autistic people, openness to experience, and reduced acceptance of inequality predicted lower stigma. Collectivism was *not* associated with heightened stigma.

Stigma surrounding autism is common in many LMICs and often attributed to lack of knowledge regarding autism and can have a restricting impact on the lives of autistic individuals and their families, resulting in lack of support and services, mistreatment and even abuse. In India and Pakistan, Minhas et al. (2015) found that poor awareness of the condition in both family members and front-line health-providers leads to delay in recognition and appropriate management, alongside considerable stigma and discrimination affecting children with autism and their families. Tang and Bie (2016) carried out a systematic analysis of Chinese newspapers' coverage of autism for stigma-causing content and found that while the reportage of autism increases over time, which might contribute to the public's heightened awareness of the condition, such reportage is often biased. The most common stereotypes about autism in Chinese newspapers are autistic people as children, as patients, or as savants.

Grinker et al. (2012) suggest that stigma is generally defined as a form of branding of an individual in which a community devalues his or her social identity. In Korea, for example, despite dramatic changes in autism awareness in all segments of society, autism (chap'ae) continues to be a highly undesirable disability. Other cultures provide pathways that minimise stigma. In India, the recent positive portrayal of autistic people on television and in films, even if inaccurate, has opened dialogue about disability and has provided a point of cultural reference and, in some cases, pride (Singhal, 2010).

In the US, many people who have both autism and above-average intelligence, while facing social challenges, still find gainful employment in the fields of engineering, computers, or mathematics. Kediye et al. (2009) described challenges faced by Somali parents, such as the language barrier in communicating with key professionals; a perception of racism and being judged; misguided advice from the public who assume poor parenting; and a sense of estrangement in the absence of extended family. Hussein et al. (2019) found that Somali parents living in the UK identified key sociocultural factors that either helped or hindered the inclusion of families with autistic children within the community, including the Somali community's perceptions of disability, beliefs about the causes of autism in the Western world and a strong reliance on religious beliefs in understanding and accepting an autism diagnosis.

Gona et al. (2015) examined parents' and professionals' perceptions on causes and treatment options for autism in a multicultural context on the Kenyan Coast. Preternatural causes were mentioned and included evil spirits, witchcraft, and curses. Biomedical causes comprised infections, drug abuse, birth complications, malnutrition, and genetic-related problems. Treatment varied from traditional and spiritual healing to modern treatment in health facilities, and included consultations with traditional healers, offering prayers to God, and visits to hospitals. The results suggest that regardless of cultural backgrounds, people on the Kenyan Coast have similar views on perceived causes and treatment of autism.

Stigma related to autism can be associated with the atypical behaviour itself. Heys et al. (2017) conducted focus groups and semi-structured interviews with parents of autistic and non-autistic children and education and health professionals from urban and rural settings in Nepal. Overall, parents of typically developing children and professionals had little explicit awareness of autism. They did, however, use some distinctive terms to describe children with autism from children with other developmental conditions. Furthermore, most participants felt that environmental factors, including in-utero stressors and birth complications, parenting style and home or school environment were key causes of atypical child development.

Parental experiences

In a meta-synthesis of studies exploring parental experiences of autism, Ooi et al. (2016) analysed 50 studies from across the globe. They identified the impact that it had on parents, the family, socially, and health and educational services. Findings revealed that parents who have a child with autism experienced multiple challenges in different aspects of care, impacting on parents' stress and adaptation. A common theme was that caregivers reported feeling socially excluded and negatively judged by others, even within their own extended family.

Grinker and Cho (2013) describe reluctant mothers in South Korea on the brink of accepting autism spectrum disorder (ASD) as a diagnosis for their children but caught in a web of social meanings that push them to resist it. This is due to them wanting to accept that their child is 'normal'; localising their children's problems as deficits in a discrete area of development, rather than as a global or pervasive impairment; and the rejection of a label they fear will index a permanent condition. These define a new kind of child that mothers and teachers increasingly call 'border children' (gyonggye-seon aideul). An ethnographic study carried out in Hanoi, Vietnam found that autism has been culturally and socially constructed as a 'disease', 'karmic demerit' and 'family problem' rather than a life-long developmental disorder that needs support from government (Ha et al., 2014, p. 278) and that autistic children and their families experienced various forms of stigma and discrimination.

Most cases of autism are idiopathic, and this uncertainty may add to the plethora of perceived causes reported by parents of autistic children. In the US and UK, the most common perceived causes reported by parents are genetics and environmental risk factors, including heavy metals, food, pesticides, pollution, and other exposures. Chaidez et al. (2018) found that environmental and genetic factors were most often believed to be the cause or one of the causes by mothers across all ethnic groups studied. However, some cultures attribute the causes of autism differently. For example, Decoteau (2017, p. 169) states that Somali refugees and immigrants have high rates of autism and call autism the 'Western disease' because there is no word for autism in the Somali language and because many believe it does not exist in Somalia. In Toronto, the Somali community support the theory that gut bacteria is a causal factor and argue that it is the diet and medical environment in North America, such as the use of preservatives and antibiotics in both health care and food production, that explain the high rates of autism.

———————————— Key research in the field ————————————

Cardon, A. and Marshall, T. (2021). To raise a child with autism spectrum disorder: A qualitative, comparative study of parental experiences in the United States and Senegal. *Transcultural Psychiatry*, 58 (3), pp. 335–50.

Objective

No known ASD studies have explored parental experiences from a cross-cultural perspective. This research used Interpretative Phenomenological Analysis to analyse in-depth, semi-structured interviews with Senegalese and American families to investigate parental experiences within the Senegalese community with further illustration by cross-cultural comparison.

Method

This study employed the Interpretative Phenomenological Analysis (IPA) method to gain an increased understanding of parents' experiences raising children with ASD in the United States and Senegal. Semi-structured interviews with seven Senegalese and seven American families were carried out to gain personal perceptions and interpretations of their experience. Thematic comparison across subjects and culture groups within this study only began once an in-depth understanding of the individual's lived experience was reached.

Findings

Analysis identified 10 themes in four interview categories: (1) diagnostics and care: the diagnostic journey and securing services; (2) daily life: daily experiences and emotional needs; (3) social relationships: social isolation, spousal tension, social tension, and sources of social support; and (4) introspection: role as a caregiver, and visions of the future.

Conclusion

This study identified cultural and contextual variables that may affect parental experience of caring for a child with autism in Senegal and the US. Most Senegalese participants first sought treatment from local spiritual or traditional healers. The findings also suggested that social support among the Americans may be weak compared to the Senegalese. Although internal support within the family and community was strong among the Senegalese, this study revealed a strong need for external services for those affected by ASD in Senegal and their families, such as therapy.

Religious and supernatural explanations

Religious and supernatural explanations are also evident in some cultures. Shaked and Bilu (2006) interviewed Jewish ultraorthodox mothers of autistic children in

Israel and outline a dual system of illness perception in which biomedical and spiritual-religious frames of references coexist. Metaphysical accounts, and especially the notion of the transmigration of souls, serve as meta-accounts, bridging the epistemological gap between God's mysterious intention and the specific bodily mechanisms underlying the disorder. Hersinta (2012) found that in Indonesia religious perspective also affects parents' childrearing goals and practices. Parents viewed the developmental disorder faced by their children as a test and challenge to their own spiritual and moral qualities, whether they could be caring and patient enough in accompanying and raising the child to achieve their potential.

Jegatheesan et al. (2010) interviewed three multilingual Muslim families from South Asia, living in a large Midwestern city in the United States, and found that families understood the task of raising a child with autism in religious terms. Their overarching goal was to raise their children as normally as possible, incorporating them into ordinary social, linguistic, and religious practices at home and in the community. However, parents strongly contested experts' understandings of autism, which they believed undermined rather than promoted their children's development. Autism and intellectual disabilities are often attributed to supernatural causes such as curses, possession by evil spirits and punishment from God for the sin that the child's family may have committed. In Ghana, although mothers reported on the medical basis for their children's condition, often related to their age at pregnancy or the presence of convulsions in the child, they did not debunk the possibilities of these spiritual connotations even though they created the impression that they did not believe in evil interpretations society associated with their children's condition (Oti-Boadi, 2017).

Reporting

The fourth level of the conceptual framework focuses on the process of reporting symptoms to a health worker or clinical professional. Two underlying processes can be distinguished at this level: (a) barriers to help-seeking and (b) when help is sought, which are factors influencing the quality and quantity of clinical information received by the clinician (de Leeuw et al., 2020). There are various dimensions of barriers to access to health care in low-income countries including geographical access, availability, affordability, and acceptability which focus upon socioeconomic factors. People in poor countries tend to have less access to health services than those in better-off countries, and within countries, the poor have less access to health services (Jacobs et al., 2012).

Studies from India and Pakistan highlight how a limited number of specialists concentrated in big cities means it is prohibitively difficult for caregivers of autistic children to seek help, and that specialist services are rare, concentrated in urban areas, and inaccessible to the majority (Minhas et al., 2015). In Ethiopia, similar barriers were reported; Tekola et al. (2016) identified four types of autism service providers: clinics; autism centres; schools with inclusive education programmes; and community-based rehabilitation organisations. However, most of these service providers were in Addis Ababa and inaccessible to most of the population living in rural areas. Also, gender inequality can form a barrier to accessing services in some cultural contexts.

Manor-Binyamini and Shoshana (2018) examined how Bedouin mothers in Israel describe, perceive, and interpret their experiences raising a child with autism. Data were collected using semi-structured ethnographic interviews with 18 Bedouin mothers of children with autism, aged 6–16, living in recognised and unrecognised settlements in the Negev. The Bedouin mothers report not only stigmatisation, a lack of social support and loneliness but also structural-cultural characteristics that prevented them from obtaining information and participating in decision-making about the child with autism and that restrict their agency in dealing with and coping with their child's autism and the phenomenology of autism. In India, research found that families who live in remote, low-resource areas typically must travel considerable distances. Also, parents consulted multiple professionals or travelled long distances to confirm the diagnosis they need (Mahapatra et al., 2019).

Kumm et al. (2022) suggest that digital technologies have the potential to empower autistic individuals and their families, but that 95 per cent of individuals with autism live in LMICs where access to electricity, internet and the ever-increasing range of digital devices may be highly limited. The World Bank coined the term 'the digital divide' to describe the disparities in access to digital technologies between high-income and LMIC contexts. In a comprehensive review of technologies for autism, Kientz et al. (2013) identified six main emerging interactive technology platforms: personal computers, robotics, virtual reality, shared active surfaces, sensing technologies, and mobile devices. Digital technologies may therefore have utility for identification, diagnostic procedures, intervention, training, and research in HIC and LMIC settings. Taking together all implementation-related constructs, consensus ratings for overall feasibility in LMICs were 'very high' for smartphone-based technologies, 'high' for personal computers, 'low' for sensing technologies, shared active surfaces and virtual reality technologies, and 'very low' for robotics.

Barriers in accessing autism services

Across different geographical contexts, the access to and quality of autism services is associated with income. Alnemary et al. (2017) reported that in Saudi Arabia the age at the initiation of services and the type of treatments used differed by parents' income among other factors. Also, most parents reported utilising non-medical treatments followed by biomedical treatments and cultural and religious treatment. Bishop-Fitzpatrick and Kind (2017) suggest that race, culture, socioeconomic status, and neighbourhood disadvantage play a significant role in autism diagnosis. In the US, Vohra et al. (2017) found that caregivers of autistic children were significantly more likely to report difficulty using services, lack of sources of care, inadequate insurance coverage, lack of shared decision making and care coordination, and adverse family impact as compared to caregivers of children with developmental disabilities, mental health conditions, or both.

Nearly half of the world's population live in countries with less than one psychiatrist per 100,000 persons (WHO, 2015). Lack of diagnostic and intervention materials or instruments; poor quality or lack of experience of practising clinicians; and long wait times for access to services have also been identified as barriers to receiving support. Durkin et al. (2015) identify that one of the barriers perpetuating this imbalance is the high cost of proprietary tools for diagnosing autism and for delivering evidence-based therapies, along with the high cost of training of professionals and paraprofessionals to use the tools.

In Africa in particular, a shortage of basic knowledge about autism among health professionals has been reported. Eseigbe et al. (2015) state that information relating to Nigeria indicates a poor level of awareness and knowledge of the disorder even among health care workers, lack of therapeutic services, and a negative attitudinal disposition towards persons with autism. In Ethiopia, Tekola et al. (2016) suggest that diagnostic and educational services for children with autism are scarce and largely confined to Ethiopia's capital city, with little provision in rural areas. The lack of culturally and contextually appropriate autism instruments was also an important problem to be addressed. Ruparelia et al. (2016) state that from a list of 14 African countries there was a huge variability in services, the numbers of specialists assessing and managing autism spectrum disorder were small relative to populations served.

A key barrier is the lack of validated screening and diagnostic tools with the primary roadblock being that the development of most tools has been from within nondiverse populations in high-income countries (Franz et al., 2017). Marlow et al. (2019) state that there is a lack of consensus around which screening tools are most effective, especially where tools are used in cultures other than those in which they were created. Stewart and Lee (2017) found 18 different autism spectrum disorder screening tools have been used in low- and middle-income settings and although clinical-based screening was the most widely reported method, community-based screening was shown to be an effective method for identifying autism spectrum disorder in communities with limited clinical resources. In a review of screening tools for autism, Marlow et al. (2019) suggest that three tools (M-CHAT-R/F; PAAS; TIDOS) could be used in LMICs. However, despite its potential benefits, screening presents numerous challenges. In LMICs, many children do not regularly see medical or mental health professionals in the early years, making regular screening or surveillance difficult (Biasini et al., 2015).

──────────────────────── Exercise ────────────────────────

Identify two countries from different regions of the world. Compare their response to educating autistic children and young people with respect to the following:

- Low/high-income factors.
- How far the two countries compare with fulfilling relevant global conventions related to disabilities, such as UN Convention on the Rights of the Child (1989), UN Convention on the Rights of Persons with Disabilities (2006), UNESCO Education 2030: A Framework for Action (2015).
- Outline and compare how the two countries are similar or differ in their approach towards the notion of inclusivity/integration and the issues that this has for practice.
- How do these two countries approach issues such as: categorisation/labels, special schools, funding, teacher training, parent/carer choice and voice?

International Classification of Functioning, Disability and Health (ICF) Core Sets for Autism Spectrum Disorder (ASD)

There is a considerable variation in individual levels of functioning and consequent outcomes for autistic individuals. Factors known to contribute to variable outcomes in autism include intelligence, socio-demographic background and accessibility to services such as evidence-based treatments and family support. Research findings endorse the necessity to appraise autism from a broader perspective than a behavioural definition, considering personal, social, and environmental factors of health-related functioning. Beyond the diagnosis, the International Classification of Functioning, Disability and Health (ICF) (WHO, 2021) offers a tool to describe the lived experience of an autistic person in a comprehensive and standardised way.

It is vital to recognise the importance of functional disabilities to the understanding and definition of mental disorders in general, as well as specifically for certain diagnoses. Autism research has shown that, irrespective of cognitive level, outcome is often poor in terms of employment, establishment and maintenance of social relationships, physical and mental health, and quality of life (Howlin and Moss, 2012). There is also evidence that autism is not exclusively characterised by deficits but also certain strengths (Happé and Frith, 2009) which may have a positive impact on an individual's overall functioning and satisfaction with life.

The ICF seeks to classify disability and ability in mental health or autism and is universally accepted by all 191 WHO member states as a classification and description of functioning, disability and health. The ICF is rooted in the interactive biopsychosocial model of functioning and provides detailed classifications of ability and disability in the areas of Body functions (i.e. physiological functions of body systems), Body structures (i.e. anatomical parts of the body), Activities (i.e. execution of tasks),

Participation (i.e. involvement in life situations), and Environmental factors (i.e. physical, social and attitudinal environment). Personal factors are also included in the biopsychosocial model but are not yet classified in the ICF given the large social and cultural variance associated with them (WHO, 2021). The World Health Organization is encouraging application of the ICF internationally not only as a classification tool, but also as a framework for social policy, research, education and clinical practice.

A comparative study in Sweden and South Africa (Viljoen et al., 2019) compared parent/caregiver perceptions of functioning in two divergent countries that participated in the International Classification of Functioning, Disability and Health (ICF) Core Sets for Autism Spectrum Disorder development study. The researchers hypothesised that environmental factors would most frequently be reported as barriers to functioning in low-resource settings. However, only three ICF categories (immediate family, attention functions, products and technology for personal use) differed in content with few differences in perspectives about environmental factors. The study supports the global usefulness of the recently developed ICF Core Sets for Autism Spectrum Disorder.

Case study

Tomeika is aged 8 and she does not have a diagnosis of autism. She attends primary education and is enjoying school and spends time with friends and family. She communicates well with her siblings but finds it difficult to make friends, share toys and gets anxious if her routines are altered. Her parents are keen to not only find out more about autism but are interested in the ICF Core Sets for Autism Spectrum Disorder. They know that these include areas such as:

- activities, including communication, doing chores and learning;
- participation, including playing with peers and attending school;
- personal factors such as motivation and personal interests.

How could they go about gathering evidence for these factors?

Teachers' attitudes towards autism and inclusion

Pause for reflection

- Why is it important to review the impact of teachers' attitudes in a comparative focus?
- How might attitudes relate to concepts such as stigma, understanding and self-efficacy?

Given the high prevalence rates, there is a high probability that teachers find they will be working with autistic students at some point in their careers. Although there are many benefits in inclusive education, this situation may also cause multiple challenges for teachers, due to the needs of the children with this disorder, their special characteristics, the disruptive and unusual behaviour, and the lack of time and resources to educate them in mainstream schools, among other factors.

Past research regarding teachers' attitudes towards inclusion has been contradictory and inconclusive since teachers have reported both positive attitudes towards the inclusion as well as strong negative feelings regarding having students with various disabilities in mainstream classrooms.

Avramidis et al. (2000) carried out a survey of 81 primary and secondary teachers in one Local Education Authority in the south-west of England and revealed that teachers who have been implementing inclusive programmes, and therefore have active experience of inclusion, possess more positive attitudes. Moreover, the data showed the importance of professional development in the formation of positive attitudes towards inclusion. Teachers with university-based professional development appeared to hold more positive attitudes.

Singaporean teachers demonstrated more negative attitudes while English teachers hold more positive attitudes (Thaver and Lim, 2012). The attitudes of Singaporean teachers are likely fuelled by the constraints within the Singapore system which Thaver and Lim believe militate against the inclusion of children with disabilities, such as the competitive outcomes-oriented culture, issues with support structures, class sizes and expectations. Singaporean parents feel that educational provisions for their child are to be pushed for by themselves, such as engaging private tutors and external practitioners to supplement what the child lacks so that he or she is 'good' enough to be included in the mainstream.

Alamri and Tyler-Wood (2015) compared teachers' attitude towards autism in Saudi Arabia and the US, among general education and special education teachers in both countries. Although the educational regulations governing autism in Saudi schools were introduced and modelled after the US, teachers in Saudi Arabia tend to teach students with autism separately and not in an inclusive environment and there were negative responses which seemed to relate to a fear of possible problem behaviour from students and insufficient awareness of the characteristics of autism. In a meta-analysis of inclusive practices in 18 countries, Curcic (2009) suggests that it is futile to standardise inclusive practices internationally due to the wide diversity of history, levels of economic, social and educational development, and uniqueness of culture represented. Hence, the concept of inclusion is predominantly subjected to socially constructed meanings within different communities. Based on international research, positive attitudes and beliefs of teachers are most critically and consistently associated to the success of any inclusive policy or practice (Avramidis et al., 2000). While most teachers possess supportive attitudes towards inclusion, they have concerns about the implementation (Hwang and Evans, 2011). In an Australian context, Forlin et al. (2008) summarised three groups of concerns: administration, classroom-based and personal.

───────────────── **Case study** ─────────────────

Due to work commitments, the Smith family are having to relocate from the UK to a European destination. Their family consists of two parents and an autistic son, Johnny, aged 11, who has been attending a mainstream secondary school. He does not have an EHC plan but has some support in lessons, such as Science. The family, including Johnny, are keen that he should be able to continue his education in a similar setting in their new country.

As a student studying autism as part of your degree, they have asked you to suggest suitable destinations for them to relocate to within the European Union.

• Where would you look to find suitable information?

A critical factor in inclusive education is the readiness of schools in implementing the inclusive education itself; particularly important are teachers' attitudes towards students in schools that provide inclusive education (see Chapter 8). Despite regular international recommendations, the inclusion rate of autistic students in mainstream educational systems is far from satisfactory. In France, Rattaz et al. (2020) found that although many autistic children and adolescents were attending school, those with more severe adaptive and cognitive deficits were less likely to attend school and challenging behaviours and sensory processing difficulties were associated with partial inclusion. Jury et al. (2021) also found that in France, teachers' attitudes towards inclusive education were the least positive for autistic students, in comparison with students with cognitive disorder (CD) and students with motor impairment (MI).

Hofman and Kilimo (2014) examined teachers' experiences of inclusive primary education in Tanzania and found that demographics like gender, class size, type of disability and training in special needs education did not relate significantly to teachers' attitudes and self-efficacy towards inclusive education. What the results did reveal was that teachers face several issues specifically in managing pupils with different disabilities: shortage of teaching and learning materials, lack of training and poor working environments, and that teachers with low self-efficacy face more problems with the implementation of inclusive education. Researching inclusive primary schools in Indonesia, Tarjiah and Riyanti (2019) showed that most classroom teachers in their study who conduct inclusive education to students with autism have positive attitudes to the students. The classroom teachers were good at understanding the academic, social and emotional aspects of autism and Tarjiah and Riyanti concluded that the attitude towards autistic students in inclusive education is good. However, contrary results were also found in other research of the same issue.

In Canada, Lindsay et al. (2014) asked about teachers' challenges regarding creating an inclusive environment within their classroom. Teachers reported several challenges, including understanding and managing behaviour, socio-structural barriers, and a lack of understanding from other teachers, students, and parents. Humphrey and Symes (2013) examined the experience, attitudes and knowledge of school staff in relation to inclusive education for pupils with autistic spectrum disorders in mainstream secondary schools in the north-west of England. Findings showed that senior managers and Special Educational Needs Co-ordinators (SENCos) reported greater self-efficacy in teaching autistic pupils and in coping with behaviours associated with autism than did subject teachers and concluded that social inclusion was both a potential benefit and challenge for autistic pupils.

In the UK, Cook and Ogden (2021) suggest that teachers generally agree inclusion is important for reasons of social justice, but many have little confidence in their capacity to support students with SEN, especially autism. They found potential differences in experiences, thoughts, and beliefs between mainstream and special school teachers. While factors such as staff training/expertise and resources are understandably more evident in specialist settings, other factors such as educational ideology, teacher attitudes, and attention to the physical environment varied widely. There was a tendency in mainstream settings to adopt generic approaches such as time-out cards, quiet spaces, and diversity week. Lindsay et al. (2014) found that secondary school subject teachers are reported to have significantly lower self-efficacy – beliefs about their capabilities to successfully teach autistic pupils – than school senior managers or SENCos.

In a systematic review, Gómez-Marí et al. (2021) reaffirmed that special education teachers have higher levels of knowledge than mainstream teachers, probably because special education teachers spend more time with autistic students or have had specific training. The differences in knowledge between mainstream and special education teachers could have repercussions on practices that segregate and exclude mainstream educators from their responsibility to educate autistic children. The authors concluded that culture does not affect knowledge of autism, which contradicts research by Ballantyne et al. (2019), who investigated the role of experience and culture on teachers' knowledge of autism in China and the UK. Results showed that teachers who had experience of working with autistic children demonstrated a higher level of knowledge relating to the disorder and that teachers in the UK had significantly more knowledge of autism than teachers in China.

Key points

- There are similarities and differences in how low/middle- and high-income countries respond to issues surrounding the nature of autism
- It is important to examine how culture and other factors are involved in differences surrounding the expression, recognition, interpretation and reporting in autism

(Continued)

- The International Classification of Functioning, Disability and Health (ICF) Core Sets for Autism Spectrum Disorder (ASD) aims to evidence the personal, social, and environmental factors of health-related functioning issues relating to autism
- Irrespective of cognitive level, outcome for autistic individuals is often poor in terms of employment, establishment and maintenance of social relationships, physical and mental health, and quality of life. It is important to examine the reasons behind these headlines
- Teachers play a pivotal role in the education of autistic children and young people

Questions to consider

- Why is it important for students studying autism to undertake a comparative approach in their research?
- How can low- and high-income countries work collaboratively with respect to some of the issues raised in this chapter?
- How do we assess the impact of globalisation on education and SEND in particular?

Further reading

Hume, K., Jordan, R. and Roberts, J. (Eds) (2019). *The SAGE Handbook of Autism and Education*. London: SAGE.

This Handbook explores the key concepts, debates and research areas in the field of autism and education. Contributions from a wide range of countries and cultures are organised into six key sections: Part 1: Learning Needs and Educational Responses; Part 2: Early Intervention, Education in Core Domains and Family Support; Part 3: School-Based and Academic Education: Access and Support; Part 4: Collaborative Working in Education; Part 5: Education for Life and Barriers to Education; Part 6: Data Collection in Education and Measurement of Progress. It is a valuable resource for researchers, postgraduate students, reflective practitioners and teachers who wish to know and understand current views of the nature of autism, and best practice in educational support.

Uwaezuoke, S. N. (2015). Autism spectrum disorder in children: The disparities between the developed and developing countries. *Autism Open Access*, 5 (3), 152.

This review appraises the disparities in the prevalence and management of childhood autism in developed and developing countries and discusses strategies that will possibly close the gaps. Unlike in developing countries, more research work has been conducted in the developed world where advanced support services and use of standardised screening and diagnostic instruments are the norm. Thus, disparities exist in the prevalence rates as high figures are reported from developed countries while the rates from developing countries are low.

van Kessel, R., Steinhoff, P., Varga, O., Breznoščáková, D., Czabanowska, K., Brayne, C., Baron-Cohen, S. and Roman-Urrestarazu, A. (2020). Autism and education – Teacher policy in Europe: Policy mapping of Austria, Hungary, Slovakia and Czech Republic. *Research in Developmental Disabilities*, 152.

This report maps autism and special education needs (SEN) policies, alongside teacher responsibilities in the education of children with SEN in Austria, Hungary, Czech Republic, and Slovakia. A policy path analysis using a scoping review as an underlying methodological framework was performed. The end of communism and accession to the European Union were critical for the countries under study. They passed crucial policies after international policies and adopted a three-stream approach towards providing education: (1) special schools; (2) special classes in mainstream schools; or (3) mainstream classes. Special schools remain for children that cannot participate in mainstream schools. The education systems aim for inclusion, though segregation remains for children that cannot thrive in mainstream schools. Teachers are pivotal in the education of children with SEN, more so than with typical children.

References

Alamri, A. and Tyler-Wood, T. (2015). Teachers' attitudes towards children with autism: A comparative study of the United States and Saudi Arabia. *Journal of the International Association of Special Education*, 16 (1), pp. 14–25.

Alnemary, F. M., Aldhalaan, H. M., Simon-Cereijido, G. and Alnemary, F. M. (2017). Services for children with autism in the Kingdom of Saudi Arabia. *Autism*, 21 (5), pp. 592–602.

Avramidis, E., Bayliss, P. and Burden, R. (2000). Student teachers' attitudes towards the inclusion of children with special educational needs in the ordinary school. *Teaching and Teacher Education*, 16 (3), pp. 277–93.

Ballantyne, C., Gillespie-Smith, K. and Wilson, C. (2019). Comparison of knowledge and experience of autism spectrum disorder among teachers in the United Kingdom and China. *International Journal of Disability, Development and Education*, 68 (2), pp. 160–71.

Begeer, S., Bouk, S. E., Boussaid, W., Terwogt, M. M. and Koot, H. M. (2009). Underdiagnosis and referral bias of autism in ethnic minorities. *J Autism Dev Disord*, 39 (1), pp. 142–8.

Biasini, F. J., De Jong, D., Ryan, S., Thorsten, V., Bann, C., Bellad, R., Niranjana, S., Mahantshetti, S. M., Dhaded, O. P., Chomba, E., Goudar, S. S., Waldemar, A. C. and McClure, E. (2015). Development of a 12 month screener based on items from the Bayley II Scales of Infant Development for use in Low Middle Income countries. *Early Human Development*, 91, pp. 253–8.

Bishop-Fitzpatrick, L. and Kind, A. J. H. (2017). A scoping review of health disparities in autism spectrum disorder. *Journal of Autism and Developmental Disorders*, 47 (11), pp. 3380–91.

Blacher, J. B., Cohen, S. R. and Azad, G. (2014). In the eye of the beholder: Reports of autism symptoms by Anglo and Latino mothers. *Research in Autism Spectrum Disorders*, 8 (12), pp. 1648–56.

Bornstein, M. H. (2006). On the significance of social relationships in the development of children's earliest symbolic play: An ecological perspective. In A. Göncü and S. Gaskins (Eds), *Play and Development: Evolutionary, sociocultural, and functional perspectives*. New Jersey: Lawrence Erlbaum Associates Publishers, pp. 101–29.

Bornstein, M. H. (2013). Mother-infant attunement: A multilevel approach via body, brain, and behavior. In M. Legerstee, D. W. Haley and M. H. Bornstein (Eds), *The Infant Mind: Origins of the social brain*. New York: The Guilford Press, pp. 266–98.

Brett, D., Warnell, F., McConachie, H. and Parr, J. R. (2016). Factors affecting age at ASD diagnosis in UK: No evidence that diagnosis age has decreased between 2004 and 2014. *J Autism Dev Disord*, 6 (6), pp. 1974–84.

Brohan, E., Slade, M., Clement, S. and Thornicroft, G. (2010). Experiences of mental illness stigma, prejudice and discrimination: A review of measures. *BMC Health Serv Res*, 10 (80), pp. 1–11.

Cardon, A. and Marshall, T. (2021). To raise a child with autism spectrum disorder: A qualitative, comparative study of parental experiences in the United States and Senegal. *Transcultural Psychiatry*, 58 (3), pp. 335–50.

Chaidez, V., Fernandez, Y., Garcia, E., Wang, L. W., Angkustsiri, K., Krakowiak, P., Hertz-Picciotto, I. and Hansen, R. L. (2018). Comparison of maternal beliefs about causes of autism spectrum disorder and association with utilization of services and treatments. *Child Care Health Dev*, 44 (6), pp. 916–25.

Cook, A. and Ogden, J. (2022). Challenges, strategies and self-efficacy of teachers supporting autistic pupils in contrasting school settings: A qualitative study. *European Journal of Special Needs Education*, 37 (3), pp. 371–85.

Curcic, S. (2009). Inclusion in PK-12: An international perspective. *International Journal of Inclusive Education*, 13 (5), pp. 517–38.

Daley, T. C. (2002). The need for cross-cultural research on the pervasive developmental disorders. *Transcultural Psychiatry*, 39 (4), pp. 531–50.

Daley, T. C. (2004). From symptom recognition to diagnosis: Children with autism in urban India. *Soc Sci Med*, 58 (7), pp. 1323–35.

Decoteau, C. L. (2017). The 'Western disease': Autism and Somali parents' embodied health movements. *Soc Sci Med*, 177, pp. 169–76.

de Leeuw, A., Happé, F. G. E. and Hoekstra, R. A. (2020). A conceptual framework for understanding the cultural and contextual factors on autism across the globe. *Autism Research*, 13 (7), pp. 1029–50.

de Vries, P. J. (2016). Thinking globally to meet local needs: Autism spectrum disorders in Africa and other low-resource environments. *Curr Opin Neurol*, 29 (2), pp. 130–6.

Durkin, M. S., Elsabbagh, M., Barbaro, J., Gladstone, M., Happé, F., Hoekstra, R. A., Lee, L. C., Rattazzi, A., Stapel-Wax, J., Stone, W. L., Tager-Flusberg, H., Thurm, A., Tomlinson, M. and Shih, A. (2015). Autism screening and diagnosis in low resource settings: Challenges and opportunities to enhance research and services worldwide. *Autism Research: Official Journal of the International Society for Autism Research*, 8 (5), pp. 473–6.

Edwards, C. P. (2000). Children's play in cross-cultural perspective: A new look at the six cultures study. *Cross-Cultural Research*, 34 (4), pp. 318–38.

Elsabbagh, M., Divan, G., Koh, Y. J., Kim, Y. S., Kauchali, S., Marcín, C., Montiel-Nava, C., Patel, V., Paula, C. S., Wang, C., Yasamy, M. T. and Fombonne, E. (2012). Global prevalence of autism and other pervasive developmental disorders. *Autism Res*, 5 (3), pp. 160–79.

Ertem, I. O., Krishnamurthy, V., Mulaudzi, M. C., Sguassero, Y., Balta, H., Gulumser, O., Bilik, B., Srinivasan, R., Johnson, B., Gan, G., Calvocoressi, L., Shabanova, V. and

Forsyth, B. W. C. (2018). Similarities and differences in child development from birth to age 3 years by sex and across four countries: A cross-sectional, observational study. *Lancet Glob Health*, 6 (3), pp. 279–91.

Eseigbe, E. E., Nuhu, F., Sheikh, T. L., Eseigbe, P., Sanni, K. and Olisah, V. (2015). Knowledge of childhood autism and challenges of management among medical doctors in Kaduna State, Northwest Nigeria. *Autism Research and Treatment*, 1, 892301.

Forlin, C., Keen, M. and Barrett, E. (2008). The concerns of mainstream teachers: Coping with inclusivity in an Australian context. *International Journal of Disability, Development and Education*, 55 (3), pp. 251–64.

Franz, L., Chambers, N. and von Isenburg, M. (2017). Autism spectrum disorder in sub-Saharan Africa: A comprehensive scoping review. *Autism Research*, 10 (5), pp. 723–49.

Gillespie-Lynch, K., Daou, N., Sanchez-Ruiz, M. J., Kapp, S. K., Obeid, R., Brooks, P. J., Someki, F., Silton, N. and Abi-Habib, R. (2019). Factors underlying cross-cultural differences in stigma toward autism among college students in Lebanon and the United States. *Autism*, 23 (8), pp. 1993–2006.

Gómez-Marí, I., Sanz-Cervera, P. and Tárraga-Mínguez, R. (2021). Teachers' knowledge regarding autism spectrum disorder (ASD): A systematic review. *Sustainability*, 13 (9), 5097.

Gona, J. K., Newton, C. R., Rimba, K., Mapenzi, R., Kihara, M., Van de Vijver, F. J. R. and Abubakar, A. (2015). Parents' and professionals' perceptions on causes and treatment options for autism spectrum disorders (ASD) in a multicultural context on the Kenyan coast. *PLoS ONE*, 10 (8), e0132729.

Grinker, R. T. and Cho, K. (2013). Border children: Interpreting autism spectrum disorder in South Korea. *Ethos: Journal of the Society for Psychological Anthropology*, 41 (1), pp. 46–74.

Grinker, R., T. Daley, T. and Mandell, D. (2012). Culture and autism. In F. Volkmar (Ed.), *Encyclopaedia of Autism Spectrum Disorders*. New York: Springer Verlag.

Ha, V. S., Whittaker, A., Whittaker, M. and Rodger, S. (2014). Living with autism spectrum disorder in Hanoi, Vietnam. *Social Science & Medicine*, 120.

Happé, F. and Frith, U. (2009). The beautiful otherness of the autistic mind. *Philos Trans R Soc Lond B Biol Sci*, 364 (1522), pp. 1346–50.

Hersinta (2012). *How Religious Beliefs Influence Understanding on Disability: A study of Muslim family's perception on autism*. Jogja International Conference on Communication: Communication in Culture; Whose Culture? UPN Yogyakarta.

Heys, M., Alexander, A., Medeiros, E., Tumbahangphe, K. M., Gibbons, F., Shrestha, R., Manandhar, M., Wickenden, M., Shrestha, M., Costello, A., Manandhar, D. and Pellicano, E. (2017). Understanding parents' and professionals' knowledge and awareness of autism in Nepal. *Autism*, 21 (4), pp. 436–49.

Hoekstra, R. A., Bayouh, F. G., Gebru, B. T., Kinfe, M., Mihretu, A., Adamu, W., Carmo, E. and Hanlon, C. (2018). *The Face of Autism in Ethiopia: The expression, recognition, reporting and interpretation of autism symptoms in the Ethiopian context*. International Society for Autism Research (INSAR) meeting, Rotterdam.

Hofman, R. H. and Kilimo, J. S. (2014). Teachers' attitudes and self-efficacy towards inclusion of pupils with disabilities in Tanzanian schools. *Journal of Education and Training*, 1 (2), pp. 177–98.

Howlin, P. and Moss, P. (2012). Adults with autism spectrum disorders. *Can J Psychiatry*, 57 (5), pp. 275–83.

Humphrey, N. and Symes, W. (2013). Inclusive education for pupils with autistic spectrum disorders in secondary mainstream schools: Teacher attitudes, experience and knowledge. *International Journal of Inclusive Education*, 17 (1), pp. 32–46.

Hussein, A. M., Pellicano, E. and Crane, L. (2019). Understanding and awareness of autism among Somali parents living in the United Kingdom. *Autism*, 23 (6), pp. 1408–18.

Hwang, Y. and Evans, D. (2011). Attitudes towards inclusion: Gaps between belief and practice. *International Journal of Special Education*, 26 (1), pp. 136–46.

Jacobs, B., Ir, P., Bigdeli, M., Annear, P. L. and Van Damme, W. (2012). Addressing access barriers to health services: An analytical framework for selecting appropriate interventions in low-income Asian countries. *Health Policy Plan*, 27 (4), pp. 288–300.

Jegatheesan, B., Fowler, S. and Miller, P. J. (2010). From symptom recognition to services: How South Asian Muslim immigrant families navigate autism. *Disability & Society*, 25 (7), pp. 797–811.

Jury, M., Perrin, A. L., Rohmer, O. and Desombre, C. (2021). Attitudes towards inclusive education: An exploration of the interaction between teachers' status and students' type of disability within the French context. *Front Educ*, 6.

Kediye, F., Valeo, A. and Berman, R. C., (2009). Somali-Canadian mothers' experiences in parenting a child with autism spectrum disorder. *Journal of the Association for Research on Mothering*, 11 (1), pp. 211–23.

Kientz, J. A., Goodwin, M. S., Hayes, G. R. and Abowd, G. D. (2013). Interactive technologies for autism. *Synthesis Lectures on Assistive, Rehabilitative, and Health-preserving Technologies*, 2 (2), pp. 1–177.

Kumm, A. J., Viljoen, M. and de Vries, P. J. (2022). The digital divide in technologies for autism: Feasibility considerations for low- and middle-income countries. *J Autism Dev Disord*, 52 (5), pp. 2300–13.

Lai, M. C., Lombardo, M. V., Auyeung, B., Chakrabarti, B. and Baron-Cohen, S. (2015). Sex/gender differences and autism: Setting the scene for future research. *J Am Acad Child Adolesc Psychiatry*, 54 (1), pp. 11–24.

Lindsay, L., Proulx, M., Scott, H. and Thomson, N. (2014). Exploring teachers' strategies for including children with autism spectrum disorder in mainstream classrooms. *International Journal of Inclusive Education*, 18 (2), pp. 101–22.

Madipakkam, A., Rothkirch, M., Dziobek, I. and Sterzer, P. (2019). Access to awareness of direct gaze is related to autistic traits. *Psychological Medicine*, 49 (6), pp. 980–6.

Mahapatra, P., Pati, S., Sinha, R., Chauhan, A. S., Nanda, R. R. and Nallala, S. (2019). Parental care-seeking pathway and challenges for autistic spectrum disorders children: A mixed method study from Bhubaneswar, Odisha. *Indian J Psychiatry*, 61 (1), pp. 37–44.

Manor-Binyamini, I. and Shoshana, A. (2018). Listening to Bedouin mothers of children with autism. *Cult Med Psychiatry*, 42 (2), pp. 401–18.

Marlow, M., Servili, C. and Tomlinson, M. (2019). A review of screening tools for the identification of autism spectrum disorders and developmental delay in infants and young children: Recommendations for use in low- and middle-income countries. *Autism Research*, 12 (2), pp. 176–99.

Minhas, A., Vajaratkar, V., Divan, G., Hamdani, S. U., Leadbitter, K., Taylor, C., Aldred, C., Tariq, A., Tariq, M., Cardoza, P., Green, J., Patel, V. and Rahman, A. (2015). Parents' perspectives on care of children with autistic spectrum disorder in South Asia – Views from Pakistan and India. *Int Rev Psychiatry*, 27 (3), pp. 247–56.

Norbury, C. F. and Sparks, A. (2013). Difference of disorder? Cultural issues in understanding neurodevelopmental disorders. *Developmental Psychology*, 49 (1), pp. 45–58.

Ooi, K. L., Ong, Y. S., Jacob, S. A. and Khan, T. M. (2016). A meta-synthesis on parenting a child with autism. *Neuropsychiatric Disease and Treatment*, 12, pp. 745–62.

Oti-Boadi, M. (2017). Exploring the lived experiences of mothers of children with intellectual disability in Ghana. *SAGE Open*, 7 (4), pp. 1–12.

Rattaz, C., Munir, K., Michelon, C., Picot, M. C., Baghdadli, A. and ELENA study group (2020). School inclusion in children and adolescents with autism spectrum disorders in France: Report from the ELENA French cohort study. *Journal of Autism and Developmental Disorders*, 50 (2), pp. 455–66.

Ruparelia, K., Abubakar, A., Badoe, E., Bakare, M., Visser, K., Chugani, D. C., Chugani, H. T., Donald, K. A., Wilmshurst, J. M., Shih, A., Skuse, D. and Newton, C. R. (2016). Autism spectrum disorders in Africa: Current challenges in identification, assessment, and treatment: A report on the International Child Neurology Association Meeting on ASD in Africa, Ghana, April 3–5, 2014. *J Child Neurol*, 31 (8), pp. 1018–26.

Samms-Vaughan, M. E. (2014). The status of early identification and early intervention in autism spectrum disorders in lower- and middle-income countries. *Int J Speech Lang Pathol*, 16 (1), pp. 30–5.

Sell, N. K., Giarelli, E., Blum, N., Hanlon, A. L. and Levy, S. E. (2012). A comparison of autism spectrum disorder DSM-IV criteria and associated features among African American and white children in Philadelphia County. *Disability and Health Journal*, 5 (1), pp. 9–17.

Shaked, M. and Bilu, Y. (2006). Grappling with affliction: Autism in the Jewish ultraorthodox community in Israel. *Culture, Medicine and Psychiatry*, 30, pp. 1–27.

Singhal, N. (2010). *The Impact of the Popular Media on Awareness*. Aap Ki Antara. Conference: International Meeting for Autism Research, May 2010.

Stewart, L. A. and Lee, L. C. (2017). Screening for autism spectrum disorder in low- and middle-income countries: A systematic review. *Autism*, 21 (5), pp. 527–39.

Tang, L. and Bie, B. (2016). The stigma of autism in China: An analysis of newspaper portrayals of autism between 2003 and 2012. *Health Commun*, 31 (4), pp. 445–52.

Tarjiah, I. and Riyanti, I. (2019). Attitude of class teachers to students with autism in inclusive education primary schools. *Journal of ICSAR, [S.l.]*, 3 (1), pp. 62–8.

Tekola, B., Baheretibeb, Y. and Roth, I. (2016). Challenges and opportunities to improve autism services in low-income countries: Lessons from a situational analysis in Ethiopia – policy and system review. *Global Mental Health*, 3 (e21), pp. 1–11.

Thaver, T. and Lim, L. (2012). Attitudes of pre-service mainstream teachers in Singapore towards people with disabilities and inclusive education. *International Journal of Inclusive Education*, 18 (10), pp. 1–15.

Viljoen, M., Mahdi, S., Griessel, D., Bölte, S. and de Vries, P. J. (2019). Parent/caregiver perspectives of functioning in autism spectrum disorders: A comparative study in Sweden and South Africa. *Autism*, 23 (1), pp. 2112–30.

Vohra, R., Madhavan, S. and Sambamoorthi, U. (2017). Comorbidity prevalence, health-care utilization, and expenditures of Medicaid enrolled adults with autism spectrum disorders. *Autism*, 21 (8), pp. 995–1009.

West, E. A., Travers, J. C., Kemper, T. D., Liberty, L. M., Cote, D. L., McCollow, M. M. and Stansberry Brusnahan, L. L. (2016). Racial and ethnic diversity of participants in research supporting evidence-based practices for learners with autism spectrum disorder. *The Journal of Special Education*, 50 (3), pp. 151–63.

World Bank (2019). *Classifying Countries by Income*. [online] Available at: https://data-topics.worldbank.org/world-development-indicators/stories/the-classification-of-countries-by-income.html [Accessed 12.02.2022].

World Health Organization (WHO) (2015). *Global Health Workforce, Finances Remain Low for Mental Health*. [online] Available at: www.who.int/news/item/14-07-2015-global-health-workforce-finances-remain-low-for-mental-health [Accessed 04.02.2022].

World Health Organization (WHO) (2021). *The International Classification of Functioning, Disability and Health (ICF)*. [online] Available at: www.who.int/standards/classifications/international-classification-of-functioning-disability-and-health [Accessed 30.03.2022].

Zakirova-Engstrand, R., Hirvikoski, T., Allodi, M. W. and Roll-Pettersson, L. (2020). Culturally diverse families of young children with ASD in Sweden: Parental explanatory models. *PLoS One*, 15 (7), e0236329.

Zhang, J., Wheeler, J. J. and Richey, D. (2006). Cultural validity in assessment instruments for children with autism from a Chinese cultural perspective. *International Journal of Special Education*, 21, pp. 109–14.

Zuckerman, K. E., Sinche, B., Mejia, A., Cobian, M., Becker, T. and Nicolaidis, C. (2014). Latino parents' perspectives on barriers to autism diagnosis. *Acad Pediatr*, 14 (3), pp. 301–8.

TWELVE
Media perspectives

Introduction

There has been much written about how the written media, such as newspapers and books, have discussed autism; for example, Huws and Jones (2010) analysed articles from British newspapers that covered stories relating to autism over a 10-year span and found that sources had mostly pessimistic opinions. Jones and Harwood (2009) suggest that the development and reinforcement of stereotypes are strongly influenced by the news and entertainment media. Media outlets have the potential to increase awareness, understanding and acceptance for autistic individuals (Dyches and Prater, 2000). However, media representations sometimes develop their own realities, diverting from realistic portrayals and creating false representations about autism to mass audiences (Sarrett, 2011). Huws and Jones (2011) state how discussions and portrayals generally rely upon third-person perspectives, usually sensationalising, misusing, or sharing misconceptions about autistic behaviours. In response to the increase of autism, or perhaps in acknowledgement of the increased prevalence, media representations of autism have also increased (Conn and Bhugra, 2012). The surge of new films and television shows presenting characters with autism can extend awareness and messaging by reaching an audience that far exceeds academic journals. This chapter explores how television and films portray representations of autism, how social media are becoming a dominant outlet for autistic children, young people and adults and how videogames are being utilised.

─────────────── Learning objectives ───────────────

This chapter will:

- Invite you to review the role films and television have had in the representation of autism
- Help you to consider if stereotypical representations have changed over time
- Invite you to review the relevance of social media platforms for autistic individuals and their allies and families
- Help you to consider the impact that social media may have in the rise of cyberbullying in relation to autism
- Invite you to evaluate the role that videogames have in the life of players

──────────────── Key terms ────────────────

Feature films and television, social media, cyberbullying, videogames, autistic stereo-types, portrayal in media

──────────────── Pause for reflection ────────────────

• Can you think of any examples of how the media have portrayed autism?
• Are these realistic representations? If not, why?
• What are the advantages and issues associated with the use of social media?

Portrayal of autism in feature films

Prochnow (2014) states that autistic characters are generally portrayed in one of the following categories: magical/savant, different/quirky, undiagnosed/unlabelled, and realistic. With so many different types of autism diagnoses, it would be impossible to perfectly depict each aspect of autism through television and film characters. However, she suggests that it is media's responsibility to at least attempt to make their portrayals as accurate as possible.

──────────────── Rain Man ────────────────

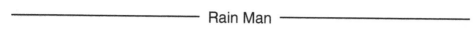

Connor and Bejoian (2006) state how most adults and children spend more time learning about the world through TV and film rather than print media. Osteen (2007) notes how audiences with no experience, use the characters in on-screen media to acquire their knowledge about autism.

The film *Rain Man* was released in 1988 and for a long time, the Oscar-winning drama was the best-known representation of autism on film. After living in an institution for several years Raymond Babbitt returns to live in Cincinnati with his brother, Charlie Babbitt, who takes him home after discovering that his late father left three million dollars to his brother. Throughout the film, Raymond is portrayed as having difficulties in expressing emotions, he adheres to rigid routines and has the savant ability to mentally calculate hundreds of objects.

Disability has also been used in narratives as a tool to create drama. Conn and Bhugra (2012) suggest that autism is often used as an entertainment tool with little regard for accurately depicting the condition and the media select mesmerising autistic behaviours that neurotypical viewers consider pleasant, including superhuman abilities and extremely awkward social deficits. Usually, autistic characters are paired with psychologically troubled neurotypical characters so that the former can heal the latter and, in the case of *Rain Man*, Raymond's autism contributes to making his brother a better person, where at the end of the film Charlie no longer wants to 'take care' of Raymond to have access to his inherited money. A study by Young (2012) carried out a content analysis of the generic stereotypes and myths associated with autism (see Table 12.1).

Table 12.1 Myths associated with autism

Myths	Reinforced Myth	Dispelled Myth	N/A
Never make eye contact	94 per cent	6 per cent	0 per cent
Unable to communicate verbally	0 per cent	100 per cent	0 per cent
Unable to respond to or show affection	16 per cent	0 per cent	84 per cent
Do not smile	6 per cent	18 per cent	76 per cent
Not perceptive to cues	24 per cent	76 per cent	0 per cent

(Young, 2012, p. 21)

The overall notion of reinforcement of stereotypes in *Rain Man* popularised unrealistic stereotypes, with many autistic people subsequently typecast as savants and incapable of functioning in normal society. Young (2012) also states how stereotypical portrayals of savant autistic characters were still present in the 1998 film *Mercury Rising*, with Osteen (2007) suggesting that films such as *Bless the Child* (2000), *Molly* (1998), Stephen King's *Rose Red* (2002), and *Cube* (1997) helped to perpetuate stereotypes. Prochnow (2014) argues that autistic representations in TV and film are so hyper-positive to the point that they are unrealistic, with Redden (2018) pointing out that actors portraying autistic characters usually aren't autistic themselves and that better inclusion of autistic actors could greatly benefit the overall positive portrayal of autism via on-screen media.

Before *Rain Man*, there was no popular conception of what autism looked like, among the public or on-screen. At that point autism was an abstraction, understood only by dedicated parents or specialised clinicians; but 30 years later autistic people are still being perceived as socially naïve or as having 'special abilities' like Raymond Babbitt (Knights, 2018). Skudra (2018) suggests while *Rain Man* delivers a powerful message of understanding and personal transformation, it is also characterised by a significant number of errors in the characters' perception of autism and fails to delve into the ability of autistic individuals to live successful independent lives. Osteen (2007) details how *Rain Man* still exists as the public's view, with many still using the term 'rain man' to refer to those with autism.

Hannam (2014) finds that autistic characters in American films were depicted only in relation to other characters who had no disabilities, such as being secondary to them, defined by them, being a hindrance to them, or of use to them in some way. Characters with autism were also presented as being asexual or isolated, their lives ultimately not undergoing much change by the end of the films.

The increasing number of international film and television productions with autistic characters (Conn and Bhugra, 2012) highlights a growing cultural diversity of autistic representations. Ejaz (2019) used content analysis to compare the films *Rain Man* and *I am Sam* to their respective Indian Hindi-language remakes. Analysis revealed differences in how disability was constructed across the original films and their remakes, indicating the influence of culture on the construction of disability.

Specifically, the Indian remakes depicted characters with autism in more romantic interactions, interactions with children, and with more occupational abilities than the original American films. Religion also featured more in the Indian films in relation to autism. The study suggests that there is a social construction of autism as a disability. However, in a systematic review Dean and Nordahl-Hansen (2021) suggested that characters were culturally and linguistically diverse, and portrayals of autism appear to be moving away from typical disability-tropes. Autism receives mostly reductive and condescending treatment in film, with characters displaying eccentricities, dazzling mathematical or musical genius.

Portrayal of autism in television

Over the past three decades, a growing number of television shows have depicted autistic individuals with varying degrees of accuracy. Generally, these shows have propagated false beliefs and stereotypes and have failed to capture the rich range of phenotypes across the spectrum (Conn and Bhugra, 2012). In the ABC *Good Doctor* television series, Shaun Murphy (played by Freddie Highmore) is a surgeon with near-perfect recall, a photographic memory, and savant-like diagnostic abilities. In the series *The Bridge* (a co-production between Sveriges Television and Danmarks Radio), Saga Noren was widely diagnosed by viewers as being on the autistic spectrum; she is lauded not just because she is a leading character with the condition, but – more unusually – because she is a woman with it. She is blunt, doesn't understand jokes and struggles to build relationships. She strips down to her underwear to get changed in the office without embarrassment and asks and answers questions with often excruciating honesty. While the writers of *The Bridge* have never confirmed that Saga has Asperger syndrome, it has been generally assumed to be the case (Townsend, 2015).

Atypical, the Netflix comedy series, is about Sam, an 18-year-old American high school student. He is observed trying to engage in 'typical' adolescent activities. He is interested in dating and works at a technology store. Joo-Young Lee and Deng (2020) state that the series more accurately captures the diversity and experience of autistic individuals. It depicts the chronic clinical trajectory of autism through Sam's recurring anxiety attacks in the context of his sister's transfer to another school, sensory overload, and rejection by his peers. Unlike autistic characters who are usually portrayed as having an interest in areas related to Maths or Science, Sam enjoys a creative activity, that of illustration. It stresses that autistic individuals may yearn for relationships and endeavours to convey more thoughtful representations of autistic individuals by incorporating voices from the autism community and bringing additional actors, consultants, and an autistic playwright into the production.

Atypical moves away from the dominant belief that all autistic people are unable to voice their views as seen in *Rain Man* (Green, 2018) and focuses on exploring disability from the social dimension (Mitchell and Snyder, 2000). However, *Atypical* received negative feedback from the autism community: that a neurotypical actor plays Sam and there is a lack of autistic actors, and that Sam is totally the higher functioning autistic stereotype – except he isn't obsessed with trains (Nordahl-Hansen et al., 2018). There is also concern that comical scenes in *Atypical* might make its viewers laugh at rather than with Sam.

Felperin (2017) argues that often it feels like *Atypical's* writers have combed through the literature – the many academic accounts, memoirs and so on – and extracted, intensified, and amplified all the most obvious autistic behaviours, particularly those that would have been described as signs of Asperger syndrome before that latter diagnosis was brought under the autism umbrella in DSM-5. Reception of the first season and the backlash it received led to changes in the second and third seasons, providing an excellent example of how autistic advocacy can shape popular culture (Brady and Cardin, 2021).

Rourke and McGloin (2019) examined the portrayal of a fictional character suspected of having Asperger syndrome, Sheldon Cooper, played by Jim Parsons, in the TV series *The Big Bang Theory* (CBS, 2007–2019). Sheldon is depicted as having obsessive and specific interests; he struggles with social cues, avoids physical contact, and is a genius and former child prodigy. While it is not explicitly mentioned that he is autistic, his idiosyncratic behaviours have led many fans to speculate or conclude he is indeed autistic (Soraya, 2009).

Sheldon is frequently perceived to be the most obviously autistic character on television (Heilker, 2012) by TV critics, psychologists, and even autistic self-advocates and activists, usually because of his obsessiveness, immersion in fictional worlds of science fiction, frequent avoidance of eye contact, and difficulty in handling emotions and social niceties. Walters (2013) suggests that the series offers new and unexpected ways of understanding and blurring categories such as autistic and neurotypical, as well as non/disabled. Labels such as autistic and neurotypical are dependent upon each other for meaning; however, Sheldon's character can be seen to normalise cognitive difference.

Nordahl-Hansen et al. (2018) investigated whether portrayals of characters with autism spectrum disorder in film and TV series align with DSM-5 diagnostic criteria. Most of the characters evaluated obtained a very high score against DSM-5 criteria for autism and this suggests that portrayals of autism on screen closely meet autism diagnostic criteria and that screen representations do have potential educational value.

Television needs to show legitimate autistic characters instead of just characters who are autistic but aren't named as such and they need to show a wider variety of perspectives of autism, as portrayals on screen may not truly represent the lived experiences. For example, nonverbal characters and those with sensory issues deserve to be shown. It is important that as autism is becoming more widely portrayed in the media, writers should approach autistic people when researching their characters instead of just asking neurotypical experts. Media representations such as the ones discussed in this chapter invite us to gaze, even stare at autism, but not to acknowledge the condition.

--- **Exercise** ---

There have been several studies with respect to the representation of autism on American television. However, recently, there have been television programmes in the UK exploring the lived experience of families with an autistic child. Two such programmes are *The A Word* and *Paddy and Christine McGuinness: Our Family and Autism*.

The A Word is a BBC drama (2016–2020) and follows an extended family with an autistic child at its centre. When 5-year-old Joe is diagnosed with autism, it brings to the surface the tensions and fault lines that run throughout his family, as they struggle to adapt to the changes in their lives and, more importantly, to learn to communicate.

In partnership with the Open University, the documentary *Paddy and Christine McGuinness: Our Family and Autism* (BBC, 2021) follows Paddy McGuinness, his wife Christine and their three children, eight-year-old twins Leo and Penelope, and five-year-old Felicity. All three have been diagnosed with autism and the documentary observes Paddy and Christine at home, as well as meeting other parents, experts, and people on the autism spectrum.

- Do these programmes differ in their portrayal of autism in comparison with other television accounts?
- How important is it to examine the impact that autism has on family relationships in real life?

Social media

With the rise of the internet and ownership of a smartphone now commonplace, it is likely that social media (and similar online resources) are now prominent in the day-to-day lives of children, young people and adults. Belcher and Maich (2014) state that technology is the purveyor of the future, especially among younger generations, and those with autism demonstrate significant difficulties socially and emotionally yet show strengths in screen-based technology. Mazurek (2013) notes how in using social media those with autism are more likely to develop closer social connections. van Schalkwyk et al. (2017) undertook a cross-sectional study, assessing social media use, anxiety and friendship quality in 44 autistic adolescents and 56 clinical comparison controls and they note how social media might offer those with autism the chance to improve friendships without developing significant anxiety. They suggest that autistic adolescents are well suited to capitalise on the unique features of social media, which require less decoding of complex social information.

Stendal and Balandin (2015) note how online communication networks offer a uniquely safe setting in which autistic individuals can communicate to others while still being physically located in a safe and known environment and that increasing the number of friends online does not necessarily transpire to increasing the number of friends in the physical world. van Schalkwyk et al. (2017) note that although social media seem to facilitate social engagement, they may in fact displace offline social activities. Ward et al. (2018) noted that from a sample of 106 autistic individuals, 84 per cent used Facebook and were reported as being happier than those who didn't use the social networking site. However, this greater degree of happiness was not observed regarding Twitter. They also found that whereas Facebook users wished to maintain their social network, Twitter users valued anonymity. Ward et al. (2018) note how Facebook sees users seeking/maintaining their known social network, posting interpersonal and emotional messages whereas Twitter users tend to value anonymity and intellectual stimulation; however, the participants in the study were predominantly male (60.38 per cent).

YouTube is now one of the most popular sites accessed by those with autism (Davidson, 2008) and it could be suggested that by displaying the somewhat hidden disability of autism, video bloggers (vloggers) on YouTube are now at the forefront of the modern era of autistic media representation. Angulo-Jiménez and DeThorne (2019) note how YouTube has become a prominent online platform that offers insight and experience into the lives of people living with autism and that 44 per cent of autistic vloggers portrayed their lives as being 'normal'. They found that the predominant narrative about autism incorporated features of both the medical model of disability and the neurodiversity paradigm to varying degrees, with a trend towards more medical model features across most content areas. However, Brownlow et al. (2013) suggest that we need to be cautious about assuming that just because a more divergent range of autistic voices and representations can be seen and heard on YouTube, this does not necessarily mean that this will be mirrored in wider face-to-face society.

When it comes to adults with autism, most of them used social networking sites to seek social connections (Mazurek, 2013), suggesting that social media appear to be beneficial for individuals with autism in communicating and engaging with others in a comfortable way. One possible reason Facebook users were happier than Twitter users in this population is because Facebook requires the user to accept friend requests, which may help social connections, but on Twitter, no interaction is needed and retweeting, a main feature of Twitter, requires knowledge of online social norms and can often lead to negative social interactions. Also, Facebook profiles provide information on others' hobbies and interests, which can help improve trust between users.

Social media, especially social networking sites, have become significant online venues for the exchange of health-related information and advice. Roffeei et al. (2015) analysed two autism support groups on Facebook and found that the highest percentage of messages were about informational support and emotional support. Most of the discussions are related to challenges and difficulties in caring and raising autistic children, as well as children's social life and self-care routines. Zhao et al. (2019) found that autism support groups on Facebook offer companionship and emotional support to autism-affected users. In addition, social, informational and emotional support appear to provide a supportive and grateful atmosphere for group members.

Roffeei et al. (2015) found that Facebook also offers support between parents and/or caregivers of autistic children. Their findings indicated that the highest percentage of messages offered informational support followed by emotional support, network and esteem support. Most of these messages discussed and addressed challenges and difficulties associated with caring and raising autistic children, as well as issues such as their child's social life and self-care routines.

Case study

In this videoclip, Joe suggests that there are many reasons why autistic people love and loathe social media and he discusses why he enjoys using them, as well as several issues he has with social media platforms.

The videoclip is available at: www.youtube.com/watch?v=QfTu1lFpvN8

- Do his views match with what the research is saying about the benefits and issues in using social media, identified in this chapter?
- What are his key messages?

Social media are the favoured and least anxiety-provoking means of social communication for many autistic people, but the internet is a dangerous 'rabid rat' looking for an opportunity to wreak havoc and mayhem onto communities and ruin lives (Sims, 2017). Abel et al. (2019) found almost one million members of autism Facebook groups created for support, social companionship, advocacy, treatments, sales or fundraising. The stated purpose for the majority of groups is support for parents and families, followed by social companionship groups for autistic people. While just over one tenth of all groups were specifically targeted at women, only two groups were targeted at men and most groups targeting autistic people used identity-first language, while those targeting parents and families used person-first language. The increased risk of internet use could be an additional stressor for parents of autistic children, who may feel concerned over their child using social media platforms to engage with others. Parents of typically developing children and young people often report that they are concerned about online risks.

———————————— Key research in the field ————————————

Gillespie-Smith, K., Hendry, G., Anduuru, N., Laird, T. and Ballantyne, C. (2021). Using social media to be 'social': Perceptions of social media benefits and risk by autistic young people, and parents. *Research in Developmental Disabilities*, 118, 104081.

Objective

Autistic individuals are reported to struggle with aspects of social interaction. Past research has shown that social media use can help to facilitate social functioning, however the perceptions of risks and benefits when engaging on social media platforms remain unclear. This study aimed to explore perceptions of social media participation in terms of online risk and online relationships in both autistic young people and parents.

Method

Eight autistic young people and six parents of autistic young people took part in semi-structured interviews, with the resultant data being transcribed and analysed using Braun and Clarke's (2006) inductive thematic analysis.

Findings

Both parents and young people showed an awareness of social media being used as a platform for socialisation and connecting with others, facilitating the formation and maintenance of friendships. Two themes were identified in relation to the impact social media have on autistic young people's relationships (Socialisation; Communication) and two themes were identified in relation to the perceived barriers and risks to engaging online (Abusive interactions; Talking to strangers). These findings show that social interaction is of value to young autistic people, in terms of affording them easier social interactions than there would be in 'real life.'

Conclusion

Online social interactions were particularly valuable to autistic young people since they allowed them to interact more easily with others by removing some of the perceived social barriers.

The findings indicated that there are risks to such online engagement that the autistic young people may encounter, however rather than showing social naivety online, the autistic young people in the study indicated awareness of such risks.

Social media hold promise as a technology to facilitate social engagement and autistic adolescents are well suited to capitalise on the unique features of social media in that they require less decoding of complex social information (van Schalkwyk et al., 2017). Burke and Kraut (2016) suggest that the characteristics of autism such as the need for structure and difficulties with nonverbal cues, e.g. facial expressions, are supported through the use of computer-mediated communication (CMC). Many autistic individuals have difficulty making eye contact, interpreting nonverbal cues such as facial expressions, processing non-literal language, thinking flexibly, and understanding others' perspective. Text-messaging, email, and Facebook wall posts all provide a highly structured environment without extraneous stimuli, and their asynchronicity allows users additional processing time. However, many report feelings of loneliness and isolation due to difficulties in social interaction. One key issue related to the use of social media is that of cyberbullying.

Pause for reflection

- Do you think that cyberbullying is an issue for autistic individuals?
- What could be done to monitor and support individuals who may be at risk?

Cyberbullying

Computer-mediated communication (CMC) has both benefits and drawbacks; for example, chat rooms quickly switch speakers and topics, making it difficult to follow a conversation thread. Concerns have been raised about social networking platforms, including the potential for cyberbullying; Kowalski and Limber (2007) refer to it as electronic bullying, or online social cruelty, which includes bullying through email, instant messaging, in a chat room, on a website, or through digital messages or images. From a study of 181 autistic adolescents, Iglesias et al. (2019) note how the most common type of cybervictimisation faced by autistic people was verbal bullying, with 38.7 per cent of respondents stating they have been cold called (received a call on a mobile but the caller stays silent). Additionally, 22.6 per cent detailed how they have been picked on through social media, with 30 individuals concluding that they have been removed or not accepted on a social network simply because they were autistic.

Malecha (2021) suggests that autistic children experience social communication challenges and have difficulties with identifying hidden nonverbal signs of bullying including identifying and recognising own and someone's intentions, expressing and detecting emotions and suspecting signs of bullying. Adults may also face cyberbullying, Triantafyllopoulou et al. (2021) found that high levels of social media use were associated with an increased risk of cybervictimisation; whereas self-esteem was positively correlated with feelings of belonging to an online community and negatively correlated with feelings of being ignored on social network sites and chat rooms. A meta-analysis (Park et al., 2020) was carried out on cyberbullying in East Asia, where peer pressure based on collectivistic ideals and rigid cultural scripts for social interactions remain strong. They also suggest that the countries represented in this review (China, South Korea, Japan, Hong Kong and Taiwan) are amongst the top globally for internet usage. They reported that the risk of victimisation in autistic students was significantly higher than that in other students.

Liu et al. (2020) found that social anxiety increased the risk of being a victim of cyberbullying and that cyberbullying victimisation was a positive predictor of depression and posttraumatic stress symptoms (PTSS). However, Campbell et al. (2017) surveyed 104 autistic students on their experiences with respect to physical, verbal, social and cyberbullying and their roles as victim, perpetrator and bully-victim. When comparing them with a group of typically developing students matched for age and gender, it was found that autistic students reported significantly more traditional victimisation (physical, verbal and social) than their typically developing peers, but that cyberbullying victimisation was similar for the two groups.

Videogames and autism

─────────────── Pause for reflection ───────────────

- Why do you think videogames are appealing to autistic players and can you think of any advantages and issues in playing videogames for autistic players?
- What impact might extensive playing have on families? Would there be any difference for autistic players in comparison with neurotypical ones?

Despite their limited engagement in social and community activities, many autistic individuals seem to have strong interests in videogames (Mazurek and Wenstrup, 2013) and they may help overcome isolation and some of the social barriers that are typical (Stendal and Balandin, 2015). One potential reason why autistic individuals may have pronounced interests in videogames is that such games offer visually stimulating virtual environments, which may provide opportunities to utilise their visual processing skills and preferences. Because videogame play often requires visual-spatial skills and immediate attention to visual cues, videogames may also be inherently rewarding. Most videogames provide a well-defined structure and framework, while simultaneously offering players imaginative experiences. Videogames are often designed to provide clear visual and/or auditory cues, clearly defined expectations, and immediate and frequent reinforcement for in-game behaviours. Instead of a situation where a person must carefully read the people around them, they are instead surrounded by avatars that have an element of emotive simplicity. There are rules, players can only use a set number of expressions and emotes in games, with others having none.

―――――――――――――――――― Case study ――――――――――――――――――

In this videoclip, a father with two autistic sons, aged three and four, suggests that one of the hardest things about having kids with autism is not being able to communicate with them properly or know how they're feeling. However, his son Gavin found a passion that allows him to express himself in ways his dad never expected and he gives a reason why videogames are such an important part of his relationship with his son.

The videoclip can be found at: www.youtube.com/watch?v=xdRIsj4FI0A

- What are the main points that Gavin's dad raises?
- What does this tell you about listening to families and how does it support research findings?

Mazurek et al. (2015) examined the preferences and motivations for game play among autistic adults. Importantly, positive and negative aspects of game play were understood from the direct perspectives of autistic adults themselves. Not surprisingly, fun/entertainment was the most common motivation for videogame play. Related to this, autistic adults reported several different game features that relate to their overall enjoyment – achievement and challenge, allowing for creativity or autonomy, containing interesting story elements, and emphasising visual graphics or artistic elements. Other game design elements that contributed to worsen user experiences included technical problems, glitches, poorly designed graphics, and movement control difficulties. Content-related issues, specifically violence and sexual content, were also perceived negatively by several participants. Many reported that games provide a way for them to interact and share enjoyment with both friends and family, offer a shared activity and topic of discussion.

Mazurek and Engelhardt (2013), through a study of 169 autistic males, argue problematic videogame use correlated with the display of inattention and oppositional behaviour, with role-playing games highlighted as the genre most associated with increases in such conduct. They go on to suggest that the characteristics of those with autism might mean that they are more subject to developing problematic and addictive gaming patterns However, Orsmond and Kuo (2011) suggest that in using such media, those with autism might enhance undesired behaviours that further alienate peers while reinforcing previously mentioned stereotypes. Laurie et al. (2019) concluded that parents of autistic children worry about their child's use of technology, particularly the time spent on such devices and the impact regarding social consequences. Stendal and Balandin (2015) detail how the online role-playing game 'Second Life' enhances the social skills independence of someone. In their case study, an individual was able to efficiently portray nonverbal communication via the medium of textual descriptions, such as eye rolling and tail wagging, this in turn developing into real-world relationships. Subsequently, it is possible to suggest that the gaming platform allows for individuals with autism to develop their understanding and demonstration of social skills while also tackling stereotypes.

Coutelle al. (2022) reviewed the literature on videogame use to examine the role of vulnerability for videogame addiction and the role of restricted interest in videogaming. They found that the high rates of videogame use in autistic boys and young males can be predominantly explained by gaming addiction. Engelhardt et al. (2017) suggest that excessive play in autistic adults may be deleterious; problematic game use was associated with poor sleep and poorer behavioural functioning. They found that autistic adults endorsed more symptoms of videogame pathology than did typically developing adults and that risk for pathological game use appears larger. Qualitative findings suggest that while autistic adults report several positive aspects of videogame use, including stress reduction and social connection, autistic children and adolescents have difficulty disengaging from video games.

Mazurek and Wenstrup (2013) found that autistic children spent more hours per day playing videogames (2.4 vs. 1.6 for boys, and 1.8 vs. 0.8 for girls), and had higher levels of problematic videogame use and spent little time using social media or socially interactive videogames. Pathological game use is defined by its symptoms: preoccupation with videogames, salience, euphoria/relief, tolerance, withdrawal symptoms, mood modification, conflict, relapse and reinstatement, unsuccessful attempts to control videogame play, continued excessive use, deceiving others as to the amount of time spent gaming, and loss of interest in hobbies (American Psychiatric Association, 2013). Their findings suggest that autistic adults may be at higher risk for pathological game use due to aspects of the behavioural phenotype of autism than neurotypical adults.

Mazurek and Engelhardt (2013) found a greater risk for problematic videogame use for autistic boys than for boys with typical development. Inattentive symptoms were strongly associated with problematic videogame use for both groups, and role-playing game preferences may be an additional risk factor for problematic videogame use among autistic children. They may have trouble focusing on videogame play, have trouble while transitioning from videogame play to other activities, and may become argumentative and oppositional, particularly when they want to play more games. Role-playing games like Pokémon that have high reward schedules and social rewards may lead to increased preoccupation or an overly intense interest in the game.

Experts remain divided over whether we should be wary of gaming because of alleged concerns around addiction, or whether we should embrace it because of its possibilities in facilitating social interaction. On the flipside, some say videogames can be a uniquely safe place for autistic people to socialise. While some research looks at social interaction between autistic and neurotypical people, it's been suggested videogames, by virtue of high autistic participation, can also increase the potential of autistic people interacting with other autistic people. Such interactions can lead to rapport and mutual understanding. A good example is the autistic-only Minecraft server 'Autcraft' that has fostered a safe anti-bullying community with clear and consistent rules.

Autcraft

Minecraft is an open-ended virtual world with no goals or play requirements with players building and creating new objects by manipulating blocks in the game. The free Minecraft server 'Autcraft' is an example of how communities can be formed online to support autistic people and their families. It is a semi-private server on Minecraft and includes modifications and add-ons to the software to allow for the safety of community members and to enhance their socialisation. In addition to the Minecraft virtual world, the community uses other social media platforms in tandem including YouTube, Twitch, Twitter, Facebook, and a community-maintained website. Ringland (2019) argues that othering of their sociality means that both gamers and autistic individuals must search for places where they can be social, and their sociality is given validity. However, those who are autistic gamers may find themselves othered twice – first, by society at large and, second, by gamers.

Gamer discourse hypermasculinises the act of gaming, making the activity only acceptable (and socially accessible) to those who identify as heteronormative white men. There are currently two broad narratives about game play and use in mainstream media: games are addictive and problematic, or games can be 'good' by being 'serious' or educational. It could also promote community building. The actions of the members of the 'Autcraft' community demonstrate videogames do not necessarily have to be profoundly negative nor do they require the player be 'productive', but rather game spaces can be places of sociality that are more accessible to the participants than other places. Sites such as 'Autcraft' can foster a sense of community, create access to social play previously inaccessible to the players and create a space to empower players.

Key points

- There has been much research undertaken about how media can perpetuate or challenge the autistic stereotype
- There has been increasing interest by television and film makers to depict the lived experience of living with an autistic member of the family
- Social media platforms are becoming more and more important for autistic individuals and their social interaction with others, but there are benefits and drawbacks
- Many autistic adults and children experience social communication and social anxiety challenges and have difficulties with communication, which can lead to cyberbullying
- Many autistic individuals seem to have strong interests in videogames and there are both risks and benefits in their use

—————————— Questions to consider ——————————

- How can media producers be encouraged to work with the autistic community to portray autism in a realistic manner?
- Who should take responsibility to ensure that social media platforms do not perpetuate inaccuracies and harmful content?
- If you were to produce a videogame in which autistic gamers would feel comfortable and enjoy playing, what would you include in the gameplay and why?

—————————— Further reading ——————————

Lisgou, M. E. and Tsibidaki, A. (2021). Characters with autism spectrum disorder in cinema. *Film International*, 19 (2), pp. 95–104.

A search of the literature on the subject showed that the number of representations of ASD in cinema is limited and that most research is recent and focuses mainly on characters with ASD, while there are fewer references to their family. Besides, not all aspects of the depictions of ASD are analysed and family environment remains a remarkably under-researched area. In an analysis of 16 films, this study found single-parent families to be the norm, while nuclear families were rarer. The main cause of single-parent family formation in the sample was divorce and the estrangement of one partner. Most of the parental behaviour in the films studied could be described as supportive, while overprotective behaviour was less frequent. This conflicts with studies of actual ASD families, who point out that overprotective behaviour was more common regarding children with disabilities (Seligman and Darling, 2007).

Carrington, S., Campbell, M., Saggers, B., Ashburner, J., Vicig, F., Dillon-Wallace, J. and Hwang, Y. (2017). Recommendations of school students with autism spectrum disorder and their parents in regard to bullying and cyberbullying prevention and intervention. *International Journal of Inclusive Education*, 21 (10), pp. 1045–64.

Accumulating evidence suggests that the prevalence of bullying is significantly higher for autistic students than for typically developing students. Additionally, the prominence and growth of social networking and resultant focus on cyberbullying in the last 10 years has added a new dimension to the traditional definitions, environments, and experiences of bullying. This paper describes current anti-bullying strategies and the legal climate regarding bullying in Australia. It then reports on interviews with 10 autistic students and their parents, and discusses recommendations based on their perceptions for dealing with bullying in schools.

Alhujaili, N., Platt, E., Khalid-Khan, S. and Groll, D. (2022). Comparison of social media use among adolescents with autism spectrum disorder and non-ASD adolescents. *Adolescent Health, Medicine and Therapeutics*, 13, pp. 15–21.

The goal of this study was to compare the time spent as well as to identify the purpose of social media use in adolescents with ASD compared to non-ASD adolescents. This was a cross-sectional study of adolescents between ages 13 and 18 who were attending a hospital-based

(Continued)

child and adolescent psychiatry clinic. Participants completed a self-report 18-item questionnaire to assess the pattern and reasons for using social media sites. The researchers found that the time spent on social media among adolescents with ASD was comparable to those without ASD diagnosis. However, participants with ASD differed from their non-ASD counterparts in both preferred social media sites as well as reasons for use. The most favourable social media site for ASD adolescents was YouTube. In contrast, the preferred social media site among adolescents without ASD was Snapchat. Participants without ASD reported using social media sites for primarily social interactions. In contrast, participants with ASD reported entertainment purposes as their primary reason for choosing a social media site.

References

Abel, S., Machin, T. and Brownlow, C. (2019). Support, socialise and advocate: An exploration of the stated purposes of Facebook autism groups. *Research in Autism Spectrum Disorders*, 61 (1), pp. 10–21.

American Psychiatric Association (APA) (2013). *Diagnostic and Statistical Manual of Mental Disorders* (5th edition). Arlington, VA: American Psychiatric Association.

Angulo-Jiménez, H. and DeThorne, L. (2019). Narratives about autism: An analysis of YouTube videos by individuals who self-identify as autistic. *Am J Speech Lang Pathol*, 28 (2), pp. 569–90.

Belcher, C. and Maich, K. (2014). Autism spectrum disorder in popular media: Storied reflections of societal views. *Brock Education*, 23 (2), pp. 97–115.

Brady, M. J. and Cardin, M. (2021). Your typical atypical family: Streaming apolitical autism on Netflix. *TOPIA: Canadian Journal of Cultural Studies*, 42 (1), pp. 96–116.

Braun, V. and Clarke, V. (2006). Using thematic analysis in psychology. Qualitative Research in Psychology, 3 (2), pp. 77–101

Brownlow, C., O'Dell, L. and Rosqvist, H. B. (2013). Commentary: Challenging representations of autism – exploring possibilities for broadcasting the self on YouTube. *Journal on Developmental Disabilities*, 19 (1), pp. 90–5.

Burke, M. and Kraut, R. E. (2016). The relationship between Facebook use and wellbeing depends on communication type and tie strength. *Journal of Computer-Mediated Communication*, 21 (4), pp. 265–81.

Campbell, M. A., Hwang, Y. S., Whiteford, C. and Dillon-Wallace, J. (2017). Bullying prevalence in students with autism spectrum disorder. *Australasian Journal of Special Education*, 41 (2), pp. 1–22.

Conn, R. and Bhugra, D. (2012). The portrayal of autism in Hollywood films. *International Journal of Culture and Mental Health*, 1, pp. 54–62.

Connor, D. J. and Bejoian, L. M. (2006). Pigs, pirates, and pills: Using film to teach the social context of disability. *Teaching Exceptional Children*, 39 (2), pp. 52–60.

Coutelle, R., Weiner, L., Paasche, C., Pottelette, J., Bertschy, G., Schröder, C. M. and Lalanne, L. (2022). Autism spectrum disorder and video games: Restricted interests or addiction? *Int J Ment Health Addict*, 20, pp. 2243–64.

Davidson, J. (2008) Autistic culture online: Virtual communication and cultural expression on the spectrum. *Social & Cultural Geography*, 9, pp. 791–806.

Dean, M. and Nordahl-Hansen, A. A. (2021). A review of research studying film and television representations of ASD. *Review Journal of Autism and Developmental Disorders.*

Dyches, T. T. and Prater, M. A. (2000). *Developmental Disability in Children's Literature: Issues and annotated bibliography.* Reston, VA: Council for Exceptional Children, Division on Mental Retardation and Developmental Disabilities.

Ejaz, K. (2019). By any other name: Portrayals of autism across international film remakes. *Disability & Society*, 35 (1), pp. 1–28.

Engelhardt, C. R., Mazurek, M. O. and Hilgard, J. (2017). Pathological game use in adults with and without autism spectrum disorder. *Peer J*, 26 (5), e3393.

Felperin, L. (2017). What Netflix comedy Atypical gets right and wrong about autism. [online] Available at: www.theguardian.com/tv-and-radio/2017/aug/14/atypical-netflix-autism-spectrum-depiction-cliches [Accessed 25.02.2022].

Gillespie-Smith, K., Hendry, G., Anduuru, N., Laird, T. and Ballantyne, C. (2021). Using social media to be 'social': Perceptions of social media benefits and risk by autistic young people, and parents. *Research in Developmental Disabilities*, 118, 104081.

Green, E. (2018). *Opinion: Why accurate representation of autism is so important in film, TV.* Carlsbad: ProQuest.

Hannam, K. (2014). The portrayal of autism in film, post Rain Man. *Good Autism Practice (GAP)*, 15 (1), pp. 91–9.

Heilker, P. (2012). Autism, rhetoric, and whiteness. *Disability Studies Quarterly*, 32, pp. 193–204.

Huws, J. and Jones, R. S. (2010). 'They just seem to live their lives in their own little world': Lay perceptions of autism. *Disability & Society*, 25, pp. 331–44.

Huws, J. C. and Jones, R. S. (2011). Missing voices: Representations of autism in British newspapers, 1999–2008. *British Journal of Learning Disabilities*, 39 (2), pp. 98–104.

Iglesias, O. B., Sánchez, L. E. G. and Rodríguez, M. Á. A. (2019). Do young people with Asperger syndrome or intellectual disability use social media and are they cyberbullied or cyberbullies in the same way as their peers? *Psicothema*, 31 (1), pp. 30–7.

Jones, S. C. and Harwood, V. (2009). Representations of autism in Australian print media. *Disability & Society*, 24, pp. 5–18.

Joo-Young Lee, M. D. and Deng, Z. (2020). *Atypical: A novel portrayal of individuals with autism spectrum disorder.* [online] Available at: https://psychiatryonline.org/doi/10.1176/appi.ajp-rj.2020.150309 [Accessed 13.03.2022].

Knights, K. (2018). Rain Man made autistic people visible. But it also entrenched a myth. [online] Available at: www.theguardian.com/commentisfree/2018/dec/17/rain-man-myth-autistic-people-dustin-hoffman-savant [Accessed 17.02.2022].

Kowalski, R. M. and Limber, S.P. (2007). Electronic bullying among middle school students. *J Adolesc Health*, 41 (6 Suppl 1), pp. 22–30.

Laurie, M. H., Warreyn, P., Uriarte, B. V., Boonen, C. and Fletcher-Watson, S. (2019). An international survey of parental attitudes to technology use by their autistic children at home. *J Autism Dev Disord*, 49 (4), pp. 1517–30.

Liu, C., Liu, Z. and Yuan, G. (2020). The longitudinal influence of cyberbullying victimization on depression and posttraumatic stress symptoms: The mediation role of rumination. *Arch Psychiatr Nurs*, 34, pp. 206–10.

Malecha, V. (2021). *Ways to Protect a Child with Autism from Cyberbullies.* [online] Available at: www.autismparentingmagazine.com/protect-autism-child-from-cyberbul lies/ [Accessed 03.04.2022].

Mazurek, M. O. (2013). Social media use among adults with autism spectrum disorders. *Computers in Human Behavior,* 29 (4), pp. 1709–14.

Mazurek, M. O. and Engelhardt, C. R. (2013). Video game use in boys with autism spectrum disorder, ADHD, or typical development. *Pediatrics,* 132 (2), pp. 260–6.

Mazurek, M. O., Engelhardt, C. R. and Clark, K. E. (2015). Video games from the perspective of adults with autism spectrum disorder. *Computers in Human Behavior,* 51 (Pt A), pp. 122–30.

Mazurek, M. O. and Wenstrup, C. (2013). Television, video game and social media use among children with ASD and typically developing siblings. *J Autism Dev Disord,* 43 (6), pp. 1258–71.

Mitchell, D. and Snyder, S. (2000). *Narrative Prothesis: Disability and the dependencies of discourse.* Ann Arbor, MI: University of Michigan Press.

Mohd Roffeei, S. H., Abdullah, N. and Basar, S. K. (2015). Seeking social support on Facebook for children with autism spectrum disorders (ASDs). *Int J Med Inform,* 84 (5), pp. 375–85.

Nordahl-Hansen, A., Øien, R. A. and Fletcher-Watson, S. (2018). Pros and cons of character portrayals of autism on TV and film. *J Autism Dev Disord,* 48 (2), pp. 635–6.

Osteen, M. (2007). *Autism and Representation.* New York: Routledge.

Orsmond, G. I. and Kuo, H.-Y. (2011). The daily lives of adolescents with an autism spectrum disorder: Discretionary time use and activity partners. *Autism,* 15 (5), pp. 579–99.

Park, I., Gong, J., Lyons, G. L., Hirota, T., Takahashi, M., Kim, B., Lee, S. Y., Kim, Y. S., Lee, J. and Leventhal, B. L. (2020). Prevalence of and factors associated with school bullying in students with autism spectrum disorder: A cross-cultural meta-analysis. *Yonsei Med J,* 61 (11), pp. 909–22.

Prochnow, A. (2014). An analysis of autism through media representation. *ETC: A Review of General Semantics,* 71 (2), pp. 13–49.

Redden, M. (2018). Keep the change: Actors with autism get the chance to shine in romcom. [online] Available at: www.theguardian.com/film/2018/mar/16/keep-the-change-actors-with-autism-get-the-chance-to-shine-in-romcom [Accessed 05.02.2022].

Ringland, K. E. (2019). *How a Minecraft world has built a safe online playground for autistic kids.* [online] Available at: https://theconversation.com/how-a-minecraft-world-has-built-a-safe-online-playground-for-autistic-kids-124492 [Accessed 02.04.2022].

Roffeei, S. H. M., Abdullah, N. and Basar, S. K. R. (2015). Seeking social support on Facebook for children with autism spectrum disorders (ASDs). *Int J Med Inform,* 84 (5), pp. 375–85.

Rourke, B. and McGloin, R. (2019). A different take on the Big Bang Theory: Examining the influence of Asperger traits on the perception and attributional confidence of a fictional TV character portraying characteristics of Asperger syndrome. *Atlantic Journal of Communication,* 27, pp. 127–38.

Sarrett, J. C. (2011). Trapped children: Popular images of children with autism in the 1960s and 2000s. *J Med Humanit,* 32 (2), pp. 141–53.

Seligman, M. and Darling, R. B. (2007). Ordinary Families, Special Children: A Systems Approach to Childhood Disability (3rd edition). New York: Guilford.

Sims, P. (2017). *Autism and the internet: Risks and benefits*. [online] Available at: www.autism.org.uk/advice-and-guidance/professional-practice/autism-internet [Accessed 11.02.2022].

Skudra, N. (2018). *A look back at the movie Rain Man and how our views of autism have changed*. [online] Available at: https://the-art-of-autism.com/a-look-back-at-the-movie-rain-man-andhow-are-views-of-autism-have-changed/ [Accessed 21.02.2022].

Soraya, L. (2009). *Sheldony or Aspergery?: The Big Bang Theory Sheldon Cooper of The Big Bang Theory...Asperger's or no?* [online] Available at: www.psychologytoday.com/us/blog/aspergers-diary/200904/sheldony-or-aspergery-the-big-bang-theory [Accessed 13.02.2022].

Stendal, K. and Balandin, S. (2015). Virtual worlds for people with autism spectrum disorder: A case study in Second Life. *Disabil Rehabil*, 37 (17), pp. 1591–8.

Townsend, L. (2015). *How the Bridge's heroine became a role model for women with autism*. [online] Available at: https://www.bbc.co.uk/news/disability-34995327 [Accessed 12.03.2022].

Triantafyllopoulou, P., Clark-Hughes, C. and Langdon, P. E. (2021). Social media and cyber-bullying in autistic adults. *J Autism Dev Disord*, 19, pp. 1–9.

van Schalkwyk, G. I., Marin, C. E., Ortiz, M., Rolison, M., Qayyum, Z., McPartland, J. C., Lebowitz, E. R., Volkmar, F. R. and Silverman, W. K. (2017). Social media use, friendship quality, and the moderating role of anxiety in adolescents with autism spectrum disorder. *J Autism Dev Disord*, 47 (9), pp. 2805–13.

Walters, S. (2013). Cool aspie humor: Cognitive difference and Kenneth Burke's comic corrective in The Big Bang Theory and community. *Journal of Literary and Cultural Disability Studies*, 7 (3), pp. 271–88.

Ward, D. M., Dill-Shackleford, K. E. and Mazurek, M. O. (2018). Social media use and happiness in adults with autism spectrum disorder. *Cyberpsychology, Behavior, and Social Networking*, 21 (3), pp. 205–9.

Young, L. S. (2012). Awareness with accuracy: An analysis of the representation of autism in film and television. *Research Papers*, Paper 256.

Zhao, Y., Zhang, J. and Wu, M. (2019). Finding users' voice on social media: An investigation of online support groups for autism-affected users on Facebook. *Int J Environ Res Public Health*, 16 (23), 4804.

Index